EXPERIMENTAL PSYCHOLOGY

EXPERIMENTAL PSYCHOLOGY

DONALD H. McBURNEY
University of Pittsburgh

WADSWORTH PUBLISHING COMPANY
Belmont, California
A Division of Wadsworth, Inc.

Psychology Editor: Kenneth King

Production: Greg Hubit Bookworks

Text Designer: Marvin R. Warshaw/Design

Cover Designer: Henry Breuer

Copy Editor: Jerilyn Emori

Technical Illustrator: Art by Ayxa

Printed in the United States of America

1 2 3 4 5 6 7 8 9 10—87 86 85 84 83

Library of Congress Cataloging in Publication Data

McBurney, Donald H., 1938–
Experimental psychology.

Bibliography: p.
Includes index.
1. Psychology, Experimental. 2. Psychological
research. I. Title.
BF181.M38 1983 150'.72 82-17533

ISBN 0-534-01319-8

ISBN 0-534-01319-8

CONTENTS

PREFACE

This book is intended to serve as a text for courses in research methods in psychology at the undergraduate level. I have kept several goals in mind as I worked on the manuscript.

First is to put psychological research into a larger scientific context. Other books on the topic provide too little emphasis on how psychology fits into the scientific approach to understanding the world. Given the debate that exists among the behavioral, dynamic, humanistic, Marxian, and other types of psychologies, as well as the confusion about the nature of science evidenced by the many popular and fringe psychologies, it is not surprising that undergraduate students have questions about how scientific psychology is done. The first section of the book therefore deals with psychology as a science, emphasizing the similarities between psychology and the other sciences on the one hand and the differences between science and pseudoscience on the other.

A second goal is to separate the discussion of research methods from its traditional dependence on statistical procedures. Many experimental psychology books are organized around particular statistical methods, especially the analysis of variance. In contrast, I have organized this book around the general problems of validity and how to control for the various threats to validity. The later chapters on true experiments, quasi experiments, single-subject designs, and nonexperimental research give examples of solutions to the problems of validity, rather than a catalog of statistical applications. With this goal in mind, it made sense to have an early chapter that discusses the types of variables encountered in psychological research and how data are represented graphically. For example, the concept of interaction is discussed in the chapter on variables, rather than in the traditional location in a chapter on true experiments, because the factorial designs in which interactions are seen are used widely in types of research other than true experiments. In addition, an early discussion of this topic, which many students find difficult, helps them understand the research they encounter as they progress through the book and as they do library research for their own projects.

A third goal, closely related to the second, is to convey the idea that designing and conducting research is an exercise in problem solving that can be exciting and creative. I have avoided giving the impression that psychological research involves following a set of cut-and-dried rules or selecting one of a fixed number of available designs. My belief is that the best research results from solving particular threats to the validity of a contemplated piece of research and only then asking what kind of design has resulted. Throughout the book I have emphasized the considerations that are involved in designing and conducting research.

Fourth, I have chosen from the psychological literature a wide variety of problems in research and their solutions. Generally I have avoided nonpsychological examples and artificial data.

Finally, I have tried to convey a feeling for all of the stages of research, from choosing the problem to publishing the results. I have discussed the literature search, the nuts and bolts of research protocols, research ethics, and the publication process. The only major step omitted is statistical analysis, which is left to a prerequisite or corequisite course or to supplementary material, according to the instructor's choice.

Many colleagues and friends have contributed to this project. Among others, Seymour Antelman, Anthony Caggiula, Lynn Cooper, Martin Greenberg, James Greeno, James Holland, Peter Holland, Robert Jewell, Russell Jones, John Levine, Scott Monroe, Richard Moreland, Merle Moskowitz, Valerie Shalin, Mark Strauss, and Edward Stricker all provided helpful suggestions and/or discussion. Special thanks go to Janneane Gent for drafting the boxes on statistics that appear in Chapter 7, as well as for making other important contributions to the book. The idea for the Reading Between the Lines exercises came from Schuyler Huck and Howard Sandler's book, *Rival Hypotheses: Alternative Explanations of Data-based Conclusions.* I thank the following colleagues who reviewed the manuscript and provided detailed suggestions that improved the book greatly: Mark Kinnucan, Saint Michael's College, Vermont; Nancy Kirkland, Trinity College, Connecticut; John Knight, Central State University, Oklahoma; Virgil Nylander, University of Wisconsin; Howard Orenstein, Western Maryland College; Walter Pieper, Georgia State University; Thomas Rowe, University of Washington; Timothy Salthouse, University of Missouri, Columbia; W. Scott Terry, University of North Carolina; Ronald Ulm, Salisbury State College, Maryland.

The psychology editor at Wadsworth, Ken King, provided helpful suggestions throughout the course of the project. Jerilyn Emori did a fine job of copyediting the manuscript. Barb Bennett typed much of the manuscript in various drafts; Ruth and Susan McBurney typed most of the rest. My thanks to all of these people and others whose influences I do not specifically recall.

PSYCHOLOGY AND SCIENCE

Experimental psychology is a science essentially like any other. Between psychology and biology, chemistry or anthropology, there may be considerable difference in subject matter, but the essentials are common to all. The differences are fairly obvious: Because animals are more complex than trees, psychological theories may be more complicated than botanical theories; because the behavior of animals varies more than that of rocks, psychology uses statistics more than does physics. On the other hand, the similarities may not be as easy to grasp. For this reason we will devote this chapter to discussing psychology as a science. First let us put psychology in context by talking about ways of looking at behavior.

WAYS OF KNOWING ABOUT BEHAVIOR

The point to stress here is that there is more than one way to learn about the behavior of animals. Every day all of us use several methods to learn about behavior.

Authority

We may believe something because some respected person told us it is true. Religious authorities proclaim the will of God to us about various matters, the government tells us that we should not drive over 55 miles per hour, and our parents tell us that we will catch cold if we get our feet wet. Because these authorities often disagree among themselves, we are inclined to reject authority as a way of knowing. How do you know that Neil Armstrong walked on the moon on July 20, 1969? You were not there. Perhaps you watched it on television. Yet there are people who believe that no man ever has walked on the moon and that the moon walk was a gigantic propaganda hoax perpetrated by the United States government. If you believe that Neil Armstrong walked on the moon, you do so because of your faith in the credibility of the government, the news media, and the books you have read. These sources all serve as authorities for you if you believe what they say.

Yet authority has major limitations as a way of knowing. Authorities often are wrong, even when they assert their beliefs most forcefully. Galileo suffered grievously for daring to hold that the earth goes around the sun. That the history of science is in large part a struggle for intellectual freedom from the dogmas of authority is a continuing theme in the history of science from Galileo in the sixteenth century to Soviet dissidents today. If you did not have any faith in authority, though, you would not be reading this book or taking an experimental psychology course from a college professor.

Logic

Logic is an important way of helping us know about behavior. Take the following set of statements:

> The behavior of all animals is subject to the laws of natural science.
>
> Humans are animals.
>
> Therefore, human behavior is subject to the laws of natural science.

These statements are logical. That is, if the first two are true, then the third follows logically. Use of logic often is crucial in making correct conclusions about the world.

Yet as important as reasoning logically is, logic has limitations as a way of knowing. You probably have heard the expression "I got it from the horse's mouth." Years ago, some philosophers are said to have argued at great length about how many teeth a horse had. After many logical arguments were presented on various sides of the question, someone suggested looking into a horse's mouth to find out. Although that suggestion seems obvious to us in today's scientific age, it was not clear to the scholastic mind of the Middle Ages that observation could be as good as logic in reaching a conclusion. For example, suppose that the horse was not typical in some respect: It had not yet grown all its teeth, or some had fallen out. Although today we are more inclined to say "show me," logic still has an important place in helping us decide whether we are drawing correct conclusions from our data.

Intuitive Methods

Intuition
spontaneous perception or judgment not based on reasoned mental steps

We size up strangers within the first few seconds of meeting them. We do this by **intuition**, a way of knowing based on spontaneous, "instinctive" processes rather than logic or reasoning. Intuition has a powerful effect on our beliefs about other people. We may distrust a person who seems too sincere to be true. This sizing up sometimes has been called women's intuition. Today we are more likely to say that someone gives off bad vibes. We use intuition continuously in making the myriad decisions necessary during the course of a day. Think for a moment how you decide whether to step off the curb in front of an oncoming car at a traffic light. You make a life or death decision in a split second. How do you do it? Probably your decision is based on a number of factors, including whether the traffic light has changed to red, whether the driver looks you in the eye, whether the car is decelerating, and so forth. Somehow you take all of these factors into account. The somehow we call intuition.

There are two important varieties of intuition, common sense and mysticism.

Common sense
practical intelligence shared by a large group of persons

Common sense. **Common sense** is a kind of intuition because of its dependence on informal methods. It has the additional characteristic of emphasizing the agreement of a person's judgment with the shared attitudes and experiences of a larger group of people. We are familiar with the example of a recent college graduate who starts working with people who lack formal education. The graduate wants to apply his scientific knowledge to the job. The old hands may resist the ideas that don't agree with common sense. After all, their methods worked well before the newcomer arrived.

Common sense as a way of knowing has two basic limitations. First, standards of common sense differ from time to time and from place to place according to the attitudes and experiences of the culture. Years ago a commonsense method of trying suspects for crimes was having them attempt to chew dry grain. It was believed that if they were innocent they would be able to eat the grain without difficulty; if they were guilty their mouths would be too dry to permit swallowing. In reality, this practice does have some basis in scientific fact: A guilty person is likely to be scared spitless. We now know, however, that innocent people can be just as nervous as guilty ones, so today we usually are more scientific in our trial practices. Again, common sense might tell us not to trust a person who will not look us in the eye. In another culture, though, the same behavior may be a sign of respect.

The second limitation of common sense as a way of knowing lies in the fact that the only criterion common sense recognizes for judging the truth of a belief or practice is whether or not it works. The old hand will tell the college graduate to forget his scientific ways because the old ways work well enough. According to the commonsense method, no systematic attempt is made to test the theoretical explanation of a practice and see whether it is true. As long as a certain practice works, that practice is maintained and the theory behind it considered true. This principle can be useful at times. Child-rearing practices for thousands of years were based on commonsense notions. Perhaps most children turned out reasonably well on this basis. Only in recent years have scientists advocated child-rearing methods that were an improvement over folk practices. Yet following a practice simply because it works does not permit any basis for predicting when the practice will work and when it will not. Commonsense notions of child rearing do not help in dealing with autistic children, for example.

More importantly, because common sense has only practical success as its criterion of truthfulness, it cannot predict new knowledge. Later we will discuss in some detail the idea that science aims at a theoretical explanation of phenomena. Here we will only point out that the absence of theory as a principal goal of common sense is one of the major limitations of this method of knowing.

Given that common sense has these two basic limitations—that it changes with time and circumstance and that it is pragmatic rather than theoretical—it is not surprising that scientific knowledge often contradicts commonsense knowledge. We may speak of a scientific result as being *counterintuitive;* that is, it goes against our notions of common sense. In fact, we consider a scientific theory to be good if it predicts something that we did not expect.

For example, a recent theory of obesity in humans says that overweight persons are controlled more by external cues (sight of food or a clock that indicates dinnertime) and less by internal signals (hunger pangs) than are other people. This theory makes the counterintuitive prediction that there should be situations in which overweight people eat *less* than normal weight people. True to prediction, overweight people do eat less if they have to make a special effort to obtain the food. If there is plenty of food in front of them, however, they will eat more than other people.

In one experiment by Richard Nisbett (1968), sandwiches were placed in front of subjects who were told to eat all they wanted and to help themselves to more from the refrigerator if they desired. Half of the subjects had only one sandwich in front of them and the other half had three. Subjects of average weight tended to eat about the same in either condition. That is, they would get more from the refrigerator in the one-sandwich condition but leave food on the plate in the three-sandwich condition. Overweight subjects, however, tended to eat whatever was there, either the small amount or the large amount, and not go to the refrigerator.

Even though science frequently contradicts common sense, we must not go to the extreme of concluding that we throw away common sense when we start doing science. In fact, science ultimately rests on common sense. There may be several different theories that could explain a given phenomenon. One of them may be rejected by scientists because it strains their common sense. Often scientists say that such and such a theory seems plausible, meaning that it agrees with their notion of common sense. Scientists choose among theories on a number of bases, but the theory that finally is accepted must satisfy the common sense of the scientific community. The crucial point here is that the scientist's common sense is different from the layperson's. Scientists' background in similar problems trains them to think in terms of a particular scientific theory. Laypersons have different backgrounds that may make the theory of the scientists seem ridiculous. Their ideas of common sense will differ precisely because they do not have common backgrounds.

Mysticism
belief in insight gained by means of a private experience such as an altered state of consciousness

Mysticism. **Mysticism** is a way of knowing based on direct insight, associated with an altered quality of consciousness. The mystical approach to knowing is like intuition and common sense in not using logical reasoning. In addition, the mystical experience has a quality about it that sets it apart from ordinary experience. We may describe it as an altered state of consciousness, a transcendental experience, a spiritual encounter, or, more simply, a high or a trip. Although we tend to think of mystical experiences as being the province of the yogi, medieval monk, or drug user, research shows that 36 percent of Americans have had an experience of this type (Greely, 1975). The mystical experience is triggered by such ordinary experiences as listening to music, praying, or looking at a sunset. The most common interpretation of the mystical experience is "a feeling of deep and profound peace," "a certainty that all things would work out for the good," or "a sense of the need to contribute to others" (Greely, 1975, p. 65).

The value of these experiences for those who have them should not be underestimated. Such persons may be led to dedicate their lives to serving their fellow humans. Certain problems exist, however. First, conveying the message received during the experience is hard because of the difficulty of describing the experience in a convincing way. Second, the message itself may be invalid. The person who feels that everything will work out for the good may have a serious disease that could be cured by medical care. Therefore, although mystical experiences may be significant for certain people, they have limitations as ways of knowing.

Science

Science is the fourth major way of knowing about behavior. In this section we will consider what science is, how it differs from other ways of knowing, and how psychology fits into the scientific approach to knowing.

What is science? To attempt to define science for a book of this type may seem either totally unnecessary, highly presumptuous, or both. Every reader of this book will have had exposure to science at the high school level, if not in college, which included some study of the scientific method. At this point there are three reasons why we must discuss the nature of science. First, there is not *a* scientific method; rather, there are scientific *methods*. Somewhere you probably learned that the scientific method consisted of executing the following steps: (1) defining the problem, (2) forming a hypothesis, (3) collecting data, and (4) drawing conclusions. This recipe is usable, if you understand that it is greatly simplified. Research sometimes is done according to these steps, but more often it involves modification of this procedure. As our discussion progresses, the need for modification will become apparent.

The second reason for discussing the nature of science in this book is that even persons who have developed a basic idea of how to do science that involves biology, chemistry, or physics often have difficulty seeing how to go about the science of psychology. To many people it seems that psychology should follow different rules from other sciences because psychology appears by definition to deal with mental events. If you have trouble seeing how psychology can be like the other sciences, don't be discouraged. The experts on psychology took a long time to come to a tentative consensus about how psychology should be done, and the debate is not settled by any means.

A third reason for defining science in an introductory discussion of experimental psychology is that beginning psychology students sometimes feel that they have become amateur psychologists by virtue of observing human and animal behavior for a lifetime. When you took chemistry, you probably had not spent much time thinking about how atoms combine to form molecules. Yet you may have had a lifetime interest in why people are friendly or unfriendly, moody or not moody, and so forth. Sometimes, too, you know exactly why you do things: "I wore a certain style of clothes in order to be accepted by my fellow students." So your very experience with people may make it more difficult for you to think about human behavior scientifically. Studying human behavior might seem easier if you were the mythical Martian sent to spy on the behavior of earthlings. We often are more aware of the customs of a slightly different culture than we are of our own.

Science
a way of obtaining knowledge by means of objective observations

Science is a way of obtaining knowledge based on objective observations. The key word in this brief definition is *objective*. Objective observations are those made in such a way that persons having normal perception and being in the same place at the same time would arrive at the same observation. Objectivity in science is a concept that is often misunderstood. It does not mean that the scientist is coldly detached from his subject matter. It does not mean that he treats people like objects rather than persons. Nor does it mean that what he observes necessarily is what actually happened. Objectivity simply means that other persons would have seen the same things had they been looking over the shoulder of the scientist who made the observation.

In addition, when observations are objectively made and carefully reported, they serve as a sort of recipe for others to follow. The other persons can repeat the procedures to see if they observe the same things. For this reason, careful records and clear, accurate reports are a crucial part of science. Such documentation permits others to bridge the gaps of space and time and peer over the shoulder of the scientist, making his or her observations objective.

The opposite of the objective observations are subjective observations. These are the observations that a person makes that another person is not required to accept as true. Ann may say, "I taste salt." This statement by Ann is subjective because no one else is required to believe that she actually experienced a salty taste. She might have tasted nothing, because the salt was too weak, and said "salt" out of perverseness. On the other hand, the statement "Ann reported tasting salt" is objective because anyone else present in the room could verify the fact than Ann made such a statement. So the experimenter can report *objectively* about Ann's *subjective* report. It is the experimenter's report that becomes the object of scientific discussion.

The need for objective observations explains the importance that scientists place on proper research methods. Great care is taken to specify the exact conditions under which observations are made so that other scientists can repeat the observations if they desire and can try to obtain the same results as the first scientists.

Objectivity is the single characteristic that sets science apart from all that is not science. Science deals with phenomena that are available to anyone. It cannot deal with phenomena that only one person or a few persons can observe. This fact distinguishes science from all systems of knowledge based on authority: religion, politics, nationalism, or whatever. Objectivity is what makes science the one universal means of achieving understanding, because it eliminates from consideration at the outset any phenomenon that cannot command the agreement of every person. This is not to say that there are no scientific controversies or nationalistic scientists. Far from it. But science as a whole is remarkably free from parochialism precisely because it deals only with those phenomena that are available to any person.

The relation between science and nonscience. We have emphasized that it is objectivity of the material with which science deals that makes it a unique way of gaining knowledge. At the same time, we should emphasize that this criterion does not make it necessary to reject other ways of knowing. In fact, we pointed out that logic and common sense have important roles to play in science. Mysticism and authority, on the other hand, have sharply reduced roles in the workings of science. Mysticism can only have the role of motivating people as single individuals. The private nature of the mystical experience rules it out as evidence to be considered by the scientific community as a whole. Certainly, many scientists have been motivated by mystical experiences or religious concepts. Nevertheless, they cannot urge a mystical experience or a religious doctrine as scientific evidence for the consideration of other scientists. For example, Gustav Fechner, the founder of psychophysics and a pioneer in experimental psychology, pursued his science as a way of proving his belief in panpsychism. His scientific work, on the other hand, has been evaluated on its own merits.

Authority also has a strikingly reduced role in science. In virtually every human enterprise are people who serve as guardians of orthodoxy. Even in the most democratic organization a majority vote can render certain opinions heretical. Although a power structure is by no means absent from science, authority plays a different role than in other human activities. A clear example can be seen in almost any meeting of a large scientific organization. Anyone who meets minimal requirements—an undergraduate, graduate student, or new Ph.D.—can present a paper that challenges the theories of even the most illustrious scientist. Although the challenger may suffer trepidation, and the senior scientist's arguments may receive more careful attention, the focus of the discussion will be on the soundness of the research methods and on the logic of the challenger's position. If the challenger has presented a sound argument based on acceptable methods of observation, other scientists will be motivated to try to repeat the observations. If these repeated observations are successful, the illustrious scientist's ideas are replaced by the challenger's.

This process of challenging repeats itself so often that it is commonplace in scientific activity. Still, it is a characteristic unique to science and stems from the fact that the only basis for authority in science is the objective evidence that any person can evaluate. True, the editors of journals, the reviewers of grants and journal articles do wield authority of a sort. Their authority, though, is that of peer review; that is, review by a person's equals. No scientific courts exist where truth is established for all to accept. A scientist must convince the entire scientific community, not just a jury of authorities. That is why we often read statements like the following: "Most workers in the field believe that . . .", or, "It is generally accepted that. . . ." People who serve as reviewers for articles and grants are chosen because of their expertise, and so they are authorities in a sense. Yet they serve as authorities because, and as long as, they are able to convince their peers that they are in fact better informed on the subject than are other persons.

PSYCHOLOGY AS SCIENCE

Our discussion so far has assumed that psychology is a branch of science essentially on the same basis as any other science. This idea has not always held sway and is still somewhat controversial. Before World War I psychology often was conceived as a *mental science*, one concerned with events inside the head that were different in *kind* from those in the physical world. It followed that a mental science would need techniques different from the physical sciences. An important technique for the study of psychology by mentalistic psychologists was **introspection**: a method of examining the contents of one's own consciousness practiced by carefully trained observers. Introspection was a reasonably useful technique, but it ran into a basic problem. Two observers often would introspect about a question and come to opposite conclusions.

Introspection observation of one's own thoughts and feelings

Suppose one observer introspected about the color orange and concluded that orange was a unique sensation, different from red or yellow. Another might conclude that orange was a mixed sensation made up of red and yellow sensations. How would you decide which observer was correct? Observers could introspect about their own experience and no one else's. No one else could take an independent look at the introspection of the two observers and decide which one was correct. This situation occurred frequently enough to cause long and fruitless debates on many topics.

Eventually, psychology converted to the doctrine of **behaviorism** put forth by John Watson. Watson argued that the *behavior* of organisms, not their consciousnesses, was the basic data of psychology. Only behavior could be observed, not sensations or mental images and the like. Behaviorism was a radical doctrine in 1913 and still is widely misunderstood. Behaviorists do not deny that there is such a thing as consciousness or that it has an important role in human or even animal behavior. Behaviorism says that the events we study must be things that can be observed by anyone—they must be objective, public events.

Behaviorism a view that the objective study of behavior constitutes psychology

Recall our example of Ann tasting salt. Ann's sensation of saltiness is a private event accessible only to Ann. Ann can introspect at length about what salt tastes like, and only Ann has access to her own introspection. But Ann's saying "I taste salt" is an event that can be observed by anyone; it is objective and public rather than subjective and private. Behaviorists can count the number of times Ann *says* that a particular concentration of salt tastes salty. They can compare this with the number of times John *says* that the same solution tastes salty. They can use the frequency of the *verbal reports* as data to compare Ann with John, or Ann on Day 1 with Ann on Day 2, and so forth.

Behaviorism has been the dominant theoretical orientation in psychology up to the present time. Although mental events were not denied to have taken place, the focus was on the objective data of behavior and this led to vigorous and successful science. On the other hand, there were psychologists who felt that the baby of consciousness had been thrown out with the bathwater of introspectionism. Eventually, many psychologists returned to an interest in consciousness and the mental events that lay behind the behavior they had been studying.

Cognitive psychology the study of behavior in terms of internal processes such as perceiving or reasoning

Thus, we have seen the rise of **cognitive psychology** in the 1960s and 1970s. Cognitive psychology is characterized by the attempt to explain behavior in terms of internal events such as images, short-term memories, and other processes that cannot be observed directly. However, cognitive psychology represents an elaboration of behaviorism, rather than a rejection of it. The presence of these internal events is always inferred from the objective behavior of the subject.

A common way of inferring internal events from behavior is to measure how long it takes to perform a response. For example, suppose you show a person a list of numbers to remember. Immediately after the list is removed, you ask whether a certain number is in the list. The time required to decide whether the number is in the list is a linear function of how many numbers the list has. In other words, each additional number in the list requires a certain additional amount of time for deciding whether the asked-for number is there. From this experiment an internal, unobserved process is inferred to take place that requires about 40 milliseconds for each item in the list that must be searched (Sternberg, 1966). Although cognitive psychology is more interested in internal events than is strict behaviorism, it can be considered to be an extension of behaviorism because it relies on objective, public data.

Humanistic psychology a philosophy that emphasizes feelings, consciousness, and other human values in contrast to the objectiveness of behaviorism

Another approach to psychology is that of **humanistic psychology**, a branch that is difficult to define. Having developed in large part as a reaction to the narrowness of behavioristic psychology, it encompasses a wide variety of viewpoints. (Shaffer, 1978). As a movement, however, humanistic psychology has several characteristic features. First, it is critical of the scientific emphasis on objective behavior at the expense of feelings, fantasies, and the like. Second, it places great interest in human conscious experience. Third, it emphasizes the freedom and autonomy of human action. Fourth, it is careful to include the concerns with human values in the science of psychology. Behaviorism tends to downplay these four areas because studying them objectively is difficult.

In Chapter 12 we will evaluate humanistic psychology further by discussing some of the limitations and biases of scientific psychology. At this point, we will simply say that developing a science of psychology that can satisfy all the concerns of humanistic psychology will be an accomplishment, if it can be done. Science has been spectacularly successful in answering certain kinds of questions precisely because it has limited itself to dealing with evidence that can command the agreement of every person as meeting the criterion of objectivity. We can wish the humanistic psychologists every success, but we will stick to the methods common to all sciences because they have worked. We will cheerfully admit that this rules out many interesting questions for the psychologist to study. As someone has said: Science is the substitution of small problems that can be solved for important ones that cannot. Remember that science is one way of knowing among many. We must realize that each way has its limitations, and we must be grateful for the balance thus brought to the human understanding of ourselves and of the world.

WORKING ASSUMPTIONS OF SCIENCE

To most of us who have come through our western educational system, science seems an obvious way to learn about the world. The rise of the counterculture in the sixties, though, and the interest in nonwestern modes of thought in the present decade have reminded us there are certain assumptions about the world that lie behind the scientific approach. Let us discuss these briefly.

The Reality of the World

Realism
the philosophy that objects perceived have an existence outside the mind

Most scientists agree that one of science's fundamental assumptions is the reality of the world. Philosophers call this assumption the doctrine of **realism**, the notion that the objects of scientific study in the world exist apart from their being perceived by us. In other words, the scientist assumes, for example, that a rat does not stop being reinforced in a Skinner box simply because the experimenter fell asleep, went out for coffee, or the recorder ran out of paper. This point may seem obvious to you, but there are a number of philosophers and some scientists who would argue fiercely on this point. They are concerned with the valid and difficult question of how we know what the nature of the world really is. For example, how can we know our senses are not deceiving us when we observe that a piece of coal is black? In general scientists have little interest in philosophical debates about the reality of the world. They assume that the world is there, and they go about studying it as best they can. We must note, however, that they do avoid one variety of realism that is known as *commonsense realism*, or *naive realism*. Commonsense realism is the philosophy of the person in the street who never wondered why coal looks black because anybody knows that coal is black. Commonsense realism says that things are just the way they seem: Coal looks black because it *is* black. The failure of commonsense realism in many situations actually contributed to the development of science, psychology in particular. For example, under some conditions, coal can look not black but light gray. Students of perception devoted a good deal of energy to solving the problem of why a piece of coal can look black at one time and gray at another.

Although the scientist and the layperson both believe in the existence of a real world, the world that the scientist believes in is different from the one the layperson believes in. The layperson's world may contain persons who are lazy or hardworking, good or evil, and so forth. The scientist's world, on the other hand, is more likely to consist of people who are influenced by stimuli, reinforcers, drives, and the like. The scientist and the layperson both assume that there is only one reality, but they differ as to what that reality is.

Rationality

Rationality
a view that reasoning is the basis for solving problems

Another crucial assumption of science is that the world is **rational**; that is, it is understandable by way of logical thinking. If the world were irrational—if it could not be understood by using principles of logic—then there would be no point in trying to understand it by any means whatever. We would simply throw up our hands and try to get along as best we could without trying to understand the world around us.

Regularity

Regularity
a belief that phenomena exist in recurring patterns that conform with universal laws

Reality and rationality of the world would not be much use to science by themselves without the assumption of regularity. **Regularity** means that we assume that the world follows the same laws at all times and in all places. We pick up a book confident that it will not have become explosive since we last used it. We go to sleep at night without worrying that we will wake up in the morning as a giant cockroach. The reason regularity is so important for science is that it says that everything that happens must be capable, in principle, of being subsumed under some law of science. If we knew all of the important facts, we could know what made Lee Harvey Oswald assassinate President Kennedy. We believe that science can understand why a person converts to a religious cult, commits a murder, becomes a priest, or writes a novel. It is true that the causes of these events may be complex and that we may never have all facts necessary to explain a particular event in detail, but science assumes that nothing about human behavior falls outside the laws of nature, wherever or whenever the behavior occurs.

Causality

Determinism
the doctrine that all events happen because of preceding causes

In order to do science, it is necessary to assume that events do not just happen by themselves or for no reason. Thus the idea that every event has a cause is a basic tenet of science. In fact, some have defined science as a search for causes of events.

A belief that all events are caused is called **determinism**. A strict determinist holds that if it were possible to know all laws of behavior and the exact condition of persons, together with everything that was influencing them at a particular time, it would be possible to predict exactly what they would do next. The strict determinist denies the existence of free will. Others say that because the laws of behavior cannot be stated with certainty, the possibility of free will cannot be ruled out.

The problem of determinism and free will is a thorny one that we can leave to the philosophers. We do not have to decide whether people's behavior is strictly determined or whether we have free will, or whether both positions can be true at the same time. We are only stating that scientists use the concept of causality as a *working assumption*. People who believe in free will send their children to school because they expect the school to change the children's behavior in a predictable way. Therefore, they believe in determinism to some extent. Similarly, scientists seek causes for behavior without necessarily making the assumption that they will ever completely learn the causes of behavior, or that the idea of free will is an illusion.

While we are discussing causality, we should note that some events may be considered causes of other events even if the relationship between them is less than constant. These events may be considered *statistical causes*. The classic example is the conclusion that smoking is a cause of lung cancer even though not every person who smokes contracts lung cancer. Similarly, poverty is a statistical cause of crime. Even though every poor person does not become a criminal and not all criminals are poor, there is a statistical association between poverty and crime.

Discoverability

Not only do scientists assume that the world is real, rational, and regular, they believe that it is possible to find out how it works. There is a difference between these two assumptions. It is possible that the world is entirely rational but that we could never find the key to the puzzle unless it were revealed to us. The scientist assumes that we can discover the way the world works without having a holy person or book reveal it to us. This belief in **discoverability** is the difference between a puzzle and a mystery. A puzzle can be solved by a person using ordinary means. A mystery, using the word in the strict sense, cannot be understood by human means but must have its solution revealed by someone who knows the mystery. Science treats the world as a gigantic puzzle that is mysterious in the loose sense of leading to wonder but is not mysterious in the strict sense of not being solvable by human means.

Discoverability the belief that it is possible to learn solutions to questions posed

This belief in the discoverability of the world by scientific methods must be tempered by an appreciation of the difficulty of the task. Many scientific puzzles have intrigued people throughout recorded history. Nature gives up its secrets reluctantly. Many books on experimental methods in psychology give the false impression that by a straightforward application of simple methods, the pieces of the psychological puzzle will slowly and steadily fall into place. Far from it. Many fascinating examples exist that show how solutions to scientific problems require great ingenuity and effort. In a fascinating autobiographical article B. F. Skinner (1956) describes the processes that led him to become the founder of operant psychology. So we see one of the characteristics of science that motivates people to make the effort necessary to carry on experimental work for large parts of a lifetime.

We must not leave the topic of the assumptions of science without pointing out that these need only be methodological, or working, assumptions, not assertions of ultimate truth. All scientists operate under such assumptions in the laboratory and in their writing about science. Outside the laboratory, however, some of them make different assumptions. At home they may doubt the existence of the real world. They may believe that human behavior is irrational, that miracles sometime happen, or that the world really is mysterious in the strict sense. The point is that persons are scientists when they are doing science and in order to do science they must make the assumptions we have discussed.

SUMMARY

1. Psychology is a science essentially like any other science.
2. There are four ways of knowing about behavior: authority, logic, intuitive methods, and science.
3. Authority plays a diminished role in science compared to other social institutions.
4. Logic plays an important role in science but is secondary in importance to observation.
5. Intuitive methods of knowing about behavior include common sense and mysticism.
6. Common sense is limited in usefulness to science because it changes from time to time and place to place and cannot predict new knowledge.
7. Scientific knowledge often contradicts common sense, but ultimately it rests on a certain kind of common sense.
8. Mystical experiences are of limited usefulness in science because they are difficult to convey to another person and their insights are often invalid.
9. There is not one scientific method but many scientific methods.
10. Science is a way of obtaining knowledge based on objective observations.
11. Psychology used to be considered a science that dealt with mental events but now is usually considered to deal with observable events and those that may be inferred from observable events.

12. Humanistic psychology attempts to deal with aspects of human experience that are slighted by the rest of psychology but does so at the expense of scientific rigor.
13. Science has five major working assumptions: the reality, regularity, and rationality of the world; the operation of causality; and the discoverability of how the world works.
14. Scientists assume that the world is real, but they do not assume that it is just the way it appears to be.
15. The assumption of rationality means that the world is believed to be understandable via logical thinking.
16. The assumption of regularity means that the world is believed to follow the same laws in all times and places.
17. The assumption of causality means that all events are believed to have causes.
18. The assumption of discoverability means that scientists believe that it is possible to find out how the world works.

SUGGESTIONS FOR FURTHER READING

Campbell, N. *What is science?* New York: Dover, 1953. This book, originally published in 1921, is a classic introduction to the nature of science. It is brief and particularly clear in its discussion of the nature of scientific laws and theories.

Conant, J. B. *Science and common sense.* New Haven, Conn.: Yale, 1961. This book shows by examples from the natural sciences how science grew out of a concern with practical problems and how science differs from technology by its emphasis on speculative knowledge to satisfy curiosity about the world.

READING BETWEEN THE LINES

One of the most important goals of an experimental psychology course is to develop skills in critically evaluating published studies and other claims made on the basis of evidence. Any set of data always has alternative explanations, but some are more plausible than others. Students need to develop a healthy skepticism for claims made about data. The following problems contain conclusions that are questionable. Study each one to see what other hypotheses might account for the data.

Some of the problems are fairly easy; others are very difficult. Because all involve actual cases, they also involve questions of interpretation that authorities of one sort or another have differed on. Most of these examples have been published in the scientific literature, passing through the peer review process with their original interpretations. In some cases, the problem of interpreting was so difficult that scientists worked for years to find the proper interpretation of the results. In other cases, the results are still debated. So don't feel discouraged if you cannot see immediately what is questionable about the interpretation of the data. Study each problem to see what other interpretations might be possible. Begin to learn to read between the lines. The answers are given in Appendix A.

1. GUNS DON'T KILL PEOPLE, PEOPLE KILL PEOPLE

The gun lobby says that guns don't kill people, people kill people. This argument is used to refute the desirability of stricter gun-control laws. On the other hand, it is known that the presence of a gun makes it more likely that a given situation will result in a death. Analyze the gun lobby's slogan. What assumption does it make about the causes of human behavior? What would you suggest as an answer to the slogan?

2. REINCARNATION

Many people believe in reincarnation because they have recalled past lives under the effects of hypnosis. They may have had vivid recollections of being a soldier in the Trojan War or of being King Solomon's favorite concubine. How would you test such a claim? How would you suggest an alternative explanation?

3. PREFERENCE TESTS FOR BEER

A series of highly publicized taste tests for brands of beer was conducted live on television. The makers of Schlitz beer took groups of 100 drinkers of a competing brand and had them do blind taste tests of their favorite beer versus Schlitz. In each test approximately 50 drinkers of the competing beer chose Schlitz over their regular brand. The Schlitz brewers claimed that large numbers of drinkers of other beers would prefer Schlitz if they only gave it a chance. How valid was this test?

THE GOALS OF SCIENCE

In Chapter 1 we discussed what science is and what its working assumptions are. From this you already may have an idea of what the goal of psychology is. Broadly speaking, the goal of any science is simply to understand the world. Of course, such a broad statement requires elaboration. The purpose of this chapter is to discuss in some detail how scientists go about trying to understand the world. In order to do this, we break down the goal of understanding into two subgoals: the discovery of regularities and the development of theories.

DISCOVERY OF REGULARITIES

The subgoal of discovering regularities can be considered in two ways: description of behavior and the discovery of lawful relationships among aspects of behavior. For convenience we will consider them separately even though they are two aspects of the same subgoal.

Description

The first step in any science is to describe the phenomena considered to be important for the science to deal with. We must define events and entities such as stimuli and responses, drives and motives, or neuroses and psychoses. This step seems so modest that often we are tempted to skip it and go on to the next one, the discovery of laws. We must have some agreement, though, about just what it is that we are going to study. Before we can find out what causes a person to become a psychopath, we must carefully describe the behavior of the psychopathic person and find out what psychopaths have in common. Only when we have a fairly clear description of the psychopathic personality can we look for factors in the psychopath's background or physiology that caused him or her to become psychopathic.

The importance of description illustrates the close relationship between psychology and the biological sciences. For many years a chief occupation of biologists was the description and classification of living forms. This process is still important today, but only recently have biologists been able to get beyond the descriptive level to study the mechanisms of life processes. Because psychology is a young science, much descriptive work still remains to be done. Perhaps nowhere is this more evident than in the area of personality, where there is fundamental disagreement about the way to go about describing personality. Several quite different approaches to personality description currently exist.

Type theories attempt to classify persons into particular categories or types, much as a botanist would classify a plant. *Trait* theories, on the other hand, see people as differing in amount, rather than kind, on various traits that all persons share to a greater or lesser extent. *Social-learning* theories play down the personal causes of behavior in favor of situational causes. Besides these theories, there are others. Without judging the relative merits of the various theories, we may observe that the large number of conflicting approaches to describing personality reflects a relatively primitive state of science.

Lest anyone think we are emphasizing one area of psychology over another, let us consider an example from perception. Complete lack of agreement exists about the classification of odor qualities. Many odor classification schemes have been proposed over the centuries, but to the present none has demonstrated its superiority over the others. It is fair to say that the absence of a satisfactory odor classification has severely hampered the development of satisfactory theories of smell and lawful relationships among variables.

Description of phenomena is crucially important to a science because it defines the subject matter for which laws are sought and theories are developed. If the descriptive phase of a science is skipped or done carelessly, it may become necessary to return to square one and start over again. All too often experimenters, yielding to the temptation to skip the difficult descriptive phase, jump into the next phase of developing laws. You might say, "I have noticed that my cat seems aggressive at certain times, fighting often with other cats and killing lots of mice. I will study the conditions under which this behavior occurs and look for its causes." What you have overlooked is that fighting with other cats and killing mice are two different kinds of behaviors. The cat that is fighting hisses, arches the back, erects the fur, and so forth. The cat that is hunting and killing a mouse has sleek fur, slinks quietly, and generally shows a different behavior pattern from a cat that is fighting. A careful description of the behaviors in these two situations will reveal that they are not the same class of behaviors. This kind of mistake is made frequently in psychology. Unfortunately there is no simple way to avoid it. You must be alert to the danger and diligent in describing behavior thoughtfully.

Discovering Laws

Law
a statement that certain events are regularly associated with each other in an orderly way

As the describing of behavior progresses, various regularities appear among behavioral events. These regularities form laws of behavior. A **law** is simply a statement that certain events are regularly associated. The frustration-aggression law states that frustration causes aggression. (This law is commonly known as the frustration-aggression hypothesis for reasons that do not concern us here.) In other words, the occurrence of frustration is regularly associated with aggression. Psychology has many examples of laws, because any time a regular association between two variables exists, you have a law.

It is not necessary to have a perfect relation between the two variables in order to have a law. Some laws are statistical; that is, there is a regular relationship between two variables, but the regularity is not perfect. Frustration does not always lead to aggression. It does so with enough regularity, however, to justify calling the association a law. Because of the complexity of behavior, its laws usually are stated in statistical form.

Another important fact about laws is that they do not have to state cause-effect relationships between events; any regular relationship is a law. When we describe the behavior of a fighting cat, we note that the cat hisses, arches the back, and has the fur erect. These events are regularly associated together when a cat fights and so can be considered a law. Therefore, description and discovery of laws are actually part of a single activity. We have separated them in our discussion for reasons of exposition. For example, description of the psychopathic personality achieves the statement of a lawful relationship among the various characteristics of people we call psychopaths.

By extension of this idea, discovery of a law becomes, not the capstone of scientific activity, but one of the early steps. A science that has discovered no laws is no science at all. The meaning of the term *law* will become clearer as we constrast law and theory, below.

BUILDING THEORIES

The ultimate goal of science is the development of a theory to explain the lawful relationships that exist in a particular field. Before we can understand the importance of theory building, we must define a theory and point out some of the misconceptions surrounding the idea of theories.

What Is a Theory?

Theory
a statement or set of statements explaining one or more laws, usually including one indirect concept needed to explain the relationship

We can define the concept of **theory** either broadly or narrowly. Broadly speaking, a theory is a statement or set of statements about the relationships among variables. If the statements concern only a single relationship between variables, we are speaking of a law. However, sometimes a number of laws are tied together into a more general set of statements, which is called a theory. An example is Skinner's theory of operant conditioning that makes statements about the effects of various reinforcement schedules on response rates among other things. Skinnerian theory avoids using nonobserved concepts such as habit strength in favor of simply stating lawful relationships among directly observed variables. This is what Skinner meant when he said that theories of learning are not necessary (1950). In other words, he did not find it necessary to develop theoretical concepts that went beyond observable laws. Skinner's system, however, is a theory in the broader sense of a set of interrelated laws.

More often, the term *theory* is used in a second and stricter sense. According to this view, a theory is a statement or a set of statements about relationships among variables that includes at least one concept that is not directly observed but that is necessary to explain the relationship among the variables. Refer to Table 2–1. The statement at the bottom of the table about Elaine's ability to remember a series of numbers concerns a specific set of observations on one person at one time under particular conditions. This statement has no generality. The middle statement is about the behavior of people in general under similar conditions. This is a general statement that is true whenever certain conditions obtain, therefore we are justified in calling it a law. At the top of the table are statements that are different from the middle or the bottom ones. They depict a brief outline of a theory of memory. This theory introduces concepts, such as short-term memory, that are not present at the level of law. These new concepts are theoretical concepts because they are invoked to explain the relationship between the variables in the middle statement. Specifically, the theory introduces the concept of short-term memory, which is said to be a stage in the processing of information into permanent form. All information to be

TABLE 2–1 Relationship of fact, law, and theory.

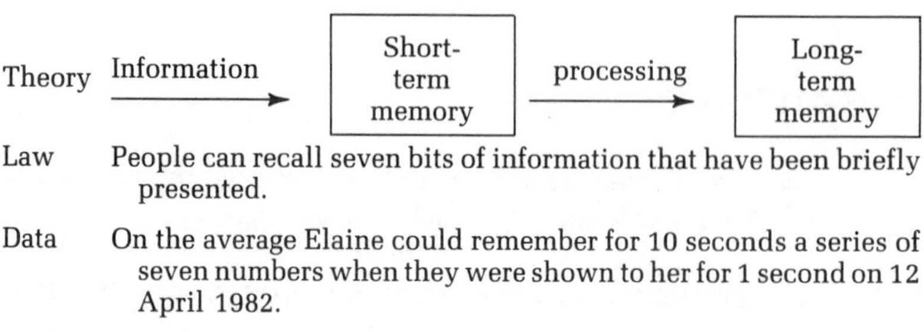

Theory	Information → Short-term memory → processing → Long-term memory
Law	People can recall seven bits of information that have been briefly presented.
Data	On the average Elaine could remember for 10 seconds a series of seven numbers when they were shown to her for 1 second on 12 April 1982.

remembered is held for a while in short-term memory before being transferred into long-term memory. Short-term memory is a theoretical concept because it is not seen or measured directly but must be inferred from behavior. This stage of processing can be inferred from several bases. Among the more important is the fact that only about seven items can be held briefly in memory after they have been presented together once, as when we remember a telephone number that we have just looked up. If more than about seven numbers are presented together, some of them are lost. In our long-term memory, on the other hand, no such limitation exists on the number of things we can recall. So short-term memory clearly is different from long-term memory in its limited capacity to hold information. Psychology makes use of a number of unobservable concepts such as short-term memory in developing theories of behavior.

Note that short-term memory is never observed directly. No single way of measuring its effects defines the concept completely. Theoretical concepts are not observed directly. They can be defined only indirectly by reference to events that are directly observed. A theoretical concept is an invention of the scientist to account for laws of behavior. To take an example from physics, no one has ever seen an electron. It is a theoretical concept invented to account for particular laws of physics.

Theories and Experiments

Talking about theories sometimes seems—well—theoretical. We do experiments in order to understand the world and to develop theories. But how do experiments and theories relate to one another? Actually, the relationship is quite close, as shown in Figure 2–1, which is based on a similar figure by Coombs, Raiffa, and Thrall (1954). We start with the real world in the top of the figure. From the real world we make two abstractions. Going to the right, we devise some theory, however primitive. Then we make predictions by logical deductions from the theory. Going to the left, we begin with the real world and abstract from it an experimental design. Then, putting the design into effect, we carry out the experiment and obtain the empirical data. The next step is to compare the results of the

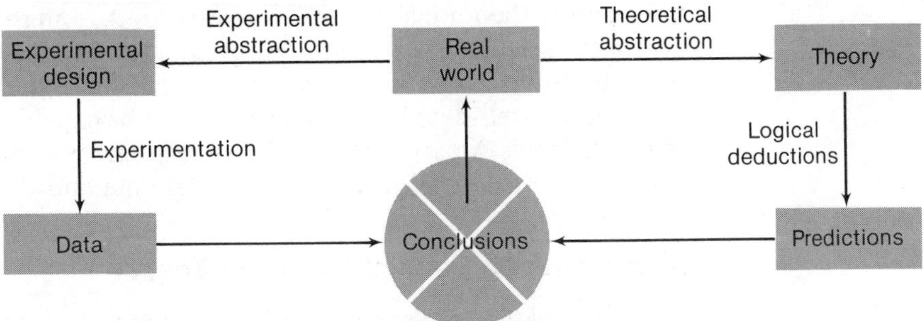

FIGURE 2–1. Illustration of the relationship between theory and experiment.

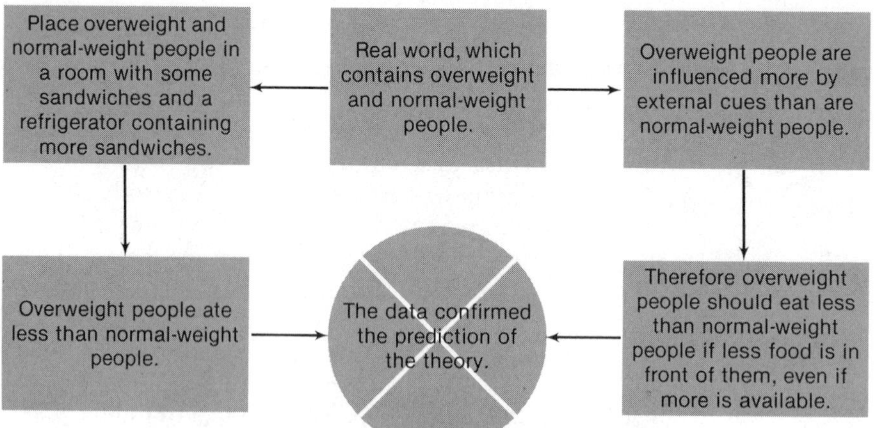

FIGURE 2–2. Application of the relationship between theory and experiment.

experiment to the predictions of the theory. If they match, we say that the theory is confirmed. If they do not, the theory is disconfirmed. Although this might seem the end of the process, ordinarily it represents only one cycle in a continuous process. If the theory is confirmed, then other predictions of the theory may be tested in another experiment. Or, the theory may be elaborated to make other testable predictions. Figure 2–2 illustrates how this model applies to Nisbett's experiment on the eating behavior of overweight people discussed earlier.

If the theory is disconfirmed, again there are two options. The theory may be modified to account for the new data, or the experiment may be changed to make it a more sensitive test of the theory. In any case we can see that after the conclusions are drawn from any experiment, the next step is to go back to the real world and decide whether to modify the theory or the experimental method or both. So the arrow going from the conclusions back to the real world represents the fact that science is a continuous process.

Seldom, if ever, does a single experiment settle all questions about a scientific problem. Scientists continuously develop theories to account for phenomena in the real world, and they continuously test these theories by conducting experiments. Figure 2–2 illustrates that science cannot be either purely theoretical or purely empirical. An interest in both must be present for science to progress. To be sure, sometimes there is very little theory to guide research and we experiment more or less randomly. At other times a well-developed theory may not be capable of being tested by today's methods. Most of the time, however, there is a continuous interplay between the development of experimental data and theory.

Other Common Uses of the Term *Theory*

It is important to contrast our definition of theory with some common ways of using the term. These uses can cause misunderstanding of the true significance of theory in science.

Theory and fact. We often hear theory used in distinction to fact. For example, someone might say, "Is it a fact that Lee Harvey Oswald acted alone in assassinating President Kennedy or is it only a theory?" This usage confuses a theory with a hypothesis, which is proved either to be a "fact" or to be wrong. Actually, theories never become facts even when they are accepted as true by everyone. Take the duplicity theory of vision. This theory was developed to account for a large number of facts about vision, having to do with the differences between the functions of rods and cones: color versus black-and-white vision, day versus night vision, and so forth. The term *duplicity* means that the retina is duplex; that is, it has two separate systems, the rod system and the cone system. Now, duplicity theory is universally accepted as true (to be a "fact"). Still, it has the status of a theory because it serves a theory's function of organizing a large body of facts (laws) into a single explanatory system. To go back to Oswald, if it were ever proved beyond a shadow of a doubt that he acted alone, we would then say that the single-assassin theory has been proved to be true.

Theory and practice. Another popular usage of the term *theory* is in statements like the following: In theory students should learn better if they expect unannounced quizzes, but in practice it doesn't work that way. This usage drives a wedge between theory and the real world, as if theories exist in books and practice in the real world. The hope of any theorist is to explain events in the real world. The problem in the quiz example arises because the real-world situation contains complications not accounted for by the theory. The theory behind giving unannounced quizzes is true, but other factors in the real classroom situation make the prediction of the theory uncertain for that case.

THE ROLE OF THEORIES

We have emphasized the development of theories as a major goal of science. But why are theories so important? Theories play two crucial roles in the development of a science: (1) organizing knowledge and explaining laws and (2) predicting new laws.

Organizing Knowledge and Explaining Laws

First, theories serve to organize knowledge and explain laws. In the absence of a theory we simply have a collection of descriptions and some laws. The theory pulls these together into a unified framework. According to philosophers of science, this relating of individual events to laws and laws to theories constitutes scientific explanation. The individual fact is explained by being shown to be an instance of a general law. In turn, the law is explained by its relation to the theory. We explain Elaine's inability to remember more than seven numbers as an instance of the law of the limited nature of short-term memory. We can go up one level and explain the limited nature of short-term memory in terms of the way information is processed from a short-term store into a permanent form according to memory theory. Explanation is a process of relating more particular concepts to more general concepts. The theory serves to explain the laws that have been found.

The better the theory the more events and laws it can explain. We would have little interest in a theory that would explain the behavior of only a few individuals under a limited set of circumstances. In addition, the more specific and precise is the explanation, the better the theory. For this reason theories that are stated mathematically are considered better than theories that state relationships only in general terms. Of course, these two considerations are often in conflict. A broad general theory can explain more laws and instances but with less precision than a less ambitious theory. During the first half of this century, psychology was characterized by many broad theories, such as those of Freud, Hull, and others, that were designed to encompass much of behavior. More recently, psychologists have devoted themselves to theories that are less ambitious in scope but have greater explanatory precision, such as theories of speech perception or problem solving.

Predicting New Laws

The second role of theories is to predict new laws. A fruitful theory not only will explain many different laws that previously were unrelated, but it will suggest places to look for new laws as well. A particularly good example of a new law or phenomenon predicted by a theory is provided in an experiment by Mark Lepper, David Greene, and Richard Nisbett (1973). According to self-perception theory, people understand their own behavior on much the same basis as would other persons—by observing the behavior and attributing it to observable causes. In a common experimental situation a person is underpaid for participating in a dull task. Afterward, this person tends to report enjoying the task more than a person who was paid adequately for doing it. According to the theory, the person says something like the following: "I did that task for only $1. It really must have been interesting." Lepper, Greene, and Nisbett concluded that the theory should also predict the opposite effect. If a person were paid to do something that was fun, it would become less fun. They had nursery school children color with Magic Markers. Some expected to be rewarded for coloring and others did not. Those who expected a reward were found in a later test to have lost interest in coloring. The others lost interest to a lesser degree. Thus, self-perception theory predicted a law that later was found to be true: Rewarding a person for having fun can make it less fun.

This example is notable because the effect was counterintuitive; that is, it would not have been predicted by common sense. For generations teachers have been giving gold stars to students for good work. The results of the experiment we've just discussed would indicate that rewarding good school work actually may make school more boring.

Other Goals

We have stressed theoretical explanation as the ultimate goal of science. On the other hand, many books say that the goals of psychology are description, prediction, and control. We have already discussed description as a goal. Prediction and control actually are part of the describing process. If we have done our job of description well, we have established laws of behavior. The knowledge of these laws will allow us to predict the occurrence of behavior. If we can predict behavior, we are also able to control it if we have control over the events that cause it. So description, prediction, and control are three aspects of the goal of discovering regularities of behavior.

HYPOTHESES IN SCIENCE

Hypothesis a provisional assertion assumed to be true for the purpose of testing its validity

If developing laws and theories is the goal of science, how do we go about that process? Let us return for a moment to the example of self-perception theory, which deals with how people interpret their own behavior. Lepper et al. said, If people are paid to do something that is fun, it will become less fun. What Lepper et al. did was to make a **hypothesis.** A hypothesis is a statement that is assumed to be true for the purpose of testing its validity. A hypothesis can be put in the form of an if-then statement: If A is true, then B should follow. The statement must be one that is either true or false: After people are paid to do something that is fun, it either will or will not become less fun; it cannot be both less fun and not less fun.

In addition to being either true or false, scientific hypotheses are always statements that can be tested empirically. A hypothesis that cannot be tested is a poor scientific hypothesis. The hypothesis that people who colonize outer space will develop a certain new form of civilization would not be a good scientific hypothesis, at least until it is possible to test it. The hypothesis is either true or false but it cannot be tested at the present time. Perhaps in the future we will test the hypothesis, but in the meantime it has little scientific value.

A scientific hypothesis is of the following form: If we make certain observations under particular conditions, and a given theory is correct, then we should find the following results. In other fields, such as mathematics, hypotheses can be tested logically, but a scientific hypothesis must be capable of empirical testing and therefore empirical confirmation or disconfirmation.

In the instance of Lepper et al. the hypothesis concerned a law that was predicted from the theory. In other cases the theory may be the focus of the hypothesis. Take an example from law enforcement: Police may hypothesize that the butler did it. This is a hypothesis that states a theory to be tested: We are working on the theory that the butler did it. In actuality, however, we must not suppose that a particular hypothesis can concern only a theory or a law, to the exclusion of the other. A hypothesis about a law involves certain assumptions about the theory underlying the law. Conversely, it is impossible to test a theory without also testing some lawful prediction of the theory. Lepper et al. might well have said, If the theory of self-perception is correct, *and* if people are paid to do something that is fun, then it will become less fun. This statement contains one hypothesis about the theory and another one about the law. If the prediction is not confirmed when it is tested empirically, either the law or the theory may be false, or both.

All scientific research, then, is designed to test at least one hypothesis. Much of the rest of this book can be considered a discussion of how one makes and tests scientific hypotheses in the field of psychology.

DEFINING THEORETICAL CONCEPTS

We said earlier that science attempts to develop theoretical explanations of phenomena that occur in the world. Developing theoretical explanations is such a complex activity that breaking down the processes into definite steps is difficult. Sometimes we start with a theory and look for phenomena that should occur if the theory were true. At other times we begin with a phenomenon for which we have no explanation and try to develop a satisfactory theory. We now take up the question of how we build theories.

The first and most important question is the one of how we go about inferring the existence of the theoretical entities, such as short-term memory, that we develop to account for the facts of behavior. On what basis are we permitted to construct theoretical concepts such as short-term memory, learning, hunger, and so forth? How do these supposedly scientific concepts differ from nonscientific concepts?

To answer these questions, we must recall that science deals with objective knowledge—those events that are available to every person. **Operationism,** which is associated with physicist Percy Bridgman, states that scientific concepts must be public in the same way that scientific data are public. According to Bridgman, a theoretical concept must be tied to observable operations that any person can observe or perform. If a concept cannot be tied to particular operations, then it is not a scientific concept. Take the concept of the will of God. If we say that everything that happens

Operationism a view that scientific concepts must be defined in terms of observable operations

is the will of God, then the concept is without operational meaning. If it should rain tomorrow, we might say the rain was God's will. On the other hand, if it should not rain tomorrow, we likewise conclude that not raining was God's will. We have no way to define which future events would be according to God's will and which would not. Few persons would say that God's will is a scientific concept.

Let us consider another example. Some people believe that psychic ability (for example, extrasensory perception) is a scientific concept. Here the problem is that the only way of defining psychic ability is for certain types of unlikely data to occur. No conditions are known that are favorable or unfavorable to the demonstration of psychic ability; that is, no operations exist that increase or decrease the probability of an event that would be defined as reflecting psychic ability. Psychic perceptions take place according to no lawful operations. Most psychologists conclude that the concept of psychic ability has no operational definition and therefore is not a scientific concept. Operationism, then, strictly limits the kind of concepts with which science can deal. If there is no way of defining the concept according to observable operations, the concept is barred from science.

Operationism has a further, more specific meaning by which scientific concepts are defined according to the operations by which they are measured. If you were to read an experiment on the effect of hunger on learning in rats, you probably would want to know what the author meant by hunger. In the methods section of the paper, you might read that rats were made hungry by being deprived of food for a certain number of hours, perhaps 23. You would say to yourself, "Ah, when the author says the rats were hungry, he means that they had no food for 23 hours." The statement of what the author did to induce hunger is called an **operational definition** of hunger. Of first and crucial importance in an operational definition is to state a procedure, or operation, that specifies what the concept means. For the purposes of the experiment, your particular way of producing hunger in the rat defines the concept of hunger.

Operational definition a statement of the precise meaning of a procedure or concept within an experiment

As important as an operational definition of a concept is, it has been misunderstood and misused in psychology. The principal misuse is to make a trivial definition of a concept, then to attempt to build a theory on it. You may believe that twiddling a button on one's clothing is a sign of anxiety. Probably this would not be as good a measure of anxiety as the Galvanic Skin Response or the Taylor Manifest Anxiety Scale. Experiments that relied on the button-twiddling measure probably would not be as good tests of an anxiety theory as those that used one of the other measures.

Another misuse of the concept of operational definition is to consider that every measure of a concept is independent of every other measure. According to this view, making a rat hungry by starving it for 23 hours is a different type of hunger from making the rat hungry by feeding it just enough to maintain 80 percent of its ad lib weight (the weight it would maintain without any restriction on its eating). It is true that these two operational definitions of hunger may produce somewhat different results in particular situations because of peculiarities inherent in the methods of depriving the animal. Yet, by using different methods of producing hunger, we hope that a common core of knowledge about hunger will result. Using different ways of homing in on a concept via different operational definitions is called **converging operations.** Each new way of producing the concept of hunger will rule out one possible objection to the explanation until a high degree of confidence can be reached. The method of converging operations is much like the way a surveyor locates a point on the ground. The point is marked from two or more independent locations in order to get a good fix on it by triangulation. The larger the number of independent locations from which the surveyor knows the distance and direction to the new point, the better it is located.

Converging operations using different operational definitions to arrive at the meaning of a concept

Today operationism no longer is adhered to in the strict sense that Bridgman advocated. Now it is appreciated that some of the meaning of a theoretical concept may be defined by its relationship to a larger theory of which it is a part. Hunger, for example, may not be defined completely by any of the ways of measuring it, or even by all of them together. Some of its meaning may come from a theory of motivation requiring that hunger have certain properties. What we must remember about operationism today is to define carefully the terms we use so that their meaning is clear with respect to events in the world that may be observed objectively and with respect to the theories we develop to explain those events.

SCIENTIFIC PROGRESS

Laypersons commonly believe that science progresses in a straightforward manner by accumulating knowledge, much as a building is built brick by brick. That this stereotype is mistaken has been shown convincingly by Thomas Kuhn (1962). Basic to Kuhn's thought is the concept of a **paradigm,** which is a pervasive way of thinking about a branch of science that includes all of the assumptions and theories that are accepted as true by a group of scientists. During what he calls normal science, nearly all scientists accept the same paradigm and work under its influence. Eventually, problems develop that cannot be explained without difficulty by the paradigm. These anomalies cause a crisis, during which other paradigms are created that compete with the original paradigm. A new paradigm will be accepted when it accounts more successfully for empirical data than did the old paradigm. According to Kuhn, the course of science is not a steady progress toward a goal. Rather, it consists of phases of normal science, each dominated by a single paradigm, alternating with revolutions that install new paradigms that last as long as each paradigm is reasonably successful in accounting for empirical data.

Paradigm a set of laws, theories, methods, and applications that form a scientific research tradition, for example Pavlovian conditioning

Kuhn's concept has gained widespread acceptance among scientists because it captures the reality of conflict among competing theories and the often acrimonious debates that take place among scientific camps. His viewpoint also accounts for some proverbs about science, such as the idea that a theory is not rejected because it is disproved but because a better theory displaces it.

More recently, Larry Laudan (1977) has taken issue with some of Kuhn's ideas. Laudan emphasizes the problem-solving nature of science. He believes that theories are developed to solve both empirical and conceptual problems. A theory comes to be preferred over another when it solves more problems than the other. Kuhn, in contrast, says a theory is accepted when it accounts for more empirical data than its predecessor. Laudan cites his view—that the ability of a theory to handle a conceptual problem is a legitimate criterion for evaluating the theory—as a factor in scientists' more frequently preferring one theory over others. Often, Laudan states, conceptual problems that scientists consider important relate to concepts that do not enter into scientific theories themselves. Social, ethical, and theological problems, for example, have been given weight by scientists in evaluating scientific theories.

Kuhn, on the other hand, believes that only empirical data can be used to evaluate theories. Therefore, much of what motivates scientists to prefer one theory over another must be considered irrational. Laudan's view seems to be more faithful to the way scientists actually go about their work. If conceptual problems legitimately influence the choice of theories, then the behavior of scientists can be considered rational in this regard.

SERENDIPITY

"Here [is] a first principle not formally recognized by scientific methodologists: When you run onto something interesting, drop everything else and study it" (Skinner, 1956, p. 223).

We said earlier that doing science does not involve mechanically applying a pat formula called *the scientific method*. Science is a creative activity that is as varied as the people who practice it. As Arthur Bachrach put it, "People don't usually do research the way people who write books about research say that people do research" (1962, p. vii). Capturing in a book exactly what doing research is like is difficult because what people write down as the way they do research often is different from how they really do it. One of the major ways in which experimental psychology books deviate from the reality of research is in not paying enough attention to the role of hunch and luck in research. Perhaps we are embarrassed to admit that our recognition rests on a stroke of luck. Perhaps it is impossible to teach people how to have hunches and follow them productively. I hope

Serendipity
the gift of finding valuable or pleasing things not sought for

not because those ideas are behind the term **serendipity,** a word heard often in discussions of research. Serendipity is defined as the gift of discovering desirable things that one was not searching for. The word comes from a Persian fairy tale *The Three Princes of Serendip* in which the characters were always stumbling onto things they were not looking for.

Rather than attempting to list rules for developing the gift of serendipity, we will simply note that serendipity plays an important role in developing scientific ideas. A breakthrough in a problem often comes because the investigator notices something peculiar happening and becomes more intrigued by exploring that than what he was working on previously. B. F. Skinner's quotation at the beginning of this section describes the process of serendipity. In the article from which the quotation is taken, "A Case History in Scientific Method," Skinner describes how he used "accidents" and curiosity to lead him to his famous discoveries.

We will mention only two of the many important discoveries that were serendipitous. In the 1950s much interest developed in the functions of a part of the brain known as the reticular formation, the importance of which for behavior was only becoming apparent. James Olds (1973) was attempting to find out whether mild electrical stimulation to the reticular formation of rats would facilitate learning. Olds permitted rats with electrodes aimed at their reticular formation to explore a large enclosure. When they approached a certain place, he stimulated them with electricity. He noticed that the rats would return to the place where they received the stimulation, as if it were pleasurable to them. Eventually, with Peter Milner, he rigged up an apparatus by which the rats could press a bar to stimulate themselves. This self-stimulation was found to be an extremely potent reinforcer (Olds & Milner, 1954). This experiment gave rise to much research on the physiological basis for reward. Not incidentally, Olds's original electrode had missed the reticular formation and instead was located in the septal area, about 4 millimeters away.

A recent example of serendipity comes from the use of tail pinch in rats as an experimental model of stress-related behaviors. For some time scientists have known that certain kinds of stressors, such as electrical shock or presence of a rival male, would cause animals to engage in certain unrelated behaviors, such as sexual behavior, grooming, and so forth. Seymour Antelman and others (for example, Antelman & Szechtman, 1975) showed that a nonpainful tail pinch reliably caused a wide range of behaviors, depending on the situation. On each of 4,000 rats they placed a padded tail clamp. Within a few seconds after placement, over 95 percent of the rats began to eat even though just before the experiment they had been given all the food they wanted. If the food was replaced by a palatable fluid, the rat began drinking. If a female rat was present, a male began copulating (Antelman & Caggiula, 1977). These tail-pinch-induced behaviors have been widely studied as models of stress-induced behavior, such as compulsive eating. The discovery of tail-pinch-induced behavior was a serendipitous finding. Antelman describes the process:*

> The ability of animals to show eating (and other motivated behaviors as well) in response to the stress of mild (nonpainful) tail pressure was first described by Henry Szechtman and me in 1973. This phenomenon was found quite by accident while attempting to induce rotation in rats following drug treatment. One of our rats not showing the desired behavior was tail-pinched, since mild stress can often induce rotation in such animals. This rat was on a cart with another animal and when pinched it did not rotate but instead began to lick the tail of the other animal each time the pinch was applied. When food pellets were substituted for the second animal, tail pinch caused stimulation-bound eating. At first we thought that tail-pinching-induced phenomena were related to the drug we had given. It soon became apparent that this was not the case. In the years since our discovery, thousands of undrugged animals have been tested and it is obvious that tail pinch can induce eating in almost 90% of them.
>
> The technique is now regularly used in laboratories throughout the world and tail-pinch-induced obesity (demonstrated by Neil Rowland and me) has gained widespread acceptance as a model for stress-related overeating in humans.

SCIENCE AS A PROBLEM-SOLVING ACTIVITY

Science often has been described as a problem-solving activity. Psychological science is a way of answering the *why* or *how* of behavior. In this sense, we can see that psychology springs from the basic curiosity about the world that is in all of us. The earliest stages of psychological science sought questions that appeared to every person: How do we gain knowledge of the world? How do we learn our way in unfamiliar places? As psychology developed, questions began to emerge from the experimental situations that had been developed in response to earlier questions. In this way existing theories suggested new findings and new findings required changes in theories.

Psychology, as every other science, has developed areas of specialization that seem far removed from the initial questions. Whereas simple curiosity about the world may motivate the initial stages of research, problems arising from trying to fit theories to data become the second motivation for scientific activity. Of course, these stages are not distinct and separate. There is some primitive theory behind the simplest curiosity,

*S. M. Antelman 1982; personal communication.

and even the most sophisticated scientists can be motivated by simple curiosity.

Even when a science no longer is in its infancy, curiosity can strongly influence its direction. For many years after the behaviorist revolution of the early 1900s, problems about consciousness were pushed into the background of psychology. Then with the rise of popular interest in consciousness and eastern philosophy during the sixties, psychologists began to look more closely at the questions of consciousness. So we see that science is never totally immune to the curiosity and interest of the average person.

Not all problems spring from simple curiosity or from conflicts between theory and data, however. Another motivation for science is the need to solve practical problems. As Alphonse Chapanis notes, "The field of mental testing started with a problem put to a French elementary school teacher; the field of speech communication started from some problems raised and first attacked by telephone engineers; . . . and some of the best work in color vision has been done to construct a usable system of specifying colors for engineers, business, and industry" (1971, pp. 950–51).

Moreover, many of the important theories of psychology developed from applied research. One of the most successful theories in recent psychology is signal detection theory, which explains how people detect weak signals in the presence of noise. This theory was developed to understand such applied problems as how sonar operators react to targets. The theory has been applied successfully not only to many areas of sensory psychology but to memory and motivation problems as well.

Finally, we should point out that some scientific psychology has no interest in theory at all. Considerable research is devoted to problems that are purely practical, such as determining which teaching method is best or what advertising campaign will be most successful. The experimenters have no intention of testing a theory, only of finding out what method works best. On the other hand, such research often gives rise to theories as conflicting data are obtained and people try to make sense out of them.

PSEUDOSCIENCE

Pseudopsychology any of various disciplines or movements regarded as psychology but not meeting the criteria of psychology

In this chapter we have been discussing several topics that put experimental psychology in context and show some of its limitations. One way to do that effectively is to contrast psychology with **pseudopsychology.** A list of all of the pseudopsychologies that exist today would be long and controversial, but many people would include parapsychology, biorhythms, astrology, and much of the human potential movement. The popularity of these pseudopsychologies merits our discussing the hallmarks of pseudoscience. We will use parapsychology, the most respectable of the pseudopsychologies, to illustrate our points. You may compare the following characteristics of pseudoscience with the discussion of the nature of science in Chapter 1. You will see that in general parapsychology fails to meet the various characteristics of science. Use these characteristics as a checklist for identifying a pseudoscience. They are not mutually exclusive; some will overlap others.

Lack of Precise Definition of Terms

A good example of imprecise definition is the term *occult* as used by many to define an area of study. The term simply means hidden or poorly understood. Those who use it do not indicate why the subject is occult or whether the information once was known and now is lost, whether it is known only to a special class, or whether nobody understands it.

Definition of Terms by Exclusion

A good example of definition by exclusion is *extrasensory perception*. Because perception, as normally understood, involves the senses by definition, the term *extrasensory perception*, strictly speaking, is absurd. If it means perception by means of receptors that now are not known or understood, such definition would include many other processes of little interest to parapsychologists, such as bird migration. Psychic scientist Thelma Moss defines parapsychology as "anything for which we do not have a material explanation" (Allan, 1975, p. 5). Taking this definition seriously would include most of the phenomena studied by scientists in all fields.

Lack of Lawfulness

As we said earlier, a science that has discovered no laws is no science at all. Extrasensory perception (ESP) is such a nonscience. In brief, there is no convincing evidence that ESP even exists. In 1882, the year of the founding of the (British) Society for Psychical Research, Henry Sidgwick, its first president, spoke of the task of finding convincing evidence for ESP. "We must drive the objector into the position of being forced either to admit the phenomena as inexplicable, at least by him, or to accuse the investigators either of lying or cheating or of a blindness or forgetfulness incompatible with any intellectual condition except an absolute idiocy" (Hansel, 1966, p. 27).

Nearly one hundred years later Martin Johnson, Chairman of the Parapsychology Laboratory of the University of Utrecht, Netherlands, speaking to an audience in Chapel Hill, North Carolina, one of the world centers of ESP research, said: "At this stage, parapsychology is badly in need of a repeatable experiment" (1976, p. 151). Similar statements can be found in almost any issue of the *Journal of Parapsychology* or the *Proceedings of the American Society for Psychical Research*. R. A. McConnell says,

"The result [of the psychological nature of ESP] is a poor record on repeatability" (1977, p. 430).

If there are no repeatable experiments, it follows that there are no lawful relationships that can be stated about the occurrence of ESP. It is not possible to state the conditions under which ESP occurs. There are no personality types, age groups, or nationalities that tend to show ESP. Distance is not a factor in ESP performance. These circumstances could be interpreted as proving that ESP does not conform to the usual physical laws as expressed, for example, by the law of the decrease in effectiveness of a signal with distance.

More reasonable is the notion that there is no regularity of any sort to be found and, hence, no stateable law. Some persons believe that a condition of quiet rest is conducive to ESP. On the other hand, others maintain that ESP works best under states of extreme stress. Some say that ESP is a primitive ability that we are evolving away from as our senses become keener. Still others believe that ESP is an evolutionarily advanced form of communication that will become more prominent over evolutionary time.

Lack of Theoretical Agreement

Theories are developed to explain lawful regularities. It follows that pseudosciences might be short on theories because they are short on facts. Actually the reverse is true. Literally dozens of theories of parapsychology exist, but they bear little relation to one another and, more importantly, to the rest of science. They are largely castles in the air. A recent handbook reviews current parapsychology theories and states: "We cannot produce a theory of psi (parapsychology) which is both comprehensive and credible. The field is strewn with dead and dying hypotheses and desperate expedients" (Chari, 1977, p. 806). The article concludes that there is "a complete lack of anything remotely like an explanatory theory of ESP (extra-sensory perception) and PK (psychokinesis)" (p. 819). This is a fair and modest assessment. Dozens of theories of ESP exist, every one as capable of explaining the data as any other. Ramakrishna Rao surveyed 20 of them and concluded: "While none [of the theories] is entirely satisfactory in explaining psi, each of them seems to contain some fruitful ideas. . . . The need of the day is for theory and research to go hand in hand" (1977, p. 344). It is unheard of for a scientific field to have dozens of theories, each of which is equally well supported by evidence. The absence of theory and empirical laws is the main reason most scientists conclude that ESP is a pseudoscience.

Exaggerated Importance of a Few People

Although there are leaders in every field of endeavor, pseudosciences are characterized by the dominance of one person or a few persons whose work is taken as revolutionary and fundamental to further progress in the field. A science that is the province of one or a few persons is almost certain to be a pseudoscience. Most sciences have a historical continuity with science as a whole and have enough people working in the field to prevent domination by one person. This characteristic of dominance is not as typical of parapsychology as it is of, say, dianetics, which is the brainchild of L. Ron Hubbard, or the orgonomy of Wilhelm Reich. Nevertheless, J. B. Rhine was the virtual guru of the parapsychology movement for many years. In addition, a few "gifted" people like Uri Geller have received attention because they have been able to produce certain effects without admitting to the use of magic.

SUMMARY

1. The goal of science is to understand the world.
2. Understanding the world can be broken down into two subgoals: the discovery of regularities and the development of theories.
3. Discovering regularities can be considered as the description of behavior and the discovery of lawful relationships among aspects of behavior.
4. Description of behavior is of crucial importance because it defines the subject matter for which laws are to be sought and theories developed.
5. A law is a statement that certain events are regularly associated with one another.
6. The ultimate goal of science is the development of a theory to explain lawful relationships that exist in a particular field.
7. Broadly speaking, a theory is a set of statements about the relationships among variables.
8. More narrowly, a theory is a set of statements about relationships among variables that includes at least one concept that is not directly observed.
9. Theories guide research and in turn are modified by research in a continuous cycle.
10. Theories should not be contrasted with facts; a theory remains a theory even if it is accepted as true.
11. Theories have two main functions in science: first, organizing knowledge and explaining laws, and second, predicting new laws.
12. A hypothesis is a statement that is assumed to be true for the purpose of testing its validity.
13. A good scientific hypothesis must be capable of empirical testing.
14. Operationism is the doctrine that scientific concepts must be tied to observable operations.
15. Although it is important to define theoretical concepts operationally, it is not held that an operational definition completely defines a concept.

16. Progress in science often involves a major shift in theories and assumptions, known as a paradigm shift, rather than a steady accumulation of knowledge.
17. Many discoveries in science come about by serendipity, rather than the application of a certain formula for the scientific method.
18. Science can be thought of as an activity that is aimed at the satisfaction of curiosity or at the solution of theoretical or practical problems.
19. Pseudoscience is activity that claims to be science but shows certain non-science characteristics, such as: the lack of precise definition of terms, definition of terms by exclusion, lack of lawful relationships among variables, lack of theoretical agreement, and the exaggerated importance of a few key people.

SUGGESTIONS FOR FURTHER READING

Hempel, C. G. *Philosophy of natural science.* Englewood Cliffs, N.J.: Prentice-Hall, 1966. This excellent brief introduction to the philosophy of science has a particularly good discussion of law, theory, and the nature of scientific explanation.

Marx, M. H., & Goodson, F. E. (Eds.). *Theories in contemporary psychology.* New York: Macmillan, 1976. This edited volume contains many of the classic papers on the philosophy of science as it relates specifically to psychological theories. The discussion is on a high level but is essential for serious students.

READING BETWEEN THE LINES

The following problems are presented for you to solve. See Reading Between the Lines in Chapter 1 for an introduction to them. The answers are provided in Appendix A.

4. IMAGINE THAT ESP DOES OCCUR

One way to evaluate the hypothesis of ESP is to imagine what the world would be like if ESP existed. What does this exercise tell you about ESP?

5. THE AUTHORITARIAN PERSONALITY

After World War II a group of researchers (Adorno, Frenkel-Brunswik, Levinson, & Sanford, 1950) were concerned to find the causes of anti-Semitism and the compliance the German population showed toward Hitler. The researchers hypothesized that a personality type existed that lent itself to authoritarianism, antidemocratic beliefs, and racism. Using specially developed questionnaires, they gave tests of "authoritarianism" to a large sample of people. Those receiving especially high or low scores were interviewed about their childhood experiences. Persons with high scores more often were found to come from families with high status concern and repressive discipline procedures. According to the authors, children in these families learned to repress their faults and to project them onto minority groups. They also repressed feelings of anger and of hatred toward their parents, and these feelings also were projected onto the minority groups. Therefore, the authoritarian persons had a tendency to be prejudiced against Jews, blacks, and so forth and to show discrimination toward them.

Can you think of another explanation of the causes of the correlation between authoritarian attitudes and childhood experiences?

3

VARIABLES

In Chapter 2 we discussed how scientists develop laws and theories to explain the phenomena they observe. In order for us to do this, we must move from general statements about broad classes of behavior to specific examples of that behavior. The phenomenon we want to study can be any event in all of its complexity and variety. When we begin to study the event experimentally, we must strip away some of this complexity. In a word, we take the phenomenon and turn it into one or more variables.

Variable
aspect of a testing condition that can change or take on different characteristics with different conditions

A **variable** is some property of an event in the world that has been measured. Variables are attributes of phenomena and thus belong to the world. Reducing a phenomenon to variables focuses the researcher's attention on specific events out of the many that may be related to the phenomenon. In the example of coloring by nursery school children discussed in Chapter 2, the phenomenon of interest was that rewards make coloring less fun. In order to study this phenomenon, it was necessary to designate a certain class of events as the variable to be measured, ignoring other events. Lepper et al. (1973) studied the amount of time spent coloring, rather than how many times the children expressed delight in coloring or the expressions on their faces while they colored and so forth.

In this chapter we will study some topics related to variables. First we will make several distinctions that are important for psychology among types of variables. Then we will discuss the concept of measurement, the depiction of variables on a graph, and the interactions among variables.

Before we discuss types of variables, we must show how the variables of a study relate to the theoretical concepts, as discussed in Chapter 2. Because the variables exist in the world, and the theory is a product of your imagination, you must make certain assumptions in order to relate the two to each other. These assumptions are guy ropes that tie a theory to the real world. The variables are tangible: for example, duration, frequency, or intensity of bar presses; items checked on a questionnaire; murders committed; or books written. The theoretical concept is intangible: hunger, motivation, anxiety, and so forth.

Suppose your theory says that increasing anxiety will increase the affiliation motive. In order to test this theory, you must take the theoretical concepts of anxiety and affiliation motive and relate them to variables in the real world. The theory is an abstract statement. You must bring it down to cases. You can measure anxiety by the Taylor Manifest Anxiety Scale and affiliation by how close subjects sit to each other in the experiment. These two measures constitute the variables of the study. It is the scores on the variables of anxiety and distance apart that are related to one another as tests of the hypothesis. The relationship between the variables is taken as providing support for or against the particular theory that generated the experiment.

TYPES OF VARIABLES

In order to understand how variables are used and discussed in psychological research, you must understand several distinctions that are made among types of variables.

Independent and Dependent Variables

Dependent variable a measure of the behavior of the subject that reflects the effects of the independent variable

Independent variable the condition manipulated or selected by the experimenter to determine its effect on behavior

The most basic distinction among variables is between independent variables and dependent variables. The **dependent variable** is a measure of the behavior of the subject. In the language of stimulus-response psychology, it is the *response*. We call it the dependent variable because it depends (we hope) on the value of another variable (the independent variable). In Chapter 2 we said that one of the goals of science is to find lawful relationships among events in the world. It is between the dependent and independent variables that these relationships are sought.

The **independent variable** is one that is believed to cause some change in the value of the dependent variable. It is the *stimulus* of stimulus-response psychology. The term *stimulus*, in its most general use, is equivalent to a *cause*. According to the famous frustration-aggression law, frustration causes aggression. If we were interested in the effects of poverty on crime, we might apply the frustration-aggression law. We might consider poverty to be a source of frustration and thus a cause of crime, even though not every poor person becomes a criminal. Poverty could be a statistical cause if the percent of poor people who commit crimes was found to be larger than the percent of nonpoor who commit crimes.

The independent variable often may be thought of as what the experimenter does to the subject and the dependent variable as what the subject does back. Although this analogy is true in many cases, sometimes there are independent variables that the experimenter does not manipulate. Examples would be poverty, as mentioned above, or the sex, age, or intelligence quotient (IQ) of the subject. These independent variables cannot be controlled by the experimenter. We will devote Chapter 8 to studies that use such nonmanipulated independent variables.

In some investigations we do not know which are the independent and dependent variables. We may think that there is a relation between violence and watching television. We may have a hard time, though, deciding whether watching violent television programs causes violent behavior or whether a predisposition to violence causes people to watch violent shows. In such investigations, the identification of the independent variable is the whole purpose of the study. This problem is typical of the nonexperimental research discussed in Chapter 10.

Continuous and Discrete Variables

Continuous variable one that falls along a continuum and is not limited to a certain number of values

Discrete variable one that falls into separate categories with no intermediate values possible

Some variables can take any value on a continuum. They are called **continuous variables** because they are not limited to a certain number of values, such as whole numbers, or to separate categories. In principle, you can measure latency, duration, or force of a bar press with any desired precision. In practice, however, the fineness of the measure is limited by the ability of the measuring instrument. **Discrete variables**, on the other hand, are those that fall into distinct categories, as the word *discrete* suggests. Persons are either male or female; subjects can be naive or informed about the experimental hypothesis; stimuli can be auditory or visual.

A variable can be discrete even though boundaries between categories may be fuzzy and classifying particular examples may be difficult. For instance, colors can be classified into red, yellow, green, or violet, even though finer distinctions can be made within colors and some colors can be considered on the border, such as blue-green. Notice that color as a psychological variable is discrete, whereas the underlying physical dimension (wavelength) is continuous.

The distinction between discrete and continuous variables can become important when we start to build theories. For example, theorists debate about taste, asking whether there are only four tastes—salty, sour, sweet, and bitter—or whether all tastes fall along a continuum, with the four basic tastes being merely convenient but arbitrary categories (McBurney & Gent, 1979). For the same reason, keeping in mind the distinction between discrete and continuous variables is necessary in making graphs, as we shall see shortly.

Quantitative and Qualitative Variables

Quantitative variable one that varies in amount

Qualitative variable one that varies in kind

The distinction that some variables are quantitative while others are qualitative is easy to state, even though it may be difficult to apply to particular cases. **Quantitative variables** are those that vary in amount, whereas **qualitative variables** vary in kind. Examples of quantitative variables would be speed of response and loudness. On the other hand, pitch or turning left versus right in a maze would be qualitative variables.

Note that loudness is quantitative, whereas pitch is qualitative. Tones differ in *amount* of loudness but *quality* of pitch. This particular example involves a subtle distinction and is not based on a single criterion. For example, loudness is coded in the nervous system by *amount* of nervous activity, whereas pitch is coded (largely) by activity in *different* neurons. Another distinction, and an important one, is that pitch and loudness follow different laws in certain psychological scaling situations (Stevens, 1975). Many variables that the layperson considers to be discrete and qualitative, the psychologist discovers to be continuous and quantitative: introversion/extroversion, normal/neurotic, or masculinity/femininity.

Physical and Nonphysical Variables

Physical variable aspect of a testing condition that can be defined in physical terms

Nonphysical variable aspect of a testing condition defined in terms of behavior or cognitive processes

Among independent variables, some are simple **physical variables**, such as the intensity of a light or the number of hours of food deprivation. It is easy to construct a graph with one of these physical variables as the independent variable. Other independent variables are of a different sort. They are **nonphysical variables**, or ones not defined directly in physical terms. Some experimenters ask questions that involve the relationship between two nonphysical variables. Suppose that you wanted to know how the preference for sugar related to its sweetness. Preference obviously is nonphysical, but sweetness might seem like a physical variable. Sweetness, however, can be measured only by *tasting* the substance. Preference and sweetness both are nonphysical dimensions and have different relations to concentration:

(1) Sweetness = *f*(Concentration)

This is read, "Sweetness is a function of concentration," where *f* stands for "a function of." For the time being, we can say that "is a function of" means that there is a particular shape of curve on a graph that relates sweetness and concentration. Other letters, g and *h*, are used to indicate other functions; that is, other shapes of curves between variables.

(2) Preference = g(Concentration)

That preference and sweetness are different is shown by the fact that for most people sweetness increases as long as concentration increases. On the other hand, preference is greater for medium concentrations and decreases for concentrations that are stronger. The relation between sweetness and preference would be between two nonphysical variables.

(3) Preference = h(Sweetness)

Sometimes kinds of variables are more difficult to distinguish. Many psychologically important independent variables cannot be specified by any physical stimulus or combination of known dimensions. For instance, what are the physical dimensions underlying the pleasantness of odors, the beauty of faces, or the hostility of an expression? In terms of the type of equations shown above, we would have to write:

Beauty = f(?,?,?,...)

Such variables obviously are important causes of behavior, but they may defy precise physical specification.

Some nonphysical variables operate via the subject's interpretation. The same event in the physical world may mean one thing to Subject A and another thing to Subject B. Remarks by the experimenter will be seen as friendly by one subject and condescending by another. The *interpretation* of the remark becomes a variable for the subject but is not under the control of the experimenter. Thus, we can see that in social psychology an area of difficulty arises that may not exist for a researcher of visual perception who asks the subject whether a light is visible or not. In the visual perception experiment the subject's interpretation of the situation is less likely to significantly affect the outcome. We will talk about subjective interpretation again under the topics of validity and conducting experiments.

MEASUREMENT

All of the types of variables we have been discussing must be measured on some scale. Often we don't give much thought to this process, assuming that it is obvious. However, when we say that a person is an 8 on a scale of 10, we are making assumptions about the scale on which the measurements are made. For example, would a 10 be twice as good looking as a 5?

On the other hand, students may shy away from the mathematics involved in measurement. Some may be uneasy about numbers, while others may be turned off because to them numbers make the subject drier and less human. We cannot escape entirely the mathematics needed to do experimental psychology. The reason is simple. As has often been said, an indication of the scientific progress of a field is the extent to which it states its laws quantitatively.

The ability to state laws quantitatively means that two things are true. First, the phenomenon is regular enough to make a reasonably precise statement of it. Data that are too variable can obscure any underlying lawfulness. It is true that many ingenious techniques exist to uncover the regularities that can lurk in data, but the scientist always strives to make the regularity of the phenomenon as apparent as possible so that the law may be stated precisely.

The second implication of stating a law mathematically is that the law is simple enough to write an equation describing it. If the law contains many qualifying statements and special conditions, it follows that the equation will be complicated in order to be accurate. Complicated equations are difficult to test. For this reason, scientists seek simplicity in the laws they use to describe their data. This fact is one of the reasons that Einstein's famous $E = mc^2$ captures the imagination: His theory is simple and elegant. In psychology an example of an elegant law is Stevens's law of sensation magnitude: $R = kS^n$. This law says that R, magnitude of response, is equal to k, an arbitrary constant, times S, stimulus intensity, raised to a power, n. Stevens's law has spurred much research and has greatly influenced the field of sensory processes, in large part because of the elegance with which the law is stated.

What Is Measurement?

Measurement the process of assigning numbers to events or objects according to rules

Measurement is the assignment of numbers to events or objects according to rules that permit important properties of the objects or events to be represented by properties of the number system. The key to the definition is that properties of the events are represented by properties of the number system. The rules by which the numbers are assigned to the events determine how useful the measurement is. For example, if we called every psychologically normal person a 0 and every disturbed person a 1, we would have done a kind of measurement: We would have assigned numbers to persons according to a rule. The rule permits us to count numbers of persons that fall into the two categories and to determine the percentage of abnormal personality in the population.

We could not do much more with this set of numbers, however. The reason is that the particular measurement permits us only to express an all-or-nothing difference between people. It is not possible, for instance, to state severity of abnormality, duration of problem, and so forth. To do this, we would need to assign numbers according to a different rule. Perhaps we might use a scale of severity from 0 to 10, with persons falling along the scale according to their symptoms. Then we could say that one person was twice as disturbed as another or that the average level of disturbance in Group A was three times that of Group B.

The rule by which you assign numbers determines the kind of conclusions you reach. For this reason, it is common to distinguish four types of measurement scales according to the rules by which numbers are assigned to objects or events.

Nominal scale
a measure that simply divides objects or events into categories according to their similarities or differences

Nominal scales. A **nominal scale** is one that classifies objects or events into categories. Suppose that Ulf is a foreign exchange student in the United States. He is learning the English names for vegetables: asparagus, broccoli, corn, green beans, and peas. He must learn that fresh peas, frozen peas, and canned peas are the same vegetable whether they are steamed, creamed, or stir-fried. What Ulf is doing is learning a simple scale of vegetables that gives each example of a kind of vegetable one name and each member of other classes different names. We will develop this rather elementary example of a nominal scale as we progress to the other types of scales.

A nominal scale is the simplest kind of scale because its rule for assigning numbers (or other labels) to objects or events is the simplest. The rule is that objects or events of the same kind get the same number and objects or events of a different kind get different numbers. A nominal scale, as the name implies, is a classification system. Each individual event or object, vegetables in this case, has been assigned to a class.

People sometimes think that a nominal scale is too primitive to be considered a proper scale. It seems to have little mathematics in it. In fact, in the vegetable example words can be used instead of numbers to identify classes. Such an attitude overlooks the importance of classification for the development of science. As we discussed in Chapter 2, defining classes of behavior is the first step in developing laws of behavior.

Ordinal scale
a measure that both assigns objects or events a name and arranges them in order of their magnitude

Ordinal scales. An **ordinal scale** is one that ranks objects or events in order of their magnitude. Suppose Ruth's mother tells her there are five vegetables in the freezer and asks her to list them in the order of her preference for them, with 5 standing for the most preferred. Ruth might give her mother the following ranking:

5 peas
4 corn
3 green beans
2 broccoli
1 asparagus

We have an ordinal scale of Ruth's preference for vegetables. The rule for assigning numbers on an ordinal scale is that the *ordinal position* (rank order) of numbers on the scale must represent the rank order of the psychological attributes of the objects or events. Notice that the scale does not tell *how much more* Ruth prefers green beans to broccoli. Perhaps she loves peas, corn, and green beans but is totally indifferent to broccoli. The scale only gives the order of preference, not the difference in preference among items.

Interval scale
a measure in which the differences between numbers are meaningful; includes both nominal and ordinal information

Interval scales. An **interval scale** is one in which the differences between the numbers on the scale are meaningful. Let us suppose that Joel's mother says to him: "I know you like peas the best and asparagus the least. On a scale of 1 to 7, with 1 standing for asparagus and 7 standing for peas, how do you rate broccoli, corn, and green beans?" Suppose Joel gives the following data:

7.0 peas
6.5 corn
6.0 green beans

5.0 broccoli

4.0

3.0

2.0

1.0 asparagus

From these data, we are able to infer that Joel's liking of green beans is halfway between that of broccoli and peas. Also, there are five units of difference between green beans and asparagus but only .5 units of difference between corn and green beans. Joel's mother knows more about his liking for vegetables than Ruth's mother does about hers. Joel's mother has developed an interval scale of his liking for vegetables. The rule for assigning numbers to events or objects on an interval scale is that equal *differences* between the numbers on the scale must represent equal psychological differences between the events or objects.

Ratio scale
a measure having a meaningful zero point as well as all of the nominal, ordinal, and interval properties

Ratio scales. A **ratio scale** is one that has a meaningful zero point as well as meaningful differences between the numbers on the scale. Suppose that Susan's mother says to her: "If your feeling toward green beans is 10 on an open-ended scale, how do you feel about broccoli, corn, and so forth? If you are neutral about a vegetable, give it a zero. If you like one twice as much as you like another, give it a number twice as large. If you dislike a vegetable, give it a negative number. A rating of –10 would indicate that you *disliked* a vegetable as much as you *liked* green beans. You may use any number that seems appropriate; there is no upper or lower limit to the numbers you may use." Now, we suppose that Susan gives the following data:

30

20 peas
15 corn
10 green beans

0 broccoli

–10

–20

–30

–40 asparagus

–50

The scale developed by Susan's mother contains the most information of the scales we have discussed. First, this scale has a meaningful zero point, which none of the other scales had. Therefore, we can know that Susan is indifferent to broccoli. Second, the ratios between numbers are meaningful. We can say that Susan likes peas twice as much as green beans or that she hates asparagus four times as much as she likes green beans. The rule for assigning numbers to events or objects on a ratio scale is that the *ratios* between the numbers on the scale must represent the psychological ratios between the events or objects.

Comparison of the Scales

As we go from nominal to ordinal, interval, and ratio scales, we are able to gain more information from the data. The nominal scale only gives information about whether two events are the same or different. The ordinal scale does that but also gives us a ranking on some variable. The interval scale conveys nominal and ordinal information and also allows us to make quantitative statements about the magnitude of the differences between events. The ratio scale contains all the information of the other three scales as well as conveying information about ratios of magnitudes. For this reason we strive to make our scales of variables ratio scales if possible. Failing that, we try for an interval scale, and so forth.

You may have noticed as we went along that each person's rating of the five vegetables was consistent with all of the others' ratings. In other words, knowing Susan's data on the ratio scale, we could derive all of the information in the other three scales. This was done purposely to show that the ratio scale is the most powerful scale, with the other scales being less powerful in the order: interval, ordinal, nominal. Thus, Susan's mother knew the most about her liking for vegetables and Ulf's hostess the least about his. Specifically, Susan's mother knows that she likes peas twice as much as green beans, she is indifferent to broccoli, and she dislikes asparagus twice as much as she likes peas. Ruth's mother, on the other hand, only knows her rank order of preferences, not the differences between them or the zero point. All that Ulf's hostess knows is that he knows one vegetable from the other.

Another way to look at the differences among types of scales is to ask: How could we have altered the assignment of the numbers to the events without violating the rule governing the type of scale? The ways that we can alter the assignment of numbers to individual events without distorting the scale are called *permissible transformations*. The permissible transformations become fewer as we go from nominal to ratio scales. In the nominal-scale example we could have called asparagus 1, broccoli 2, and so forth. Or we could have done the reverse. On the other hand, we could label them 37 and 59 and so forth. Any five numbers would do. We would not have lost any information about Ulf's ability to identify the vegetables if we had changed the labels because we were using the numbers only to put vegetables into classes.

For the ordinal scale we can change the numbers any way that would preserve the order of preference for the vegetables. We could have called Ruth's favorite vegetable 59, the second one 14, the third 13, and so forth. We would still know Ruth's order of preference for the vegetables.

We can do less to change the numbers of the interval scale because we must preserve the meaningfulness of the differences between items. But we could add or subtract a constant from all numbers or we could multiply them by a positive constant. Thus, we could add 10 to all of Joel's answers or multiply them by 100 without changing any of our conclusions about his preferences for vegetables.

In the ratio scale we can change little without distorting it. The only thing we can do is multiply all of the numbers by a positive constant. If we were to add a constant, we would destroy the significance of the ratios between numbers; we could no longer say that Susan likes corn twice as much as green beans.

Table 3–1 summarizes the points we have been making in this section. The types of scales are listed in order in the first column. The second column indicates the properties of the number system that must be represented in the rule used to assign numbers to events or objects. The third column gives the permissible transformations. The fourth column gives common examples of psychology scales.

The various psychological defense mechanisms are good examples of nominal scales. No order of severity is implied by the names for the defense mechanisms: projection, denial, intellectualization, and so forth. Common examples of ordinal scales would include any preference data of the sort we

TABLE 3–1 Summary of information on scales of measurement.

Scale	Number system properties represented by assignment rule	Permissible transformations	Example
Nominal	Similarities and differences	Any substitution of a number for another number that preserves similarities and differences, including all below	Types of defense mechanisms
Ordinal	Similarities and differences, rank order	Any change that preserves order among members, including both below	Neurosis versus psychosis, preferences
Interval	Similarities and differences, rank order, magnitude of differences between individuals	Addition of a constant, multiplication by a positive constant	IQ
Ratio	Similarities and differences, rank order, magnitude of differences, ratios of properties between individuals, meaningful zero point	Multiplication by a positive constant only	Stevens's law of sensation magnitude

have already used in our discussion. Another example would be the classification of abnormal behavior into neurotic versus psychotic. Order is implied because psychosis is considered worse than neurosis. IQ is a good example of an interval scale. The IQ tests are designed so that the amount of the differences between people can be meaningfully represented by the IQ score. However, IQ is not a ratio scale because it would be meaningless to say that a person with an IQ of 120 is twice as smart as someone with an IQ of 60. The most common example of a ratio scale is given by Steven's scale as in the example of Susan's liking for vegetables. She was told to use numbers to represent ratios of differences between vegetables.

Understanding the type of scale that the data are measured on is important so as not to draw incorrect conclusions. We already said that it would be meaningless to say that a person with an IQ of 120 was twice as smart as someone with 60. Similarly, even though many teachers when they compute grade-point averages consider an A to be worth four points, a B three, and so forth, no one would conclude that a person who received an

A had learned twice as much as someone who received a C. In reality there are relatively few scales in psychology that are measured on ratio, or even interval, scales. Therefore, we must know what kind of scale our data are measured on before we compare the magnitudes of differences between numbers.

READING GRAPHS

One thing that psychology students quickly discover is that psychologists are constantly drawing graphs. Graphs help us understand the relationships between variables. The old saying that a picture is worth a thousand words often is literally true of graphs. So you can see why it is imperative that we are able to read graphs and understand them.

A graph is a visual representation of the functional relationship between variables. Virtually all graphs used in psychology are in the form of one variable plotted at right angles to another variable. Look at Figure 3–1 for an example of a basic graph. The direction indicated by the x is called the x axis. The direction at right angles to the x axis is the *y* axis. The x axis is called the abscissa and the *y* axis is called the ordinate. A silly but simple way of remembering this is that when you say abscissa your mouth takes a horizontal shape, and when you say ordinate it becomes vertical. Ordinarily, the abscissa, or x axis, represents the value of the independent variable, while the ordinate, or *y* axis, shows the value of the dependent variable.

Bar Graphs and Line Graphs

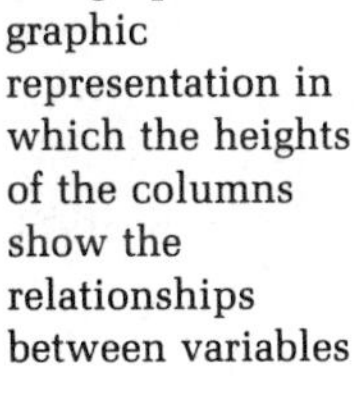

Bar graph graphic representation in which the heights of the columns show the relationships between variables

Bar graphs are used when the independent variable is categorical, or discrete, rather than continuous. If the independent variable in an experiment is sex of subject, it will be necessary to represent the data by a bar graph, as in Figure 3–2. Because persons are either male or female, the independent variable is discrete and it is impossible to have data points falling between M and F on the abscissa. Therefore, it would be incorrect to

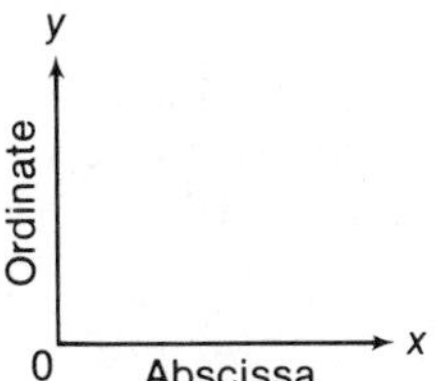

FIGURE 3–1. Format of the axes of a typical graph.

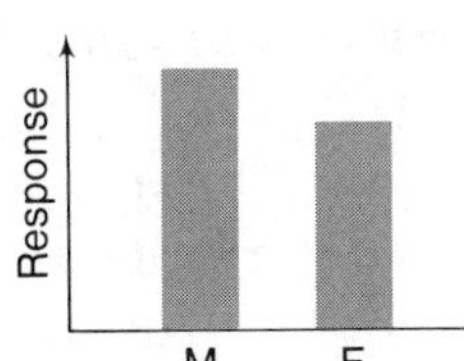

FIGURE 3–2. Format of a typical bar graph in which the abscissa represents categorical data.

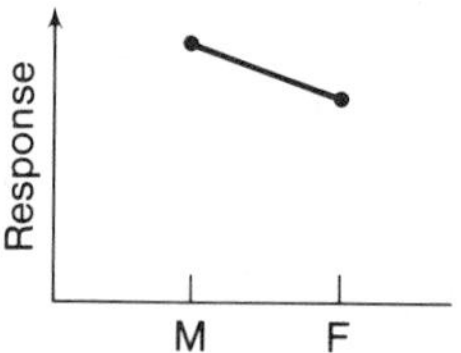

FIGURE 3–3. Incorrect format for graph of categorical data.

Line graph a graphic representation using lines to show relationships between variables

draw a line graph for the data because doing so implies that it is possible to have a data point falling anywhere along the line. See Figure 3–3. On the other hand, if the independent variable is masculinity/femininity as measured by a test, drawing a **line graph** is then possible because individual subjects could, in principle, fall anywhere along the abscissa. See Figure 3–4.

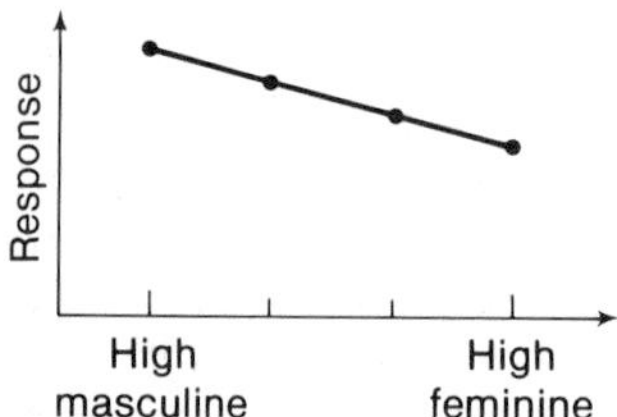

FIGURE 3–4. Correct form of graph when the variable represented by the abscissa is continuous.

We said that a graph represents a functional relationship between variables. Another way of putting this is to say that a graph shows how one variable changes as a function of another. When one variable is a function of another, it means that the value of one depends on the value of the other. This relationship can be stated in terms of an equation: $y = f(x)$. We introduce the equation to point out that any graph can be thought of as representing a relationship between two variables that could be stated in the form of an equation, if we desired. Many times the equation would be complicated; other times it might be simple. Any time we look at a graph, we should ask ourselves the basic question, "What is the function relating y and x?"

Slopes of Functions

We will take up the various types of functions in a moment. But first, in order to facilitate our discussion, we will talk about the slope of a line. Figure 3–5 shows the simplest kind of function, a linear or straight-line function. We can find the slope of this linear function by taking any convenient segment of the line and determining the ratio of change in y to the change in x for that segment. This may be expressed as follows:

$$\text{slope} = \Delta y/\Delta x$$

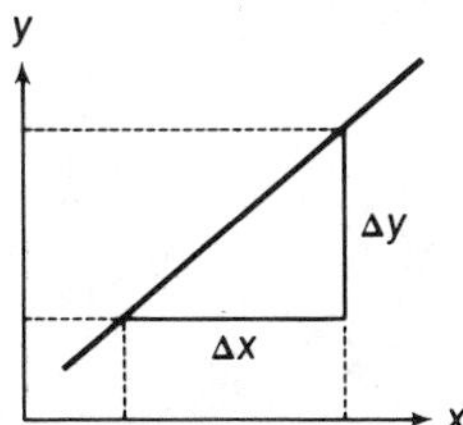

FIGURE 3–5. Graph of a simple straight-line function.

which is read, The slope equals the change in *y* divided by the change in x. The Greek letter *delta* (Δ) is used as a symbol for *change*. A horizontal line has a slope of zero because the change in *y* is zero. A 45° line has a slope of 1 because the change in *y* equals the change in x. The slope of a line may also be negative.

Talking about the slope of a curved line is more complicated. It would be misleading to talk about the slope of the entire curve in Figure 3–6,

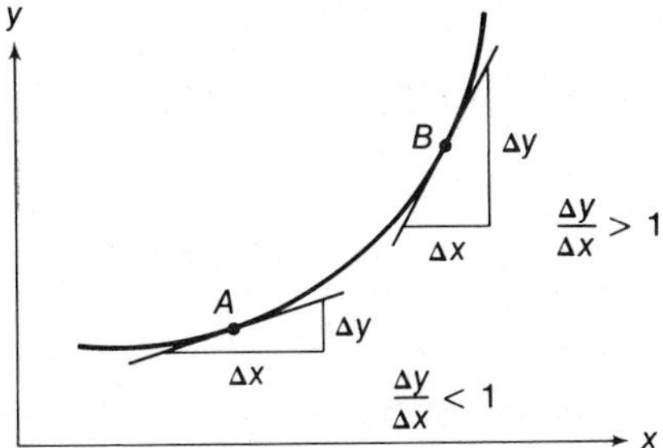

FIGURE 3–6. Graph of a curvilinear function.

because the line is not straight. We can obtain the slope of the line at a given point, however, by drawing a straight line that is tangent to the curve at that point. Thus, we can see that the slope is shallower at Point A than it is at Point B. When the slope of a line is not constant—that is, when the line is curved—we say the curve accelerates. If the slope increases, as this one does, we say that it is positively accelerated. Positive acceleration can be thought of as speeding up; negative acceleration is slowing down. Now we are ready to look at the various kinds of functions encountered in psychology.

Types of Functions

Figure 3–7 shows some common functions. Line *a* is a linear function such as we have already discussed. Because it has a positive slope, we call it a *linearly increasing* function.

Line b is curved in such a way that its slope increases as *c* increases. It is called a *positively accelerated, increasing* function. Curves like Line *b*

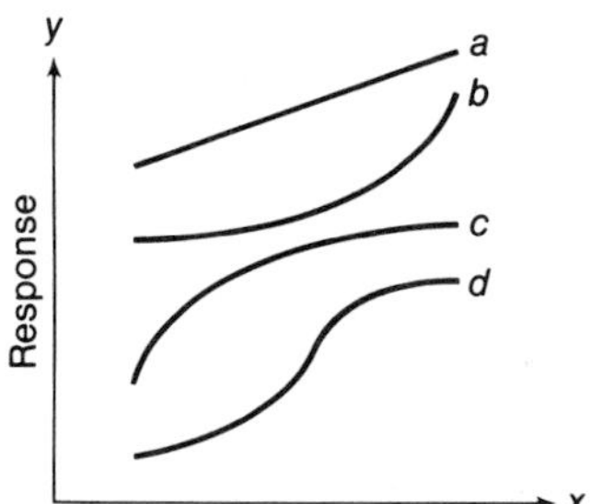

FIGURE 3–7. Some common monotonic functions.

are seen when the response grows more and more rapidly with increases in x. An example is the increase in apparent heaviness of an object with increasing weight. Doubling the weight more than doubles the apparent heaviness of an object.

Line *c* is a *negatively accelerated, increasing* function. Although *y* continues to increase with increases in x, the *slope* of the line decreases with increases in x. The growth in *y* becomes slower as x increases. Curves like Line *c* are common in psychology. For example, doubling the amount of light on a surface causes less than a doubling of the brightness of the surface.

Line *d* is called a *sigmoid* curve. Sigmoid simply means S shaped. The dependent variable, *y*, starts out low, then increases until it levels off at a high value. In contrast, the *slope* of the line is almost zero at the low end, grows rapidly for a while, then *decreases* to almost zero at high values of x. Sigmoid curves are typical of learning data. During the early part of training, learning is slow, then it becomes rapid, until eventually the subject reaches some upper limit.

Figure 3–8 is similar to Figure 3–7. In fact, every type of curve in one figure is shown in the other. The only difference is that all curves in Figure 3–8 are decreasing instead of increasing. We have presented this figure to show that curves can be either increasing or decreasing *and* at the same time also be either positively or negatively accelerated. For example, Curve *b* in Figure 3–8 is positively accelerated, decreasing. Its counterpart in Figure 3–7 is positively accelerated, increasing.

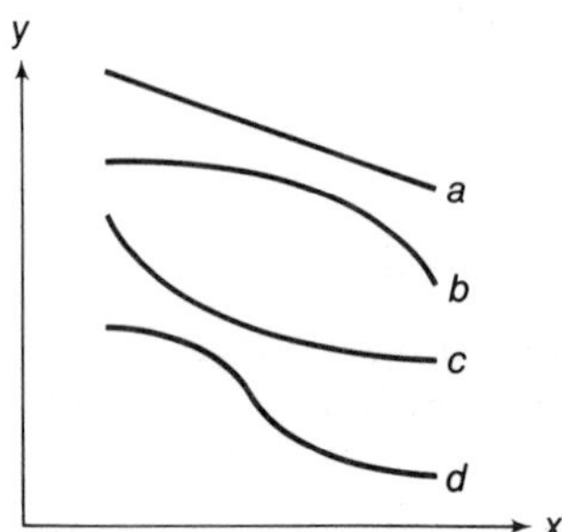

FIGURE 3–8. More common monotonic functions.

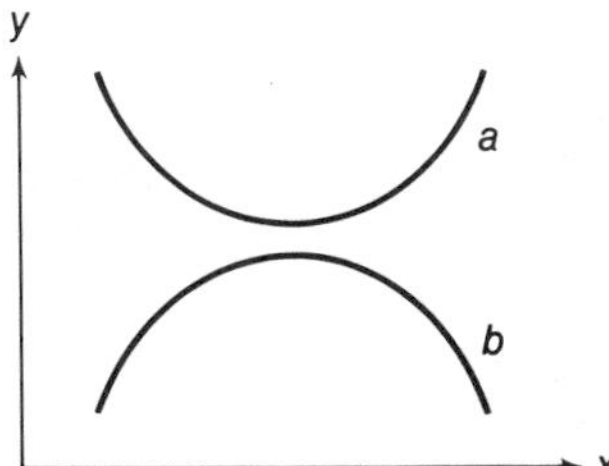

FIGURE 3–9. Two common nonmonotonic curves.

All of the curves in Figure 3–7 and Figure 3–8 have one property in common: They all either increase or decrease over their entire range. They never reverse directions. A curve that never reverses direction is called *monotonic*. All of the curves in Figure 3–7 are monotonically increasing curves. All of the curves in Figure 3–8 are monotonically decreasing curves.

Figure 3–9 shows some *nonmonotonic* curves. Curve *a* is a *U-shaped* curve. It first decreases then increases with increasing x. In this curve y might represent discomfort caused by a room's being either too cold or too hot. Curve *b*, an *inverted U-shaped* curve, is common in psychology. One use of it is to depict the effect of motivation on performance. Performance is optimal in the middle range of motivation but poor if the motivation is too low or too high.

Frequency Distributions

Frequency distribution a graph that shows the number of cases falling within specific categories

In all of the graph types we have discussed so far, the abscissa, or x axis, represented the independent variable and the ordinate, or y axis, represented the dependent variable. In another kind of graph common in psychology we find that the y axis does not represent the value of a dependent variable. This graph is known as a **frequency distribution**. You can tell a frequency distribution from other kinds of graphs because the ordinate represents a *count* of something: numbers of individuals or numbers of responses. All other graphs have some kind of *magnitude* as the ordinate: mean rate of responses, average score, and so forth. A frequency distribution, in contrast, has *number* of individual subjects or responses (number of cases, number of rats) represented on the ordinate.

Consider Figure 3–10, a frequency distribution of scores on the first quiz in a course. The abscissa represents quiz scores and the ordinate shows the number of students who achieved each score. No doubt you have seen such frequency distributions before. Notice that the abscissa does not represent an independent variable: a quiz score is a response and therefore is a dependent variable.

These same data could also become part of an ordinary graph that shows the relationship between an independent and dependent variable.

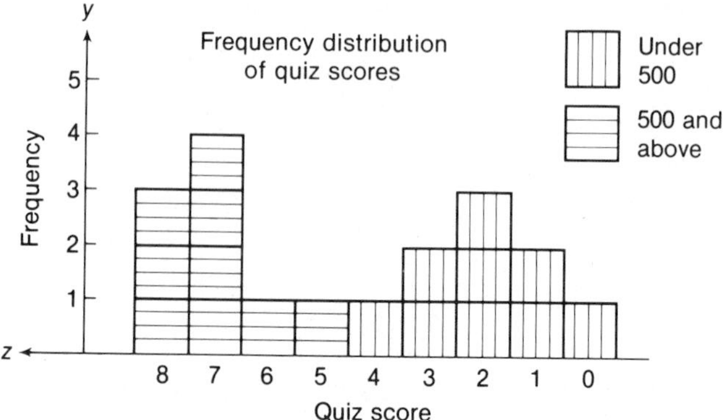

FIGURE 3–10. Graph of a frequency distribution.

Suppose the instructor knows the Scholastic Aptitude Test (SAT) scores of the students. In the frequency distribution she represents each student who has an SAT score of 500 or above by squares having horizontal stripes and those who have SAT scores below 500 by squares having vertical stripes. We can see that those who have SAT scores of 500 and above did better in the quiz than the others.

Now let us consider SAT score to be the independent variable and quiz score the dependent variable. We might want to know if SAT score can predict the score on the first quiz. To learn this, we would plot average quiz score as a function of SAT score. We do this step by finding the average quiz score for the students in each group and plotting the data as in Figure 3–11. This basic kind of graph may feel familiar: A dependent variable, quiz score, is plotted as a function of an independent variable, SAT score.

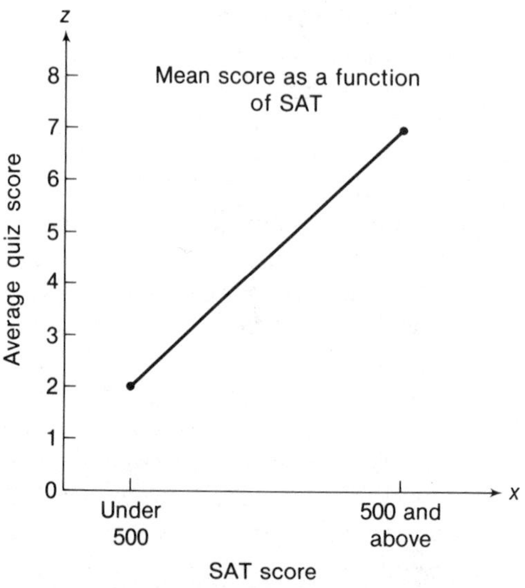

FIGURE 3–11. Graph of data shown in Figure 3.10 after computing the mean quiz score for each SAT group and plotting that value against SAT.

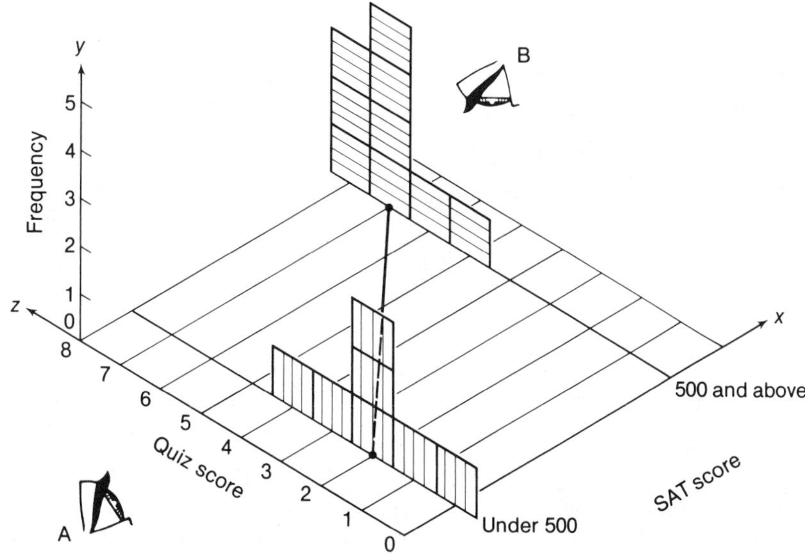

z versus x: Mean quiz score as function of SAT score
y versus z: Frequency distribution of scores

FIGURE 3–12. Three-dimensional graph combining the information in Figure 3–10 and Figure 3–11.

Figure 3–12 is a three-dimensional graph that combines the information from the two previous graphs. The x axis represents SAT score, our independent variable. The z axis represents the quiz score, which is the dependent variable. The *y*, or vertical dimension, shows frequency, or how many students achieved each score. If we mentally rotate the graph so that we take Viewpoint A in the figure and look at right angles to the z dimension, then the graph becomes identical to Figure 3–10. From this viewpoint dimension z collapses and we have frequency (*y*) as a function of quiz score (z). Now we rotate the graph again in our heads and look at it from Viewpoint B; that is, looking down at the surface defined by the x and z dimensions. If we plot the two mean quiz scores, 2.0 for those students having SATs under 500 and 7.0 for those having SATs of 500 and above, then we have Figure 3–11.

Thus we see that frequency distributions are different from other graphs but can be related to them. Remembering this distinction will help you when you are reading graphs.

Cumulative frequency distribution a graph where each plot shows the summed total of cases that fall at or below a given score

Cumulative Frequency Distributions

A common and important kind of frequency distribution is the **cumulative frequency distribution**, one that plots the frequency of cases that fall *at or below* a given score. It is called cumulative because the curve cumulates, or

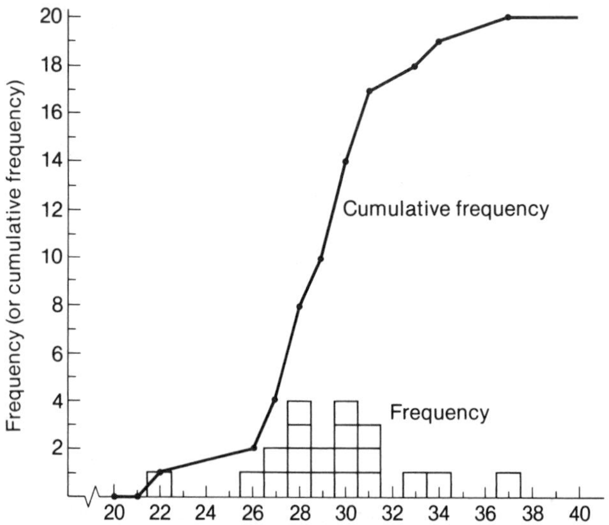

FIGURE 3–13. Cumulative frequency distribution and the histogram of scores on which it is based.

adds up, all cases that have occurred up to a certain point. Figure 3–13 shows a common type of data plotted both as a frequency distribution and as a cumulative curve. The figure represents scores on a quiz. The squares at the bottom (histogram) show the frequency distribution of scores. The line connecting the Xs is a cumulative curve because it shows how many students earned that score or lower. You will notice that the cumulative curve reaches a frequency of 20, which is equal to the number of students in the class. You can verify this by counting the boxes in the frequency distribution. The shape of the cumulative frequency distribution is sigmoidal. So, you can begin to see how the cumulative curve has properties that are useful in analyzing results of experiments.

MAIN EFFECTS AND INTERACTIONS

So far we have considered graphs that represented only one function at a time; that is, they have shown only one line relating the dependent and independent variables. Often it is helpful to show more than one curve on a single graph. Before we look at such a graph, let us consider the tabular form of some data that will be graphed in such a way shortly.

Table 3–2 shows data from an experiment that has two independent variables, A and B. We have measured the response to all possible combinations of three particular values, or levels, of the two variables. Such an experiment is known as a *factorial* experiment. Factorial experiments are common in psychology; some examples are discussed in Chapter 7. Each cell of Table 3–2 represents the response to one combination of A and B. The cell in the upper left corner, for example, shows the response to Level 1

TABLE 3–2 Table of data from a factorial experiment.

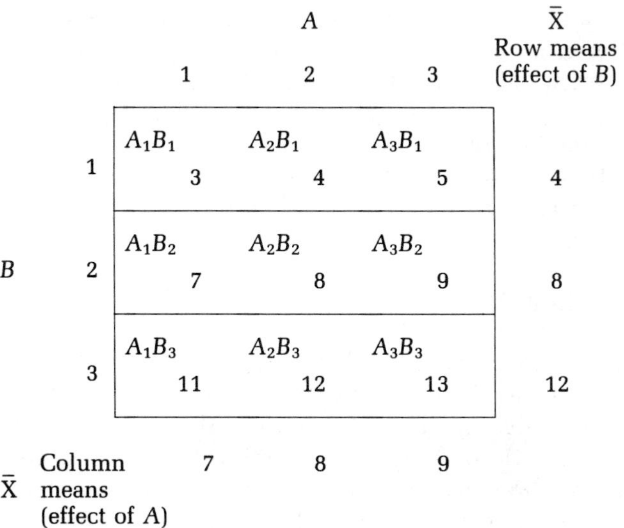

		A 1	A 2	A 3	$\bar{X}$ Row means (effect of B)
B	1	A_1B_1 3	A_2B_1 4	A_3B_1 5	4
	2	A_1B_2 7	A_2B_2 8	A_3B_2 9	8
	3	A_1B_3 11	A_2B_3 12	A_3B_3 13	12
$\bar{X}$ Column means (effect of A)		7	8	9	

of A together with Level 1 of B. We can determine what the average response is to variable A by averaging over all levels of B. We do this by finding the means of the columns of the table. Similarly, we can average over all levels of A to find the effect of the B variable. We do this by taking the row means. We can see from the row and column means that both variables A and B had some effect on the response.

Now we are ready to graph the data shown in Table 3–2. The ordinate of Figure 3–14 shows the response, R, as a function of independent variable A. The three different curves show the effect of A on the dependent variable for particular levels of the second independent variable, B. The lower curve shows the response to A when it is combined with B_1, and so forth.

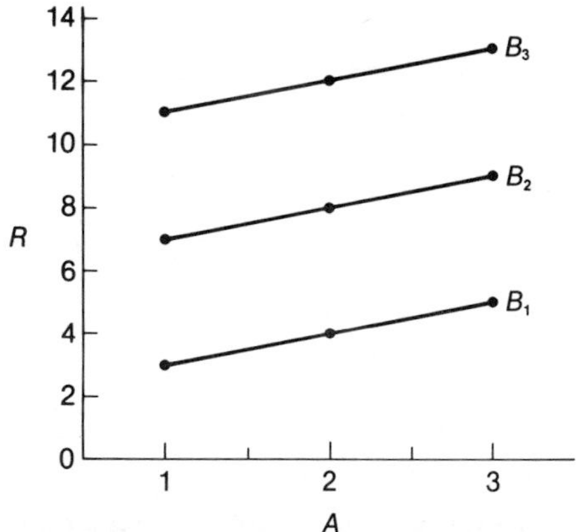

FIGURE 3–14. Graph of data shown in Table 3–2. The response is plotted against variable *A* with variable *B* as the parameter.

Parameter a constant in a curve that differs with changes in experimental conditions and defines the form of the curve

This graph is said to show a *family of curves*. The family is related by the values of *B*, which vary from one curve to another and determine the differences between the curves. Variable *B*, then, can be said to be a **parameter** of the function relating the response to variable *A*. A parameter, in this usage, is a quantity that has an effect on the exact form of the function that relates two variables. Changing the parameter *B* changes the relationship between the response and variable *A* and gives us different functions, or curves. In this case, the parameter *B* simply shifts the curves vertically.

Main Effects

Whenever we have a graph like Figure 3–14, we can plot the same data in a different way. Return to Table 3–2 for a moment. Notice that the layout of the table is completely symmetrical; there is no reason why we could not have made the table by placing the levels of *B* along the top and the levels of *A* along the side. The only difference would be that the column means would now show the effect of *B* instead of *A*, and the row means would show the effect of *A* instead of *B*. (Of course, the data would be rearranged to fall in the proper cells.)

Likewise, we can plot the figure representing the data another way. Instead of plotting the response against *A* with *B* as a parameter, we can plot the response against *B* with *A* as the parameter, as in Figure 3–15. All we have done is make the independent variable in one graph become the parameter in the other. The same data are represented (check it out), but the functions are different. Comparing the two graphs, we can see that variable *B* has a greater effect on the response than does variable *A* (over the arbitrary values chosen).

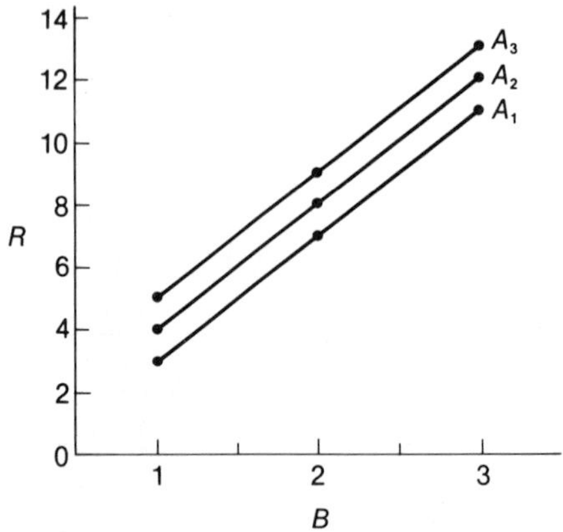

FIGURE 3–15. Graph of data shown in Table 3–2 and Figure 3–14. The response is plotted against variable *B* with variable *A* as the parameter.

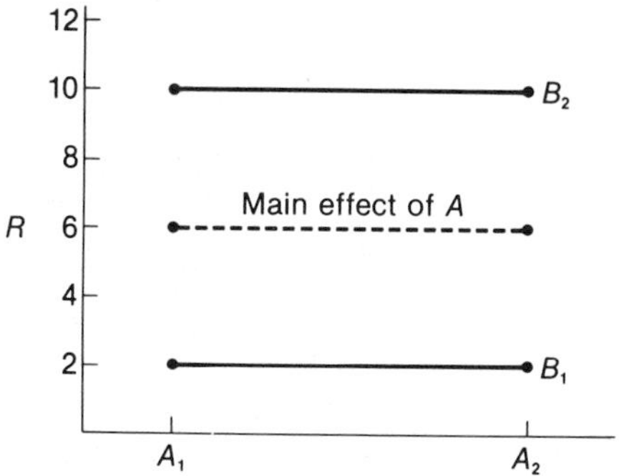

FIGURE 3–16. Graph of the response plotted agianst variable *A* with variable *B* as the parameter.

Main effect change in the dependent variable caused by changes in an independent variable, averaged over another independent variable

Another example is given in Figure 3–16, which plots a dependent variable as a function of independent variable *A*, with independent variable *B* as a parameter. If we average the response to the independent variable *A* over levels of *B*, we find the average effect of *A* on the dependent variable. This effect is called the **main effect** of the independent variable. Main effect does *not* mean the principal effect, as you might expect. The main effect of *A* is the *change* in the dependent variable caused by changes in *A*, averaged over all values of *B*. The main effect of *A* is shown in the graph by the dotted line in Figure 3–16. We can see that *A* has no main effect because the slope of the line is zero.

Figure 3–17 shows the same data, but this time the response is plotted as a function of *B*, with *A* as a parameter. Because A_1 and A_2 cause the same response for both levels of *B*, there is only one line and therefore the two sets of data points overlap completely. But we can clearly see in this graph that there is a main effect of B, because the line has a nonzero slope. Figures 3–16 and 3–17 show the same data, and so we should be able to draw the same conclusions from each. However, the different graphs make it easier to see different points in the same data.

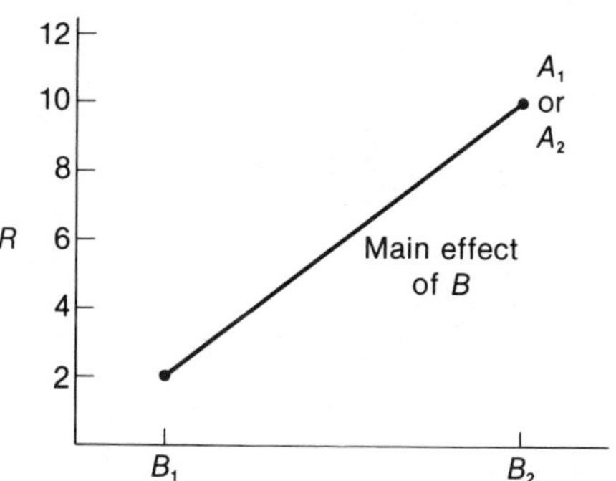

FIGURE 3–17. Graph of the data shown in Figure 3–16. The response is plotted against variable *B* with variable *A* as the parameter.

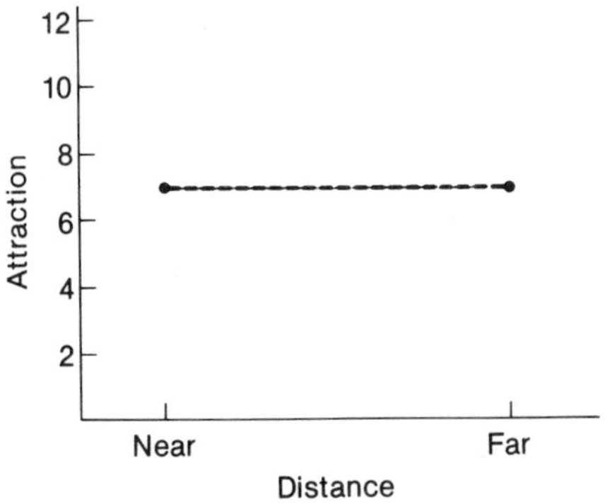

FIGURE 3–18. Data of the first test of the relationship between attraction within couples and distance.

Interactions

Suppose that you are intrigued by the apparent contradiction between the two proverbs: Absence makes the heart grow fonder, and Out of sight, out of mind. Certainly they seem contradictory, and they are often cited by psychologists as examples of the limitations of commonsense.

You decide to do an experiment in which you study the degree of attraction between members of couples that either are near to each other or separated by a distance. Let us assume that you find the results shown in Figure 3–18: Distance has no effect on the degree of attraction. Both proverbs then appear to be false. Suppose next that you have the idea that perhaps you overlooked an important variable: Maybe it makes a difference whether the members of the couples are in love or not. Suppose now that you are able to determine on some independent basis which couples are in true love and which are merely having a flirtation. You then repeat the experiment with a new group of subjects and you find the data shown in Figure 3–19. Here attraction is plotted as a function of distance, with

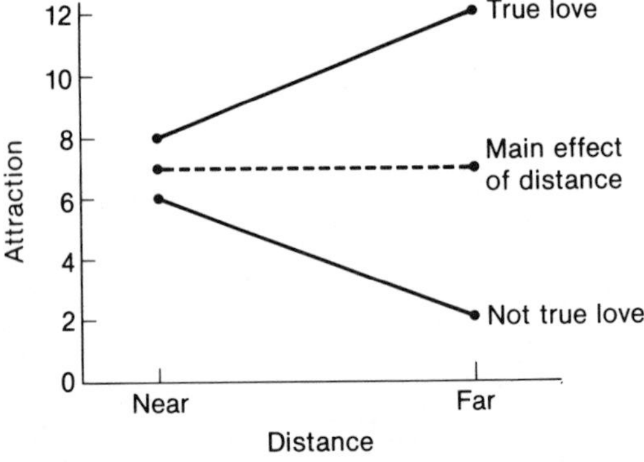

FIGURE 3–19. Graph of the relationship between attraction within couples and distance, considering presence or absence of true love as a parameter.

presence (or absence) of true love as a parameter. You find that attraction increases with distance for couples that are in true love, but that it decreases for those who are only having a flirtation.

As it turns out, both proverbs are true, but under particular circumstances. Absence makes the heart grow fonder for couples in true love; but Out of sight, out of mind is the case for those who are not in true love. In other words, there are two independent variables, distance and presence of true love, that must be considered when testing these two proverbs.

Interaction occurs when a change in the value of one independent variable changes the effects of the other

Now we are ready to define the concept of **interaction**. We say that there is an interaction between two variables when the effect of one of them on a dependent variable depends on the value of the other. Specifically, interaction means that independent variable A has a different effect on the dependent variable when it is combined with one value of independent variable B than with another value of B. By *effect*, we mean the exact shape (for example, slope) of the function between the independent and dependent variables. For example, in Figure 3–19 increasing distance causes a 4-unit increase in attraction for the true-love condition but a 4-unit decrease under the not-true-love condition.

Interaction does *not* refer to the vertical separation between the two curves, only to the shape of the curves. In other words, it refers to the *differential* effects of the distance variable, when the true-love variable differs. If you could slide one of the curves up or down so that it matched another, there would be no interaction. This is true no matter how complicated the curve. Of course, small differences may be due to chance and may require statistical evaluation. One easy way to tell if there is an interaction between two variables is to see whether the two lines in a graph of the data are parallel. If they are parallel, there is no interaction; if they are not parallel, there is an interaction. In Figure 3–19 it is easy to see that the lines for true love and flirtation are not parallel, so there is an interaction.

The Importance of Interactions

The interaction between two variables is extremely important in the interpretation of an experiment. In our example of attraction between members of a couple, contradictory conclusions could be drawn if the interaction effect is not taken into account. We could conclude that distance either decreases attraction or increases attraction, depending on whether the subjects are in true love. We must not overlook the fact that in any such experiment we often want to ask ourselves what is the effect of one independent variable by itself, not taking the other independent variable into account. We did this in Figure 3–18 where we did not take presence or absence of true love into account. In that case, there was no effect of distance on attraction. We would say that the main effect of distance was zero (see Figure 3–19).

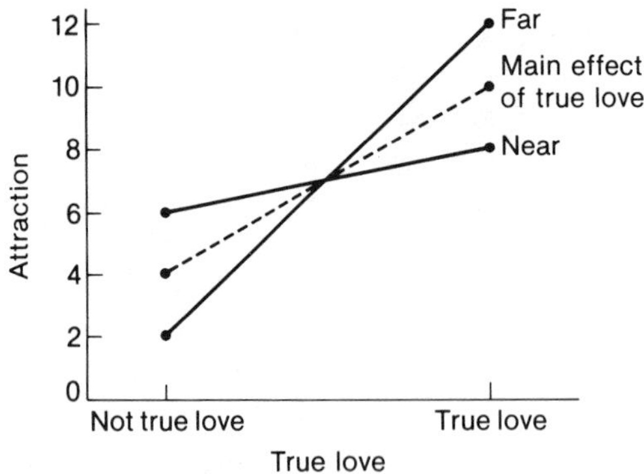

FIGURE 3–20. Graph of the data shown in Figure 3–19, except that attraction is plotted against the presence or absence of true love as the parameter.

It is instructive to replot the data of Figure 3–19 as in Figure 3–20. Now we have attraction plotted as a function of true love, with distance as the parameter. Comparing Figure 3–19 with Figure 3–20, we can see that true love has a main effect on the dependent variable (Figure 3–19), but there is no main effect of distance (Figure 3–20).

Types of Interactions

The interaction between distance and true love that we have been discussing can be called an *antagonistic interaction*: The two independent variables tend to reverse each other's effects. Distance had one effect under the true-love condition but an opposite effect under the not-true-love condition. Figure 3–21 shows an interesting case of an antagonistic interaction in which each variable completely reverses the effect of the other. The same data are replotted in Figure 3–22, with *B* as the independent variable and *A* as the parameter. Neither variable in this example shows a main effect at all.

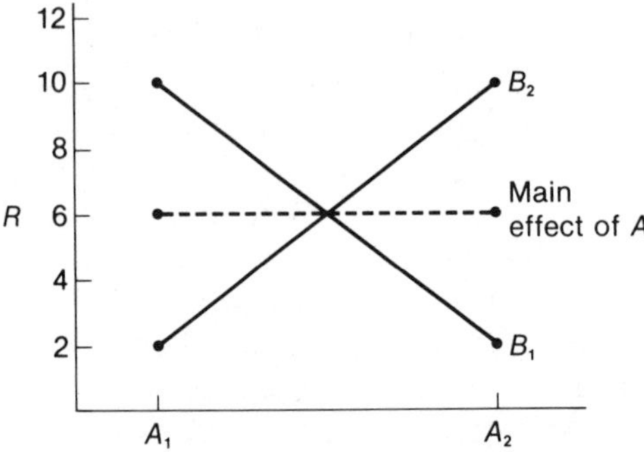

FIGURE 3–21. Example of an antagonistic interaction.

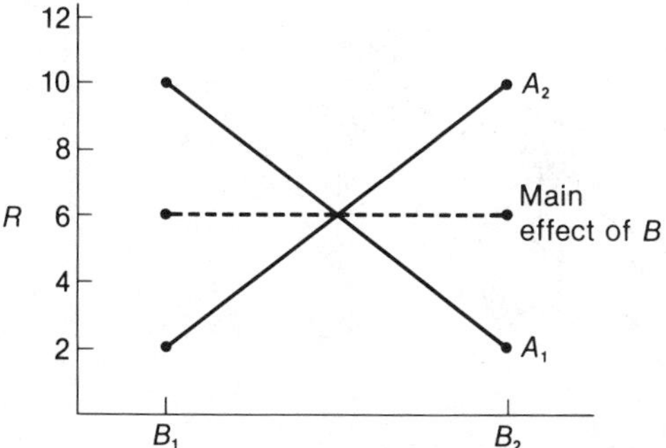

FIGURE 3–22. Data shown in Figure 3–21 replotted as a function of variable *B* with *A* as the parameter.

The interaction in Figure 3–23 can be called a *synergistic* interaction because the higher level of B enhances the effect of A and vice versa. This relationship is shown in the steeper slope of the line relating the dependent variable to A when B is larger. Figure 3–24 shows the same data replotted by making B the independent variable and A the parameter. The same type of interaction is seen either way.

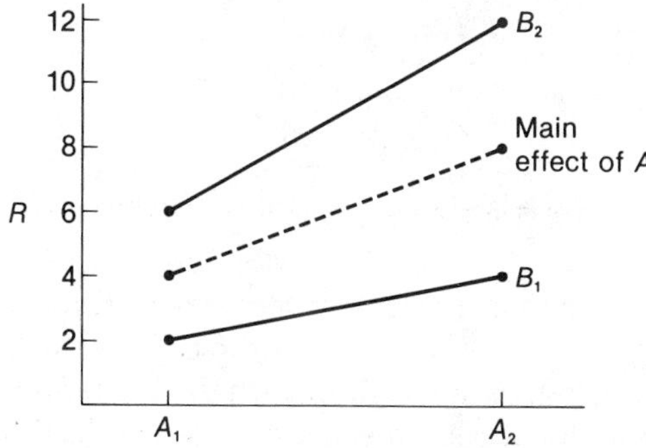

FIGURE 3–23. Example of a synergistic interaction.

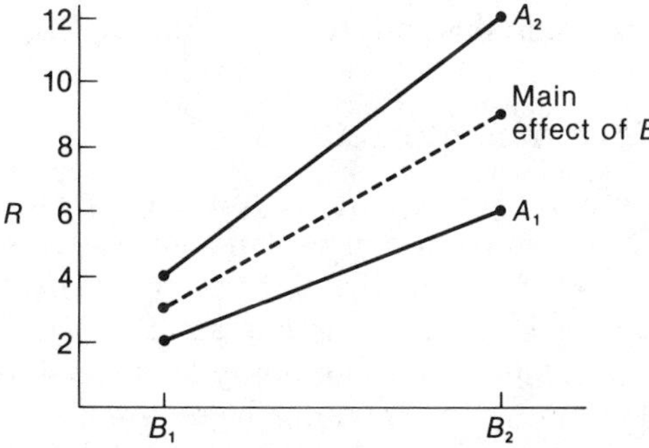

FIGURE 3–24. Data shown in Figure 3–22 replotted as a function of variable *B* with *A* as the parameter.

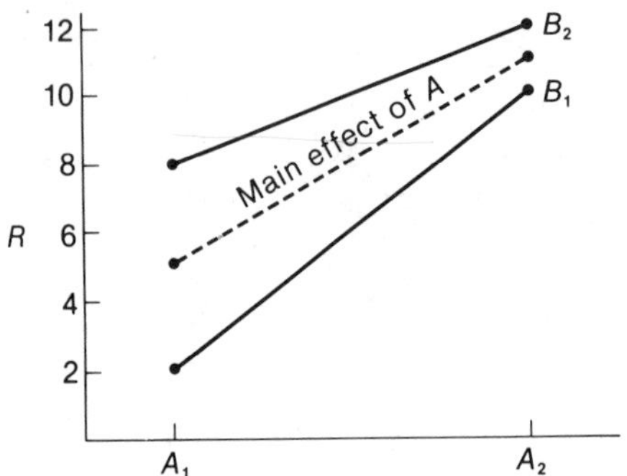

FIGURE 3–25. Example of a ceiling effect interaction.

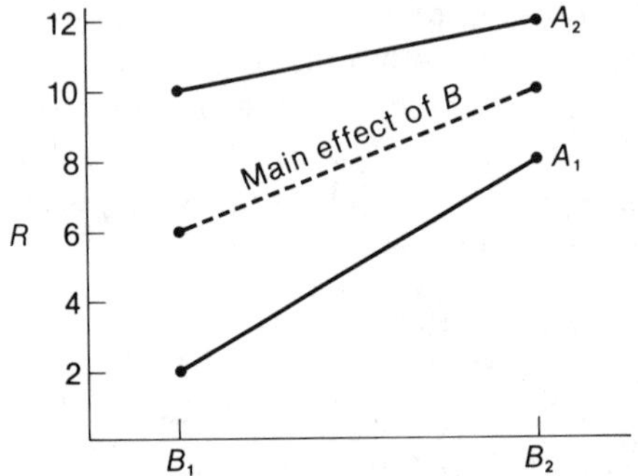

FIGURE 3–26. Data shown in Figure 3–25 replotted as a function of variable *B* with *A* as the parameter.

Figure 3–25 shows a *ceiling effect* interaction; the higher level of B reduces the differential effect of A on the dependent variable. Variable A has a smaller effect when it is paired with the higher level of B. Likewise, in Figure 3–26, which shows the same data, variable B has less effect when paired with the higher level of A.

All of these types of interactions are common in psychological research. Others are possible, but these are the principal kinds.

Transformations and Interactions

After our discussion of interactions, you may be surprised to know that whether there is an interaction in a set of data depends completely on how the data are handled. Specifically, performing a transformation on the data often will have an effect on whether an interaction is found. Certain numerical transformations are commonly made on data, such as taking the logarithm of all of the scores or taking the reciprocal of all scores. A certain transformation may produce an interaction when the untransformed data did not show one, or it may remove one that previously was there. It may even change the interaction from one type to another.

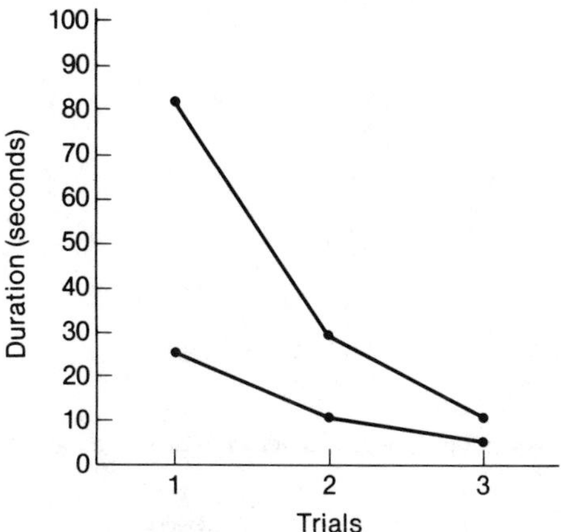

FIGURE 3–27. Duration as a function of trials with level of hunger as the parameter.

Consider Figure 3–27. Suppose these data represent a measurement of latency. Perhaps rats were running an alley for food under two levels of hunger. The upper curve might represent low hunger and the lower curve high hunger. From this figure we would conclude that an interaction existed between time to run the alley and hunger: Levels of hunger had a bigger effect during early trials. We might also conclude that learning was rapid at first and tapered off after the first two trials.

Suppose instead that we were to plot running speed instead of time. Recall that speed and duration are reciprocally related. Figure 3–28 shows running speed as a function of trials, with hunger as a parameter. Now we find that the interaction is reversed: Levels of hunger had a greater effect on speed during the later trials. Also, you might conclude that learning was slow at first and then speeded up.

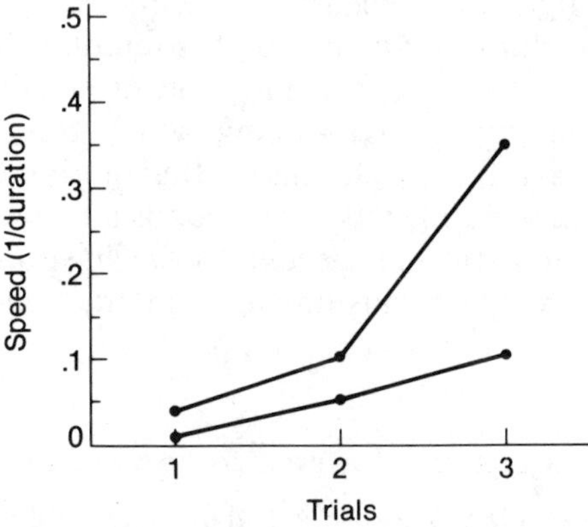

FIGURE 3–28. Data shown in Figure 3–27 after a reciprocal transformation of the data. This graph shows speed as a function of trials with hunger as the parameter.

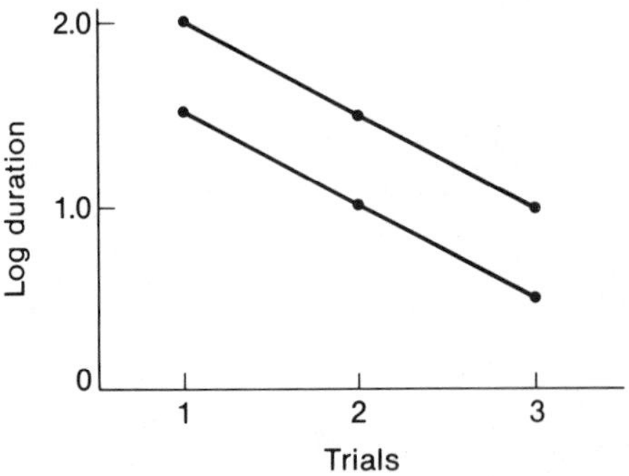

FIGURE 3–29. Data shown in Figure 3–27 and Figure 3–28 after a logarithmic transformation of duration.

How do we get out of this confusion? Before we try, let us be certain that we realize that the theoretical conclusions we reach about data can depend entirely on how we plot them. In other words, the presence or absence of an interaction and what form it takes depend on the type of transformations made of the data. An interaction exists only in a particular transformation of the data. It does not exist in the abstract or even in a particular theory. It exists only in a particular way of transforming the data. If a theory predicts an interaction, it only does so together with a prediction (or assumption) about how the data will be transformed.

Now, often there is a theoretical reason to prefer one transformation over the other. For example, we may have a theory of learning that says that learning takes place at a constant rate in terms of the *proportional* improvement from trial to trial. This theory would lead us to prefer still another transformation, the logarithmic transformation. A logarithmic transformation will cause constant *proportional* changes in the response as a function of the stimulus, to yield a straight line. Figure 3–29 shows the results of a logarithmic transformation. There we see no interaction. We would conclude from this figure that the rate of learning was constant and was the same for both groups of rats. Of course, it is circular thinking to prefer a transformation because of a theory and then to use data to confirm the theory. Other criteria exist for choosing which transformation to use. Usually, but not always, the transformation that produces normally distributed data with equal variability between conditions will be the preferred transformation for theoretical purposes as well. The point is to be aware of the problem and not make conclusions about interactions out of ignorance.

SUMMARY

1. A variable is some property of an event in the world that has been measured.
2. A dependent variable is a measure of the behavior of the subject.
3. An independent variable is one that is believed to cause some change in the value of the dependent variable.

4. A continuous variable is one that is not limited to a certain number of values.
5. A discrete variable is one that falls into a certain number of categories.
6. Quantitative variables vary in amount, whereas qualitative variables differ in kind.
7. A physical variable is one that can be defined in physical terms. A nonphysical variable is one that cannot be so defined but must be defined in terms of behavior or cognitive processes.
8. Measurement is the assignment of numbers to objects or events according to rules that permit important properties of the objects or events to be represented by properties of the number system.
9. Four scales of measurement are distinguished according to the rules by which numbers are assigned to objects or events: nominal, ordinal, interval, and ratio.
10. A nominal scale is one that classifies objects or events into categories. Objects or events of the same kind get the same number and different objects or events get different numbers.
11. An ordinal scale is one that ranks objects or events in order of their magnitude. The ordinal position of the numbers on the scale must represent the rank order of the psychological attributes of the objects or events.
12. An interval scale is one in which the differences between the numbers on the scale are meaningful. Equal differences between the numbers on the scale must represent equal differences between the events or objects.
13. A ratio scale is one that has a meaningful zero point as well as meaningful differences between the numbers on the scale. The ratios between the numbers on the scale must represent the ratios between the events or objects.
14. We are able to gain more information from the data as we progress from nominal to ordinal, interval, and ratio scales.
15. Knowing the type of scale that data are measured on is important so as to avoid drawing incorrect conclusions from the data.
16. Bar graphs are used when the independent variable is categorical; otherwise line graphs are used.
17. The slope of a curve is the ratio of the change in the Y variable divided by the change in the X variable over some portion of the curve.
18. Some common attributes of curves are: linearly increasing or decreasing, positively or negatively accelerating, sigmoid, monotonic or nonmonotonic, and U shaped.
19. Frequency distributions are graphs in which the ordinate represents a count rather than a value of a dependent variable.
20. A cumulative frequency distribution is one that plots the number of cases that fall at or below a given score.
21. A factorial experiment is one that measures the response to all possible combinations of at least two levels of at least two independent variables.

22. In a factorial experiment, the main effect of one variable is the effect of that variable averaged over all of the levels of the other variable(s).
23. An interaction exists between two independent variables when independent variable *A* has a different effect on the dependent variable when it is combined with one level of independent variable *B* than with another level of *B*. If the graph of a factorial experiment has nonparallel lines, there is an interaction between the variables.
24. If there is an interaction, the main effect is uninterpretable unless the nature of the interaction is taken into account.
25. Types of interactions include: antagonistic, synergistic, and ceiling effect.
26. The presence or absence of an interaction and the form it takes are affected by any transformations made on the data.

SUGGESTIONS FOR FURTHER READING

GUILFORD, J. P. *Psychometric methods*. New York: McGraw-Hill, 1954. This book contains a good discussion of scales of measurement as well as a mathematical introduction that covers much of the material in this chapter.

LEWIS, D. *Quantitative methods in psychology*. New York: McGraw-Hill, 1960. Valuable mathematical background for this chapter is covered.

STEVENS, S. S. Mathematics, measurement, and psychophysics. In S. S. Stevens (Ed.), *Handbook of experimental psychology*. New York: Wiley, 1951. The classic discussion of scales of measurement is presented.

READING BETWEEN THE LINES

The following problems are presented for you to solve. See Reading Between the Lines in Chapter 1 for an introduction to them. The answers are given in Appendix A.

6. TESTING FOR INDEPENDENCE OF DIMENSIONS

Robert Hamm and James Mattson (1978) wanted to test whether stimuli to which an animal had been conditioned separately would have a combined effect when the stimuli were presented together. They taught rats in a Skinner box to press a plastic bar, causing the bar to be lit up from behind. The two dimensions were the intensity of the light and the rate at which it flickered. The intensity of the light on the bar could be either high or low, and the light could flicker either once per second or ten times per second.

The duration of the light was the same each time it flickered, so that when the light flickered ten times per second, ten times as much light was presented to the rats. The rats were trained to respond either when the intensity was high (and the flicker rate was low) or when the flicker rate was high (and the intensity was low). They were trained not to respond when both the intensity and the rate of flicker were low.

Hamm and Mattson tested the hypothesis that the two dimensions, intensity and flicker rate, would have an independent effect on the response rate by presenting a high intensity, fast flicker that the rats had never seen before. The rats' response to this combination was higher than to either the high intensity or the fast flicker by themselves. The investigators concluded that flicker rate and intensity had independent effects on the response rate. Was their conclusion justified?

7. IS PRAYER EFFECTIVE?

Sir Francis Galton wanted to know whether prayer changes things. He reasoned that the royalty would be prayed for by more people and should therefore live longer than average. He found, instead, that royalty lived 64 years, intellectuals lived 68, and gentry lived 70, on the average (Webb, Campbell, Schwartz, & Sechrest, 1966). What do you think of Galton's reasoning?

8. "YOU CAN PROVE ANYTHING WITH STATISTICS"

In a televised speech to the nation in support of his tax cut program, President Reagan used the graph shown in Figure 3–30 to convince viewers of the advantage of his tax proposal over that of the Democrats. The graph shows taxes paid by a typical family under the two proposals. He said, "The lines on the charts say a lot about who's really fighting for whom" ("That Numberless Presidential Chart," 1981). What is the problem in drawing conclusions from the President's graph? What is missing from the graph that makes it impossible to interpret?

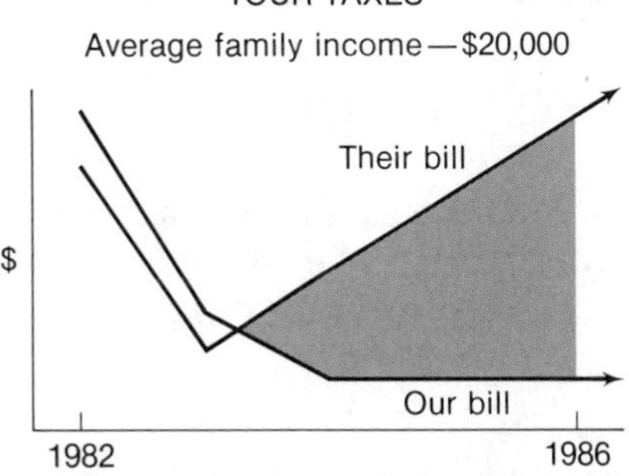

FIGURE 3–30. Graph shown by President Reagan on television in support of his tax cut proposal. © 1981 by The New York Times Company. Reprinted by permission.

VALIDITY

All research is designed to permit the researcher to draw conclusions about cause-effect relationships among variables. As we discussed in an earlier chapter, the ultimate goal is to develop a theory that explains the relationships found among variables. This chapter concerns the various problems that can threaten the validity of conclusions drawn by a researcher. By **validity**, we mean simply that the researcher's conclusion is true or correct, that it corresponds to the actual state of the world. You will probably realize that achieving the truth about the world is asking a great deal.

Validity
an indication of accuracy in terms of the extent to which a research conclusion corresponds with reality

Some of the problems of validity threaten the conclusion that a cause-effect relationship exists among the variables at all; some threaten the theoretical explanation of the kind of relationship obtained. We will discuss first, the various kinds of research validity, and second, the many threats to validity. In Chapter 5, we will consider the methods available to the researcher to control for these threats.

TYPES OF VALIDITY

Thomas Cook and Donald Campbell (1976) list four types of validity that must be considered in designing and evaluating a piece of research: internal validity, construct validity, external validity, and statistical validity.

Internal validity
extent to which a cause-effect relationship exists between the independent and dependent variables

Internal Validity

Internal validity is the most fundamental type because it concerns the logic of the relationship between the independent and dependent variables. An experiment has internal validity if there are sound reasons to believe that a cause-effect relationship really is present between the independent and dependent variables. In other words, the independent variable caused the dependent variable to change.

Suppose that you did an experiment on the effect of informational feedback on a motor learning task. Group A received a tone whenever they made the correct reponse and Group B did not. So far, so good. But you tested all of the subjects in Group A on Monday and all in Group B on Tuesday. Now, besides the difference in feedback between the groups, they also differed in the time of administration of the experiment. It is impossible to decide whether any differences in behavior should be attributed to feedback or to time of administration.

Confounding error that occurs when the effects of two variables in an experiment cannot be separated, resulting in a confused interpretation of the results

This experiment lacks internal validity because you cannot conclude that feedback caused the results. We say that time was **confounded** with feedback because its possible effects were not tested separately from the effects of feedback. We say that time covaried with feedback. When some condition covaries with the independent variable in such a way that their separate effects cannot be sorted out, the two variables are confounded. You can easily imagine a number of potentially important variables that could affect performance on a motor skills task. The Monday could have followed fraternity rush weekend, with some of the subjects feeling the aftereffects. Perhaps on Tuesday the barometric pressure was high, or the experimenter had just learned that her boyfriend was going to join a commune. Notice that none of these confounded variables enter into any theory of motor learning, even though some of them might affect behavior.

Confounding is one of the biggest threats to validity in experimentation. Great care must be taken that no important variable is confounded with the independent variable. Much of Chapter 5 concerns techniques used to avoid confounding.

On the other hand, making sure that *no* variable is confounded with the independent variable is not feasible. Among the possible confounded variables in the above example is phase of the moon. Although some people have suggested that strange behavior occurs during full moon, the evidence for this conclusion is weak. Most investigators therefore feel justified in ignoring lunar phase.

If day of the week is an important confounding variable but lunar phase is not, how do experimenters decide which variables to worry about? The fact is that many value judgments are made as the experiment is designed. For example, many taste researchers take care that no smokers serve as subjects or that no subjects smoke within one hour of the experiment. I used to routinely eliminate smokers from my taste experiments, in spite of the fact that no persuasive evidence existed that smoking affects sensation for college-age subjects. In one experiment that an undergraduate student and I did, we concluded that there was no discernable effect of smoking on taste thresholds in the college-age subjects we used. These results, together with the fact that other experiments in the literature are inconclusive, led me to quit paying attention to whether my subjects are smokers.

The problem of confounding is particularly acute in research where the experimenter cannot control the independent variable—when subjects must be selected according to the presence or absence of a condition, rather than having a condition assigned to them. A good example of a variable that the experimenter cannot assign is sex of subject. When sex of subject is one of the independent variables of an experiment, as it often is, then we have a quasi experiment (see Chapter 8) and a much greater probability of confounding. Take, for example, the lively debate about the extent of the differences in psychological processes between men and women. This debate results from the greatly differing influences in our society on males and females that begin when they leave the hospital in their pink or blue clothes. All the innumerable experiences and the resulting learned attitudes and skills are confounded in the simple term *sex differences*. The extent to which these confounded variables contribute to the sex differences found in research is the crux of the sex difference controversy.

Similarly, in research on race and IQ we find many variables confounded with race that are known to influence IQ, such as parents' level of education, family income, and quality of available schooling.

Construct Validity

Construct validity extent to which an experiment measures the theory behind the research

Construct validity concerns the question of whether the results support the theory behind the research. Is there another theory that would predict the same results?

Every experiment is designed to test some hypothesis, yet the hypothesis cannot be tested in a vacuum. Particular conditions of the experiment constitute *auxiliary hypotheses* that also must be true in order to test the main hypothesis. Suppose your hypothesis is that anxiety is conducive to learning. You may select your subjects on the basis of whether they bite their fingernails, with your goal being to see how fast they can learn to write by holding a pencil in their toes. If you find no difference in the rate of learning between groups, you might conclude that your hypothesis is false. However, you did not test just the one hypothesis that anxiety is conducive to learning. You also tested two auxiliary hypotheses: that fingernail biting is a measure of anxiety and that writing with toes is a good learning task. If either of these auxiliary hypotheses is false, you could have found negative results.

How can you ensure construct validity? Actually, you cannot, but you can plan your research so that it is more plausible. In order to improve the validity of your experiment, you might have used the Taylor Manifest Anxiety Scale to classify your subjects on anxiety, and you might have used a more standardized learning measure, such as learning a list of unrelated words. These techniques, although not perfect, have been used many times. We have more faith that they are valid than we do in fingernail biting and writing with the toes.

Another example of the problem of construct validity can be taken from psychobiology. Destruction of a particular part of the brain will cause a rat to become obese if it is allowed to eat all it wants. Researchers initially believed that the rat was hungrier than normal as a result of the operation. Later they learned that the rat would eat more only if the food was palatable and if the rat did not have to work hard for it. The result was that the rat really was not hungrier; it simply lacked the ability to tell when it had eaten enough.

Experiments like these that used destruction of part of the brain as a way of *increasing hunger* were actually *decreasing satiety*. Any research using this method to increase hunger in rats would lack construct validity, because the manipulation did not increase hunger as measured by other manipulations such as food deprivation. More recent work (Friedman & Stricker, 1976), in turn, has suggested that the injury to the brain may not be influencing either hunger or satiety directly but may be changing the rat's metabolism. The rat gains weight because it has a greater tendency to store fat, even if its food intake is restricted.

Construct validity is similar to internal validity. In internal validity you strive to rule out alternative variables as potential causes of the behavior of interest. In construct validity you must rule out other possible theoretical explanations of the results. In either case you may have to perform another experiment in order to rule out a threat to validity. For internal validity you may find it possible to redesign the experiment to control for the source of confounding. In the case of construct validity you must design a new experiment that will permit a choice between the two competing theoretical explanations of the results. When the researchers suspected that rats with brain damage really were not hungrier, they designed tests to find out how the rats responded to the food's being unpalatable or harder to obtain or to their exposure to food being limited. In each case the brain-damaged rats ate less food than normal rats, making the hypothesis of greater hunger less tenable than the alternative theory.

External Validity

External validity how well the findings of an experiment generalize to other situations or populations

External validity concerns whether the results of the research can be generalized to another situation: different subjects, settings, times, and so forth. Strictly speaking, the results of a piece of research are valid only for other identical situations: 18 sophomores at State University on a rainy 13th of April 1980 in a room with green walls and an experimenter with a beard. Such literalness is ridiculous, of course, but which variables are trivial to the validity of the experiment and which are important?

In an influential experiment in perception conducted in 1949 (McGinnies), subjects were asked to read words that were flashed on a screen. The results were interpreted as showing that a person's threshold for seeing taboo words was higher than for seeing ordinary words. Today researchers would interpret the data to reflect reluctance of subjects to utter the taboo words, rather than a truly higher perceptual threshold for them. We mention this experiment because of the particular taboo words used. You may be surprised and skeptical to learn that subjects would hesitate to say the words *belly*, *bitch*, or *rape* aloud in an experiment. We must remember, though, that this experiment was reported in 1949. The use of language in public has changed much since then. Today it is unlikely that the experiment would yield the same results. This experiment could not be generalized to today's world; it would lack external validity.

Statistical validity extent to which data are shown to be the result of cause-effect relationships rather than accident

Statistical Validity

Statistical validity is similar to internal validity. Here the question is: Was the observed relationship between the independent and dependent variables a true cause-effect relationship or was it accidental? Or, was the number of subjects so small that the results happened purely by chance?

THREATS TO VALIDITY

We have been talking about kinds of validity. Now we will consider some problems that constitute threats to validity.

Threats to Internal Validity

In essence guarding against threats to internal validity consists of learning to avoid the confounding of potentially important variables with the independent variable or variables of interest. The major sources of confounding will be considered in turn.

Events outside the laboratory. Whenever an experiment is conducted in such a way that different experimental conditions are presented to subjects at different times, it is possible for events outside the laboratory to influence the results. If you studied the effects of success and failure on feelings of depression, and all of the subjects experienced the failure condition on Monday and the success condition on Wednesday, you can imagine how the results would be difficult to interpret if it rained on Monday. This situation may sound like a threat to external validity, but it is not. External validity assumes that there is no confounding within the experiment. Rather, it is concerned with important variables that might change between the time an experiment is conducted and when it is repeated another time.

Maturation. Subjects may change between conditions of an experiment because of naturally occurring processes. Certainly they get older. If the experiment involves a significant lapse of time, for instance, changes may occur in motor coordination, knowledge, and the like that could influence the results. Suppose you were interested in studying the effect of "Sesame Street" on children's reading skills. You would want to have a control for the improvement in reading that would occur over time in children not exposed to "Sesame Street."

Maturation
a source of error in an experiment related to the amount of time between measurements

Maturation is a more critical problem in research involving children because they change more rapidly over time than do adults. Yet the fact that adults change with age is now becoming widely appreciated. Take, for example, a hypothetical long-term study of attitudes toward alternative life-styles as a function of age. To separate out changes caused by shifting attitudes in society from changes in individual persons as a result of the aging process would not be easy.

Effects of testing. Simply being in an experiment or being tested will influence peoples' performance in a later experiment or administration of the test. The subjects may become sophisticated about the testing procedure or may learn how to take tests so that their later behavior is changed by the earlier experience. This phenomenon is similar to maturation in that the subjects are changed over time but is different in that the change is caused by the testing procedure itself, rather than processes unrelated to the test.

Regression effect
tendency of subjects with extreme scores on a first measure to score closer to the mean on a second testing

Regression effect. This effect, one of the most insidious threats to validity, arises in many situations. The **regression effect** operates when subjects (or responses) are tested twice on the same variable. Individuals who performed at the extremes on the pretest will tend to score closer to the mean on the posttest.

The regression effect occurs when there is error associated with the measurement of the variable. Notice that when we say there is error in the measurement, we do not mean that recording errors are made. We mean that the test itself is not a perfect measure of what is being measured. For example, on a multiple-choice test students will make some lucky or unlucky guesses, resulting in a score that is not a perfect indicator of what they know.

Random error
change in the measurement of a variable that can be attributed to chance

The classic example of the regression effect is that of a teacher who notices that students who scored highest on the first test usually do less well on the second, whereas those who did the worst improve. The teacher often concludes that the ones who did well the first time rested on their laurels for the second test, while the ones who did poorly worked harder. In reality this is not what happened. Whenever **random error** exists in the measurement of a variable, individuals will deviate from their true score by the operation of random error. Some will be lucky, others will be unlucky. Many of the extreme scores, both high and low, will be more extreme than their true value. On the retest, the errors average out and the scores of these previously extreme individuals tend to return toward their true value, closer to the mean.

The regression effect can lead to some unfortunate conclusions. A parent may notice that praising a child for good behavior is followed by a *decrease* in the desired behavior and that the child's behavior improves after he or she is punished for bad behavior. If the bad behavior is unusual, generally it will improve anyway. The good behavior also may have been a random event that would decrease with or without praise. The parent wrongly concludes that praise is useless and that the way to teach children is to punish bad behavior and to ignore good behavior. In experiments similar results may be found where subjects are chosen on the basis of a pretest, are given a treatment, and then are retested. The treatment is found to help the low-scoring subjects but to make the high-scoring subjects worse.

Selection. Many studies compare two or more groups on some dependent variable. Any bias in selecting the groups can undermine internal validity. In the next chapter, we will discuss the foolproof remedy of randomly assigning individuals to groups. Often this is not possible, particularly in field research where it is necessary to study existing groups. You can easily imagine that the local chapter of the Veterans of Foreign Wars would not make a good group to compare with the local chapter of the Society to Protect Baby Seals. Most people would not make as poor a choice as this. But would the Veterans of Foreign Wars from Detroit, Michigan, be a good choice to compare with the chapter from Tuscaloosa, Alabama? You must exercise care and ingenuity to choose or create groups that can be considered truly comparable.

Mortality. Even if there is no bias in selecting subjects and you are able to constitute groups that are the same in every respect, your study may be invalid if all subjects do not complete all phases of it. **Mortality** as a threat to validity means that the subjects who drop out of a study may be different from those who complete it. Biases can be caused by particular kinds of subjects dropping out.

Mortality
the dropping out of some subjects before an experiment is completed, causing a threat to validity

Suppose you are studying two methods of behavior modification on weight control. Group 1 is given a diet to follow. In addition they are to keep a diary of everything they eat, weigh all foods to the nearest gram, and estimate all calories consumed. Group 2 is simply given the diet to follow. You may reasonably assume that the subjects in the group with the more demanding tasks will be more likely to drop out. At the end of the experiment that group will contain a higher proportion of highly motivated subjects who would, in turn, be more likely to succeed in losing weight.

You then might falsely conclude that the first condition was more effective than the second.

Another example concerns whether intelligence declines with age in older persons. Here the difficulty is in obtaining equivalent groups to compare across age. If you use the same group at two different ages, some individuals will become unavailable the second time because of illness or death. If you consider only those people who are available on both occasions, you may find little or no decline. Are these the appropriate subjects on which to base your conclusion, or should you make a concerted effort to retest people who are now in hospitals and institutions for the aged? The harder you try to locate subjects for retest, the more likely you are to get people who will perform poorly because of sickness, rather than old age per se. Thus, it is difficult to decide whether a true age effect on intelligence exists or whether all decline results from illness.

Threats to Construct Validity

Construct validity is perhaps the most difficult type of validity to achieve because of the indefinite number of theories that may account for a given lawful relationship. The general strategy for obtaining construct validity in a piece of research is to ask whether alternative theoretical explanations of the data are less plausible than the theory believed to be supported by the research. We will discuss two areas that pose threats to construct validity.

Loose connection between theory and experiment. The experiment described earlier for testing the effects of anxiety on learning was an extreme example of a loose connection between theory and experiment. Nail biting is a poor method of measuring anxiety, and writing with the toes is likely to be a poor measure of learning. Much psychological research suffers from poor operational definition of theoretical concepts. In a previous chapter we gave the example of hunting and fighting in cats. We said that these two theoretical concepts would not be validly tested in a situation where an example of one class of behavior was taken to belong to the other.

Take two examples of behavior that both might be called aggressive. We might say that Philip aggressively attacked his job of weeding the garden and that Willard showed aggression in deliberately being slow in carrying out his teacher's instructions. Philip's aggressive weeding may simply reflect his desire to get on with more interesting activities. Or, someone familiar with the frustration-aggression law may conclude that he was showing displaced aggression. Perhaps his sister had provoked him to hit her and then had made the hitting appear to be his fault so that he had to weed as punishment. Willard's behavior, on the other hand, may be described by clinical psychologists as passive aggression.

Frequently we use the same term, such as aggression, for behaviors that may represent different classes of behavior and relate to different theoretical concepts. Trivial operational definitions of concepts, like the nail-biting definition of anxiety, are not likely to tap directly into the nature of the concept. Therefore, they will not be helpful in relating an experiment using such a definition to research using more valid measures.

Ambiguous effect of independent variables. An experimenter may carefully design an experiment in which all reasonable confounding variables seem to be well controlled, only to have the results compromised because the subjects perceived the situation differently from the experimenter.

For example, some of my research has involved measuring taste thresholds to chemicals flowed over the outstretched tongues of subjects. The situation seemed perfectly straightforward to me. However, occasionally when the session was over a subject would say to me, "What was the experiment really about? You weren't interested in how all that junk tasted, were you?" What those subjects had done was conduct an experiment of their own instead of the one I thought I was conducting. Fortunately, in research of this type, the subjects' ideas about what is supposed to happen are not likely to influence the results that the experimenter is interested in.

Often, though, in psychological research the effect can be devastating. The classic example concerns a series of experiments conducted from 1924 to 1933 in the Hawthorne, Illinois, plant of the Western Electric Company. Management wanted to study the effects of working conditions on productivity. Many factors such as lighting, length of working hours, and the like were varied. The results showed that changes in output bore little relation to working conditions. Output went up when lighting was reduced, for example. Overall, productivity increased throughout the period of the experiment regardless of working conditions. The accepted explanation of the now-famous *Hawthorne effect* is that the workers, who were separated from the rest of the plant and thus were aware that they were being tested, reacted to the knowledge that they were in an experiment rather than to the working conditions as such. The effect of the conditions caused the workers to conduct their own experiment, so to speak. Thus, the experiment that the researchers thought they were conducting was rendered invalid.

A more recent paper (Bramel & Friend, 1981) suggests another interpretation: Workers were suspicious of management and varied their output in order to maintain control over aspects of the working conditions that were important to them, such as work breaks. In any case, the independent variables have an ambiguous effect in this experiment.

Many experiments suffer from similar ambiguity. Whenever subjects are aware that they are participating in an experiment, their behavior may be different from their everyday behavior. A commonplace example is the reaction of people to having a movie camera directed toward them. The solution to this type of problem is to keep the subjects from becoming aware that they are participating in an experiment. We will discuss the pros and cons of this technique in Chapter 10 when we discuss nonexperimental research.

The ambiguous effect of the independent variables results from the fact that any psychological experiment for which a subject has volunteered must be considered to be a social situation wherein the subject has preconceived ideas about what is expected. Such ideas lead to several tendencies on the part of the subject. Perhaps the most prevalent is for the subject to play the role of the **good subject.** That is, subjects act the way they think the experimenter wants them to act. They may deliberately feign a naive attitude about the expected results even though they can guess the true purpose of the experiment. Perhaps they have heard about the experiment or have learned of similar experiments conducted elsewhere. You may have observed this phenomenon among subjects recruited from introductory psychology classes in which many types of experiments are discussed. The subjects may pretend to be fooled by the instructions in order to be "good subjects."

Good-subject response tendency of experimental subjects to act according to what they think the experimenter wants

Another kind of subject expectancy is the concern that the experimental procedure in some way measures the subject's competence. Some subjects are convinced that the experiment is a carefully disguised measure of intelligence or emotional adjustment. This expectancy gives rise to **evaluation apprehension,** in which subjects tailor their behavior to make themselves look as normal as possible. Another name for this problem is social desirability. Researchers who develop attitude scales take care to ensure that various responses appear equally socially desirable so that subjects will not damage the results by concealing their true attitudes.

Evaluation apprehension tendency of experimental subjects to alter their behavior in order to be as socially desirable as possible

Suppose that you are conducting an experiment on the effects of pornography on sexual behavior. Subjects are asked to keep a diary of all sexual activity for a week before and after they are shown a pornographic movie. You can imagine that people would hesitate to volunteer information about deviant activities. Even if they were honest in their reporting, they might modify their behavior during the experiment in the direction of social desirability. You can see how evaluation apprehension will have the opposite effect of the good-subject tendency.

Threats to External Validity

Even if an experiment has internal validity, statistical validity, and construct validity, it may not be generalizable to other situations. There are as many threats to the external validity of research as there are dimensions along which one experiment can differ from another. We will consider the most important differences between experiments that can constitute threats to external validity.

Other subjects. A common indictment of psychological research is that it predominantly uses college students and white rats as subjects. The reasons psychologists rely on these two species is their presumed representativeness and accessibility to researchers. The problem is that over one million species of animals exist, most of them insects. However, if you accept that psychologists are interested primarily in human behavior, then the attention to rats and college students is not as unfortunate as it might seem at first. The degree to which common principles of behavior operate across species is impressive. Many years ago Skinner presented data showing that the behavior of a pigeon, rat, and monkey under certain experimental conditions was identical in all important respects (1956).

On the other hand, we must not assume that any animal can be substituted for any other in all situations. Keller Breland and Marian Breland (1961) give many examples of the need to choose the response one wishes to study and then to manipulate the variables, paying careful attention to the animal's natural behavioral repertoire. Thus it is easy to teach a chicken to dance because dancing is similar to the normal behavior of scratching for food. You would not train a rat to dance because dancing is not close to the natural behavior.

Human subjects should be chosen with equal attention to their representativeness concerning some larger population. If you are doing an experiment with college students on bargaining and negotiation, will the results validly predict what a secretary of state or a general would do?

Other times. Would the same experiments conducted at another time produce the same results? We mentioned this problem earlier in introducing the concept of external validity. The "dirty word" experiment almost certainly lacks external validity today, at least as far as the original words are concerned. Many historical trends render particular research findings invalid, whether they concern use of language, attitudes toward foreign countries, or deviant groups.

Other settings. A pervasive problem that can hinder external validity involves the question of how the phenomenon observed in one laboratory can be related to a similar phenomenon observed in another laboratory or in the real world. Many psychologists have given up laboratory work altogether in favor of field research, or even armchair speculation, for this very reason. It is not easy to decide if a certain effect is simply a laboratory effect or whether it would survive transplantation to the world outside the laboratory. Suppose that you are interested in whether letting students work at their own pace produces better learning than giving schedules, assignments, and tests. A school that would permit its students to be experimented on might be more open to innovation in general. Likewise, students, teachers, and administrators in such a school might respond more favorably to the self-paced condition than to the more regimented procedure. So your results may not be valid for more traditional schools.

Summary Note on Validity

Our review of the many threats to validity should make you aware of the kinds of problems that may arise in research. Not all of the problems discussed above will be as serious in all areas of psychology. From the examples we have used in this chapter, you may have surmised that the problems are acute in the social areas. It is true that most of the literature on validity has been contributed by social psychologists. On the other hand, an area like visual perception is much less subject to these problems. As long as subjects have normal acuity and are not color blind, one subject is much like another. Few visual experiments suffer from problems of validity.

In the next chapter we will consider how to cope with the various threats to validity.

SUMMARY

1. A conclusion based on research is valid when it corresponds to the actual state of the world.
2. Four types of research validity are commonly recognized: internal validity, construct validity, external validity, and statistical validity.
3. An investigation has internal validity if a cause-effect relationship actually exists between the independent and dependent variables.
4. Construct validity concerns the question of whether the results support the theory behind the research.
5. Every experiment tests auxiliary hypotheses in addition to the main hypothesis. These auxiliary hypotheses are that particular conditions of the experiment are valid measures of the theoretical concepts the experiment is testing.
6. External validity concerns whether the results of the research can be generalized to another situation: different subjects, settings, times, and so forth.
7. Statistical validity concerns whether the observed relationship is a true cause-effect relationship or whether it is accidental.
8. Threats to the internal validity of an experiment include: events outside the laboratory, maturation, effects of testing, regression effect, selection, and mortality.
9. The regression effect occurs when subjects are tested twice on some variable and there is error in the measurement. Individuals who performed at the extremes on the pretest will tend to score closer to the mean on the posttest.
10. Threats to construct validity include: loose connection between theory and experiment and ambiguous effect of independent variables.
11. Among the problems that cause an ambiguous effect of the independent variables are tendencies for subjects to interpret conditions differently from

the experimenter, as well as the good-subject tendency and the matter of evaluation apprehension.

12. Threats to external validity include problems arising from generalizing to other subjects, other times, or other settings.
13. Certain of these threats to validity are more prominent in particular types of research than in others.

SUGGESTION FOR FURTHER READING

COOK, T. D., & CAMPBELL, D. T. The design and conduct of quasi-experiments and true experiments in field settings. In M. D. Dunette (Ed.), *Handbook of industrial and organizational psychology*. Chicago: Rand McNally, 1976. This chapter is the standard source on validity.

READING BETWEEN THE LINES

The following problems are presented for you to solve. See Reading Between the Lines in Chapter 1 for an introduction to them. The answers are provided in Appendix A.

9. DO YOUNGER INFANTS PREFER SIMPLER PATTERNS?

Wendy Brennan, Elinor Ames, and Ronald Moore (1966) showed infants cards with black-and-white checkerboard patterns on them. All cards were the same size and the number of squares per card was either 4, 64, or 576. They found that 3-week-old infants looked longest at the simplest card, that 8-week-olds preferred the middle card, and that 14-week-olds preferred the most complex card. They concluded that there was a developmental trend in preference for complexity. Can you think of another interpretation of these results?

10. DO WOMEN FEAR SUCCESS MORE THAN DO MEN?

Matina Horner (1968; cited by Tresemer, 1977) had male and female college students write brief stories in response to the following verbal cue: "At the end of first-term finals, Anne [John] finds herself [himself] at the top of her [his] medical school class" (Tresemer, 1977, p. 32). Women saw the Anne version and men saw the John version. Horner scored the resulting stories for themes that indicated a fear of success, such as social rejection ("everyone hates and envies her") and negative affect (feeling unhappy, unfeminine, guilty). Horner found that 62 percent of the women showed fear of success in their stories, whereas only 9 percent of the men did so. She interpreted her data as indicating that females had more fear of success than did males. Can you think of alternative hypotheses to account for these results?

CONTROL

The previous chapter discussed the concept of validity and the various threats to the validity of research. In this chapter we talk about ways of counteracting those threats to the validity of psychological research. First, we define the concept of control, discussing, in turn, several general strategies for achieving control. Then we describe a number of specific control strategies.

Control is the other side of the validity coin. The heart of the experimental approach to knowledge is to ask the following two questions: First, what are the threats to the validity of a contemplated piece of research? Second, what means are available to neutralize those threats? This approach is so basic that anyone who is acquainted with research has heard of control groups. Every experiment must have a control group. Right? Wrong.

It *is* true that you must have some method of countering every plausible alternative explanation of the results of your experiment. It is also true that often this involves the use of a group of subjects who do not experience the manipulation—that is, a control group—to serve as a standard against which to compare the effect of the variable of interest. Many experiments are performed, however, in which the use of a group that does not receive the independent variable makes no sense at all. Suppose you are interested in the effect of teaching methods on learning. You might arrange for some students to receive only lectures and others to receive both lectures and discussion. You could conclude that one method of teaching was better than the other without having a group that never went to class.

Control
providing a standard against which to compare the effect of a particular variable

We will define **control** as any means used to rule out possible threats to the validity of a piece of research. In psychology the concept of control is

TABLE 5–1 Illustration of the meaning of control.

	Treatment	Test
Group 1 (experimental group)	*A* present	yes
Group 2 (control group)	*A* absent	yes

used in two ways. The fundamental meaning of the term is that of providing a standard against which to compare the effect of a particular independent variable. If two experimental conditions differ on only one independent variable, then any difference between the two conditions following the treatment may be attributed to the operation of that variable. All other explanations are ruled out by the existence of the second, or control, condition.

This meaning of the term *control* is illustrated in Table 5–1. Two groups of subjects are tested on a dependent variable. Group 1 receives Treatment *A* and therefore is called the **experimental group**. Group 2 receives no treatment and therefore is the **control group**. The control group serves as the basis of comparison for the experimental group. If the two groups were equal before the experimental treatment, then any postexperiment difference between them can be attributed to the treatment.

Experimental group
subjects in an experiment who receive treatment

Control group
subjects in an experiment who are like the experimental group in every respect except that they do not receive treatment

Although a control group is an effective way of achieving control of extraneous variables, it is not the only way. We said earlier that control can be achieved without a control group. Table 5–2 illustrates this point. We still have two groups and they both are tested after receiving treatment. However, instead of Group 1 experiencing *A* and Group 2 experiencing the absense of *A*, both groups experience some value of *A*. As in an earlier example, A_1 and A_2 could be two different teaching methods. Assuming the groups were equal before treatment, we can attribute any difference between Group 1 and Group 2 on the test to the difference between Condition A_1 and Condition A_2. Although we do not have a control group as such, each group serves as a control for the other. We have as much control in this situation as we did in the previous example where we had a control group.

Let us consider one further point. Instead of having different subjects experience each condition, in some experiments each subject experiences

TABLE 5–2 Illustration of control without a control group.

	Treatment	Test
Group 1	A_1	yes
Group 2	A_2	yes

TABLE 5–3 Illustration of a control condition in a within-subjects experiment.

All subjects	Treatment	Test
Condition 1 (experimental condition)	*A* Present	yes
Condition 2 (control condition)	*A* absent	yes

Control condition a condition in an experiment that does not contain the experimental manipulation

Within-subjects experiment research design in which each subject experiences every condition of the experiment

Between-subjects experiment research design in which each subject experiences only one of the conditions in the experiment

every condition. In such an experiment, instead of having a control group, we have a **control condition**, as illustrated in Table 5–3. When each subject experiences every condition, we say that each subject serves as his or her own control. Experiments of this kind are called **within-subjects experiments** because the differences between conditions are tested within individual subjects. Experiments in which different groups of subjects experience different conditions are **between-subjects experiments** because the differences between conditions are tested between different subjects.

A second meaning of the term *control* is distinct from the first but closely related; namely, the ability to restrain or guide sources of variability in research (Boring, 1954, 1969). This idea of experimental control is the one brought home so convincingly by the operant conditioning work of B. F. Skinner. When one has so limited the sources of variability in an experiment that the behavior becomes highly predictable, one has achieved *experimental control*. We are extremely impressed to observe a pigeon that has been trained to peck a key for food in the presence of a green light but not to peck in the presence of red. When the bird is well trained, the light virtually turns the bird on and off.

The two meanings of control are related in the following way. The primary meaning allows one to say that a dependent variable is associated with an independent variable and not with any other variable. The second usage facilitates the drawing of this conclusion by so limiting the number of variables operating in the situation and their range of values that the conclusion is more clear.

We can characterize the difference between the two meanings by use of the terms *control experiment* and *experimental control* (compare Sidman, 1960). When we have experimental control (secondary meaning), we have a much more sensitive situation in which to rule out alternative explanations of the experimental results (primary meaning).

The next section deals with the most important ways of achieving control in research. At the outset we should note that just as all types of threats to validity do not appear in all research, so it is not necessary or even possible to use every means of control in all research. The various methods of control are tools for psychologists to employ as necessary. Some will be used almost always, some less often.

GENERAL STRATEGIES

We will discuss three general strategies for achieving control in psychological research: using a laboratory setting, considering the research setting as a preparation, and instrumenting the response. Although these strategies are closely related, we will consider them separately for emphasis.

Control in the Laboratory

Laboratory research generally is preferred to field research. The reason is simple and has to do with what a laboratory is. We tend to think of a laboratory as a room with gray or black furniture, no curtains on the windows, tile floors, with all of the workers dressed in white coats. Certainly, we are describing a typical laboratory, but the description has nothing to do with the essentials. Basically, a scientific laboratory is a place set up to allow the most appropriate control over variables of interest in the particular research. Thus, a social psychology laboratory might well have rugs on the floor, curtains on the windows, pictures on the walls, and comfortable chairs—like any living room. Laboratory work in social psychology, for example, requires control over elements like choice of subjects, beginning and end of social interaction, freedom from distraction, and so forth. If someone's home or a storefront building provides these requirements, such a setting might serve just as well or better than a sterile-looking room. The results of laboratory research depend entirely on the degree and type of control that is possible.

In Chapter 10 we will discuss some methods and advantages of field research. Here we will simply say that at times field research is preferable and at times laboratory research is preferable. Much social research, for example, is done in field settings because it is not possible or ethical to manipulate certain variables. Most people would frown on mugging subjects to learn what determines whether they will call the police. Or, in some cases the effect of a manipulation may not be realistic enough in the laboratory. Simulating a riot, for instance, would be difficult to do in a laboratory. But even those people who advocate field research agree that they must give up a degree of control and that problems of validity thus become greater. Field research is warranted when ethical or practical problems preclude the degree of control that would justify calling a certain research program a laboratory experiment. Laboratory research remains the ideal simply because the maximum control consistent with the nature of the problem is the ideal.

The Research Setting as a Preparation

One of the first questions to be answered in designing research is to decide what type of setting you want to use. You may be interested in learning what determines whether people will be cooperative or competitive. You could study how children play with toys, how basketball players pass to each other, or how salespeople decide who will help a customer. Any of these might be a good study. Another way to do research on cooperation is to use a situation called the prisoner's dilemma. The name comes from the situation in which two people have been arrested for involvement in a crime. If both of them refuse to confess, both will get a modest punishment. If one confesses and the other does not, the one who confesses will be pardoned (rewarded) and the other severely punished. The dilemma arises because confession can lead either to reward or punishment, with nonconfession also leading to punishment. This situation has been adapted to the laboratory, and much research has been done on the effects of the magnitude of rewards and punishments, relationship of the two people involved, and so forth.

The idea of a preparation is familiar to anyone who has studied biology. Researchers often use the giant nerve axon of the squid to study nerve conduction. Because the squid nerve is much larger than those in other animals, it thus permits biologists to do things that they cannot do with other nerves. The concept of a preparation is not as familiar in psychology, yet one of the researcher's goals is to choose the most suitable preparation for studying a given problem. Some of the most important contributions to psychology have been made by people who devised a new preparation for studying a given phenomenon. Perhaps the best example is that of B. F. Skinner, who created the device that everyone, except Skinner, calls the Skinner box.

Before Skinner's invention a number of devices had been used to study learning in small animals. Such study began with a maze patterned after the Hampton Court maze in England, one of those people-sized hedge mazes that were popular on large estates a few hundred years ago. Researchers soon realized that this first maze was too complicated for its purpose, so mazes were made progressively simpler until the T maze was designed. Later someone made a runway with no choice points at all and measured the speed at which rats ran the "maze." Then Skinner took a box, added a lever, and the rest is familiar history. What his apparatus provided that others did not was simplicity, plus the opportunity for the rat to respond as often as it liked without waiting for someone to pick it up and return it to a starting point.

Skinner's seemingly small change made it possible to study *rate* of responding rather than *number* of correct turns or even *speed* in the runway. Having focused on an important dependent variable largely overlooked by others, Skinner went on to revolutionize the study of learning in animals. Thus the Skinner box becomes one of the most important experiment preparations in psychology.

Preparation in this sense is involved in every experiment, but hardly ever is it spoken of that way in books on research design in psychology. Nevertheless, it is one of the most important considerations in designing research: Exactly which situation will provide the most powerful relationship between the variables of interest? No amount of sophisticated design or statistical analysis will make up for a poor choice of research preparation.

Instrumentation of the Response as Control

We have discussed the research setting as a preparation that allows the sensitive analysis of a phenomenon. Another important means of increasing the sensitivity of the research is to improve the measuring of the behavior being studied. Many researchers pay little attention to the response that will be measured, but here is where a little effort can pay big dividends. Just as certain preparations have become classic in psychology, so certain methods of measuring dependent variables also have had enormous impact. We have already mentioned the Taylor Manifest Anxiety Scale. The Minnesota Multiphasic Personality Inventory, the polygraph, and Stevens's direct psychophysical scaling methods are other excellent examples. These techniques have greatly improved the sensitivity of research in their respective fields. Many scientists devote their careers to developing and honing measuring devices. Most of these people do not intend to become methodologists but do so in order to better evaluate phenomena of interest to them.

I have used the term *instrumentation* in discussing the task of improving response measurement. This use may seem strange because not all measurement methods employ mechanical means. The usage is deliberate, though. It calls attention to measuring devices as instruments for reducing behavior to numbers or to other forms convenient for data analysis. A characteristic of a good measuring instrument is that it takes the response out of the realm of casual observation and makes it reliable. In this way we can speak of measurement of behavior as *objective,* thus meeting the requirement of interobserver reliability necessary for science. Therefore, even a measure of a *subjective* state, such as the pleasantness of an odor, can be considered *objective,* provided the instrumentation of the response is adequate.

Not only can instrumentation make the measurement of a response more sensitive, it can also be thought of as *creating responses.* An example is the use of the electroencephalograph (EEG) to study dreaming. Since antiquity people had reported dreams and psychologists and others had studied them. Yet some denied that dreams were a separate stage of sleep, stating that those who reported having dreams were merely describing a mental activity that was more or less continuous throughout sleep. In 1953 Eugene Aserinsky and Nathaniel Kleitman, while studying the EEG of sleeping persons, noticed occasional periods of a distinct type of eye movement they called rapid eye movement, or REM for short. They also noted that REM was associated with particular types of EEG activity. When subjects were awakened during a bout of REM, they usually reported that they had been dreaming. When they were awakened during non-REM sleep, they generally reported they had not been dreaming. This discovery led to further research on dreaming that has been both exciting and informative. Thus the instrumentation of the response of dreaming by the measurement of REM and related EEG activity has been important in the study of dreaming, and few people today deny that there is such a state as the dream.

Many other examples exist. For years sexual behavior was not studied in the laboratory because of strong taboos. One of the widely held beliefs was that women could experience two kinds of orgasm, vaginal orgasm and the so-called clitoral orgasm, depending on the method of stimulation and other factors. William Masters and Virginia Johnson began taking photographs and other measurements of people engaged in sex. Their research made clear that only one kind of female orgasm existed. Years of myth out the window. Another belief was that women did not respond to erotica as did men. Yet when suitable measuring devices were built to record the activity of the vagina, women were shown to respond to erotic stimuli in much the same way as did men (Fisher & Byrne, 1978). The women, however, were not aware of their vaginal behavior and so did not interpret their response as sexual arousal.

SPECIFIC STRATEGIES

Subject as Own Control

We are aware that each of us is unique and varies in many ways that could be important in an experiment. One of the most powerful control techniques is to have each subject experience every condition of the experiment. In this way variation caused by differences between subjects is greatly reduced. The experimenter is wise to adopt the strategy of using subjects as their own controls whenever possible.

This control method is common in many areas of psychology, particularly sensation and perception. For example, if you are interested in the effect of adaptation to different concentrations of salt on the threshold for salt, using different subjects for each condition does not make much sense. The experimental manipulation is not likely to destroy the naivete of the subject, because the subject is unlikely to guess the purpose of the experiment even after experiencing it. In fact, the subject may not be aware that the experiment has different conditions. In addition, if enough time between conditions is allowed, there is not likely to be an important carry over between conditions. The subject will recover in a few minutes from the effect of adaptation to salt and will be ready to experience the next condition.

On the other hand, in many experiments using subjects as their own controls simply is not possible. Once the subject has learned a problem by one method, learning the same problem again using a different method is impossible.

Another situation where using subjects as their own controls is not feasible is when contrasting effects exist between the conditions of the experiment, so that experiencing one condition may influence the response to another condition. For instance, if magnitude of reward is the independent variable, then subjects who experience a large reward first may respond less to a small reward than they would if only the small-reward condition had been received. Later we will discuss in more detail particular situations in which subjects cannot serve as their own controls. For the present you should use this strategy whenever three conditions can be met: (1) Using subject as own control is logically possible; (2) participating in all conditions of the experiment will not destroy the naivete of the subject; and (3) serious contrast effects between conditions will not be present.

Randomization

Random assignment unbiased selection process that gives each subject an equal chance of being chosen for every condition

Random assignment of subjects to conditions is another powerful control method. The term **random assignment** is used in a specific sense to mean that the allocation of subjects to conditions is random when each subject has an equal chance of being assigned to every condition. The advantage of random allocation of subjects to conditions is that once subjects have been randomly assigned, the only way that confounding of subject-related variables with the experimental variable can occur is by chance alone. This advantage may not seem big, you say, because the differences could still have resulted from chance. A better way may be to rule out chance effects in an experiment as possible.

Modern statistical analysis, however, provides numerous ways of testing whether experimental results are likely to have occurred by chance alone. These statistical methods rely completely on random allocation of subjects to conditions. In other words, statistical tests make estimates of the probability that purely random allocation of subjects to the various experiment conditions might have produced the results obtained. If the subjects are not assigned to conditions randomly, then the statistical tests are not valid. One of the biggest "sins" in experimental psychology is to perform an experiment that cannot be analyzed statistically. The surest way to commit this error is to fail to randomly assign subjects to conditions.

Randomization may be achieved in a number of ways. We will mention one, simply referring to a random-number table. Random-number tables contain lists of the digits zero through nine in random order. Successive subjects are assigned to groups according to the successive numbers in the table until each group is full. If there are two experimental groups, subjects with odd numbers may be assigned to one group and subjects with even numbers to another group. If there are four groups, the digits one through four may be used and the rest ignored.

Using the procedure of randomization requires care. Students may be asked to volunteer for an experiment by signing up on a sheet for available times. The experimenter might be tempted to assume that the times are selected randomly and might place the first half of the students in one condition and the last half in the other. You can easily think of a number of ways in which the two groups could differ. The people who sign up for the early times might be more highly motivated to serve as subjects. On the other hand, all may have jobs requiring them to leave campus in the afternoon. The experimenter must randomly assign subjects to conditions *after* they have signed up.

Another example of a mistake in allocating subjects is to pull rats from a group cage and place the first batch selected in Condition *A*, the second batch in Condition *B*, and so forth. A little reflection will make it clear that the order in which the rats will be picked depends on their tendency to approach or avoid the experimenter's hand. This occurrence could reflect important differences for many experiments in learning, motivation, or social behavior. See Table 5–4 for how to conduct a randomized-groups experiment.

At first glance calling random allocation a method of control may seem improper because you appear to be throwing away a means of control and casting yourself on the mercies of chance. However, when you randomly assign subjects to conditions, you can be sure that *only* chance could cause the groups to be unequal with respect to a potential confounding variable: All sources of confounding variables are ruled out except as they become associated with the conditions by chance. Even if some variable is

TABLE 5–4 Steps in conducting a randomized group experiment.

1. Randomly assign subjects to groups.

Group A	Group B
S_1	
	S_2
	S_3
S_4	
	S_5
S_6	
S_7	
	S_8
S_9	
	S_{10}

2. Administer experimental conditions.
3. Examine differences between groups.
   What is the difference between the groups?

confounded with the independent variable by chance alone, assessing the likelihood of this happening is possible via statistical methods.

Matching

Matching
control procedure to ensure that experimental and control groups are equated on one or more variables before the experiment

Improving experiment precision sometimes is possible by **matching** subjects on a pretest before randomly allocating them to conditions. When the subjects differ among themselves on an independent variable known or suspected to considerably affect the dependent variable of interest, matching may be necessary. For example, suppose you are studying the effect of two different feeding schedules on weight gained by rats. You might expect that rats that were heavier to begin with would continue to gain more weight regardless of the schedule they were on. If subjects were allocated randomly to conditions, then more of the heavier rats could wind up in one condition than in another. By weighing the rats before the experiment, you can allocate them in such a way that the average weight in the various groups is the same.

The first requirement to justify matching is a strong suspicion that there is an important variable on which the subjects differ that can be controlled by matching. Further, you must believe that a substantial correlation will be present between the matching variable and the dependent variable. In our example of the weight-gain experiment with rats, you would find the two lightest rats and randomly place one in Group A and the other in Group B. You would repeat this procedure until you had paired off all of the rats. If you found that, in fact, those animals that were initially heavier tended to gain weight regardless of the group they were in, then you would have been justified in matching on weight. By correlating weight gain with starting weight, you would have found that weight gain correlated with beginning weight in spite of the effect of the variable of interest. On the other hand, if you found that there was little or no correlation, you would have wasted your effort matching the subjects.

In fact, you can weaken your experiment by matching the subjects if the matching variable is not substantially correlated with the dependent variable. This effect results from the fact that the statistical test appropriate for a matched-group design considers the data from *pairs* of subjects, while the randomized-group test considers *individual* subjects. You can see that there are twice as many subjects as pairs of subjects, so the randomized test has more numbers to work with and therefore is more powerful.

A second condition necessary to justify matching is that it must be feasible to present a pretest to the subjects before assigning them to the conditions. For example, weighing rats before an experiment would be a simple matter, but giving an IQ test to every prospective student in an experiment on learning may not be feasible. The experimenter's time probably would be used better simply in testing more subjects, unless the

IQ data can be obtained readily and ethically or unless the experiment is long enough to allow time for IQ testing.

Some bases for matching are better than others. Generally you try to match on the basis of some variable that has the highest possible correlation with the dependent variable. Normally the highest correlation is between the dependent variable and itself. In other words, if you are doing an experiment using reaction time, matching subjects according to their reaction times makes the most sense. You could present some practice trials and then allocate subjects to conditions based on their performance in the trials. On the other hand, if you are doing an experiment on learning and you want to control for intelligence, matching according to socioeconomic status (SES) would be a poor choice, even though there is some correlation between SES and intelligence scores. Your choice would be poor because the correlation between SES and IQ is weak. The slight control achieved by matching would be offset by the lower statistical power of a matched-group design.

Let us emphasize a final word about the mechanics of matching. Even when you have matched your subjects, you must still randomly allocate the members of the pairs to conditions. If you have ten pairs of rats matched for weight, you must flip a coin or follow some procedure that will assure that each member of a pair is put in a group at random. Otherwise, your procedure for placing them into groups could introduce confounding. See Table 5–5 for how to conduct a matched-groups experiment.

Building Nuisance Variables into the Experiment

Nuisance variable a condition in an experiment that cannot easily be removed and so is made an independent variable as a means of control

Another way to handle variables that cannot easily be removed from the experiment is to design the experiment so that these **nuisance variables** become independent variables of the study. Suppose that your subject pool consists of both day-school and night-school students in introductory psychology. These people may differ in several ways that could relate to psychological variables. Night students may be older, may have more family and work responsibilities, and so forth. If you suspect that your subjects are dissimilar on some dimension related to day- and night-student status, you have two choices. The first is to use only day or night students. This solution has the advantage of reducing the variability, but it also reduces the subject pool and the generality of the results.

The second choice is to build a nuisance variable into the experiment. Figure 5–1 shows the results of a hypothetical experiment in which night- or day-student status was designed into the experiment as a nuisance variable. If we do not consider day or night status, we find considerable overlap between the results of Conditions *A* and *B*. We might not be willing to conclude that the conditions had a differential effect on the dependent variable. (We are ignoring the possibility of using inferential statistics to help in this decision.) But let us consider day or night classes as a nuisance

TABLE 5–5 Steps in conducting a matched-groups experiment.

1. Administer pretest.
2. Rank subjects on pretest.

S_1
S_2
.
.
.
S_{10}

3. Form pairs on the basis of rankings.

S_1, S_2 } 1st pair
S_3, S_4 } 2nd pair
. .
. .
. .
S_9, S_{10} } 5th pair

4. Randomly assign members of pairs to groups.

Group A	Group B
S_1	S_2
S_4	S_3
S_5	S_6
.	.
.	.
.	.
S_{10}	S_9

5. Administer experimental treatments.
6. Examine differences between members of *pairs*.

S_1 — S_2
S_4 — S_3
.
.
.

What is the average difference between pairs?

variable; that is, let us analyze the data separately for day and night students. We find now that no overlap exists between Group A and Group B for night-school students considered alone or for day students considered alone. We have increased the sensitivity of the experiment by building a nuisance variable into the study. Note that the nuisance variable need not

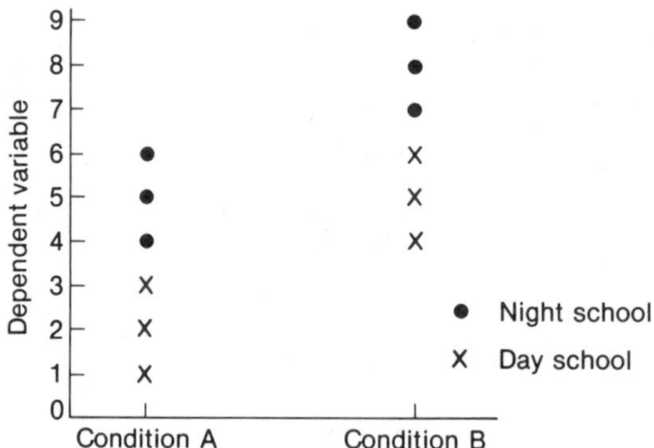

FIGURE 5–1. Example of using a nuisance variable to increase the sensitivity of an experiment.

have any theoretically important role in the experiment. We do not care why night-school students scored higher. On the other hand, the nuisance variable may suggest new theoretical questions for another experiment.

Statistical Control

Except for randomization, all of the control methods described so far can be classified as methods of achieving experimental control; they aim to reduce variability as much as possible. Sometimes these techniques can be spectacularly effective, and a very few observations on a single subject can be used to make firm conclusions. Usually, however, that old devil variability cannot be completely exorcised from the experiment. Then it is necessary to use **statistical control**.

Statistical control mathematical means of comparing subjects on paper when they cannot be equated as they exist in fact

Statistical control in the broad sense is synonymous with inferential statistics, the branch of statistics that deals with making decisions in the face of uncertainty. Suppose you have a difference between two groups on some dependent variable in an experiment. Was the effect real or did it happen by chance? The point behind the question is that statistical control is involved in designing an experiment. Are there enough subjects? How many trials should there be? Can the experiment as designed be analyzed properly by accepted statistical methods?

Such considerations are important enough to merit courses that specialize in the statistical analysis of experimental data. For now, because you are not taking such an experimental design course, you will have to answer questions of statistical control with general knowledge about statistics and with advice from your instructor. Remember, too, that in the end the question of statistical control comes down to whether you and others believe the data. If you have enough subjects to look convincing, and if you have avoided the pitfalls discussed in this chapter, you probably have a good experiment. Although you may be fooled into thinking that some effect was caused by the independent variable when it actually was random—especially when you look at your own data—at this stage of your career you should aim to design an experiment that will convince yourself and others.

In the more narrow sense statistical control refers to a means of equating subjects on paper when they cannot be equated in fact. Suppose that you are studying the effect on grades of two different teaching methods in the classroom. Because randomly constituting the classes is not feasible, you must work with existing classes. If the students in the two classes do not have the same average IQ, you will have a problem in attributing the difference in grades to the teaching methods. There is another approach. If you know the relationship between IQ and grades in the class, you then can find out how much the students' grades differed from what you would have expected, based on the prediction of the IQ/learning relationship.

This approach is best illustrated in Figure 5–2, which represents the relationship between grades and IQ. Each data point represents a single subject, the X being placed at the intersection of the person's grade with his or her IQ on the appropriate axes. The slanting line shows what grade would be predicted for persons having particular IQs. The data point circled and labeled A represents a single subject's position on the two axes. You can see that Subject A earned a higher grade than you would have expected from the relationship shown by the slanted line. Subject B, however, earned a lower grade than predicted by the line. Notice that both students received the same grade.

The basic idea of statistical control is that you are able to compare students, not on their absolute grade, but on the difference between grade and what would have been expected from the line predicting grade from IQ. Subject A would be scored as earning a grade of plus-so-many points and Subject B as earning minus-so-many points. You could conclude that A had benefited more from the condition than had B. In this way it is possible to compare groups that are made up of subjects who differ on IQ. The technical term for this comparing process is analysis of covariance, a topic beyond the scope of this book. Be aware that this method is available as a means of controlling for variability in an experiment. You may refer to one of the standard books on statistics, such as Kirk (1968), for a description.

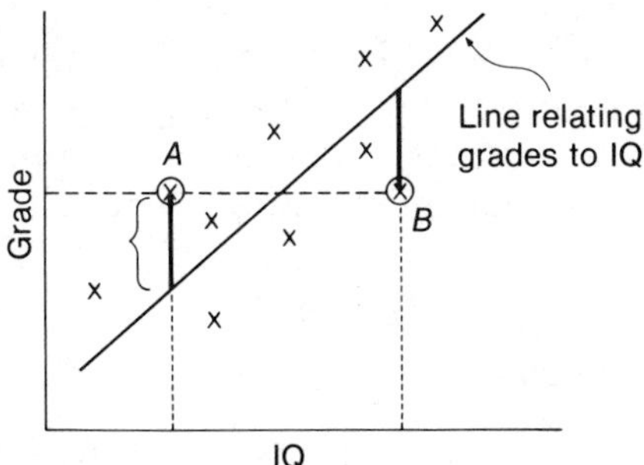

FIGURE 5–2. Example of using statistical control to compare subjects.

CONTROLLING FOR ORDER AND SEQUENCE EFFECTS

In within-subjects experiments, whenever a subject experiences more than one experimental condition, the possibility exists that some variable may influence the data as a result of the repeated testing. Some of these possible variables are related to the subjects; others are related to the conditions of testing. The subjects may get fatigued during the session, or the first condition may be tested before lunch when subjects are hungry and the second after lunch when they are sleepy. Ordinarily experimenters avoid within-subjects designs if they believe that order or sequence effects will be substantial. Then a between-subjects design probably is more appropriate.

Order effects changes in a subject's performance resulting from the position in which a condition appears in an experiment

Sequence effects changes in a subject's performance resulting from interactions among the conditions themselves

Before we discuss ways of controlling for these problems, let us note the distinction between order effects and sequence effects. **Order effects** are those that result from the (ordinal) position in which the condition appears in an experiment regardless of the specific condition that is experienced. The best example of an order effect is the warm-up or practice effect that often occurs in experiments on learning. Whichever condition is presented first will show poorer performance than later conditions simply because the subjects have not warmed up to the task. **Sequence effects**, on the other hand, are those that depend on an interaction between the specific conditions of the experiment. For example, in an experiment on judging the heaviness of lifted weights, there is likely to be a contrast effect such that a light weight will feel even lighter if it follows a heavy one and vice versa. Order effects are more general and result from warm-up, learning, fatigue, and so forth. Sequence effects are interactions between the conditions themselves.

In general, one controls for order effects by arranging that each condition occur equally often in each ordinal position; that is, first, second, third, and so forth. Sequence effects generally are controlled for by arranging that each condition follow every other condition equally often. Note that these controls are not the same. You should also note that the various methods for controlling for order and sequence effects are only effective under certain conditions, which we will discuss below. However, if you are using a within-subjects design, you are wise to control as effectively as possible for order and sequence effects.

Two basic strategies are available for controlling order and sequence effects. The first and preferable one is to arrange the order of conditions in such a way that order and sequence effects are controlled *within subjects*. When this is not possible, you must control for order and sequence effects *between subjects*.

Within-Subjects Control

Controlling for order and sequence effects within subjects is possible when each subject receives each condition. *Randomization* can be used when each condition is given several times to each subject or when a sufficient number of subjects will be tested so that one particular sequence is unlikely to have much influence on the outcome. Experiments in learning or perception typically involve presenting each stimulus many times to the subject. The best procedure is to randomize the order of conditions for each subject. Although you might prefer to be told a magic number of subjects or repetitions that are sufficient for randomizing to be effective, this determination remains a matter of your judgment.

Block randomization control procedure in which the order of conditions is randomized, with each condition being presented once before any condition is repeated

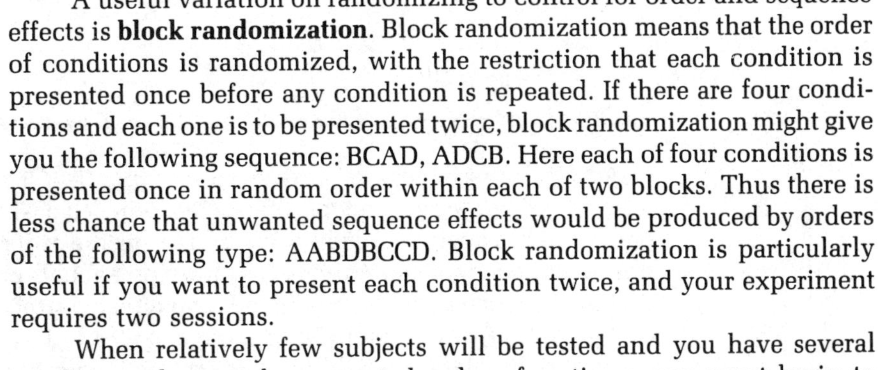

A useful variation on randomizing to control for order and sequence effects is **block randomization**. Block randomization means that the order of conditions is randomized, with the restriction that each condition is presented once before any condition is repeated. If there are four conditions and each one is to be presented twice, block randomization might give you the following sequence: BCAD, ADCB. Here each of four conditions is presented once in random order within each of two blocks. Thus there is less chance that unwanted sequence effects would be produced by orders of the following type: AABDBCCD. Block randomization is particularly useful if you want to present each condition twice, and your experiment requires two sessions.

When relatively few subjects will be tested and you have several conditions that can be presented only a few times, you must begin to exercise ingenuity. A typical example is the instance where you have three conditions, each presented twice. In this situation it is common to use **reverse counterbalancing** to control for order effects. The three conditions are presented in order the first time and then in reverse order. This technique is known as ABCCBA sequence, or ABBA for short. Counterbalancing works well when you suspect that the possible confounding variables will act in a linear manner over conditions. Figure 5–3 gives an example of ABCCBA order in which there is a linear effect. The order effect produces a large increase in the dependent variable that, since the effect is linear, averages out. The counterbalancing has done its job.

Reverse counterbalancing method of control in which conditions are presented in order the first time and then in reverse order

On the other hand, suppose that a variable has a large effect in the early part of the experiment but a smaller effect later on. The best example is a warm-up, or practice, effect that may occur in the early part of an

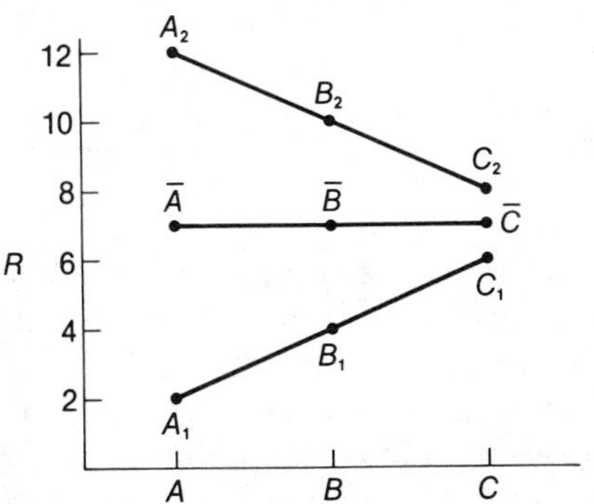

FIGURE 5–3. Example of using reverse counterbalancing to control for order effects.

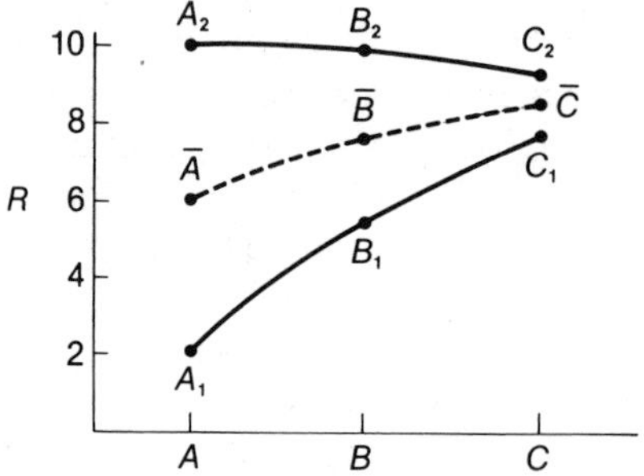

FIGURE 5–4. Example of reverse counterbalancing when the order effects are not linear.

experiment and be less important later. Figure 5–4 shows an example in which there is a large practice effect. Here you can easily see that counterbalancing has not been effective in eliminating the order effect. One way of improving such an experiment is to provide enough practice beforehand that the practice effect is eliminated. (Note that counterbalancing may do an incomplete job of controlling *sequence* effects in an ABCDDCBA experiment; the B condition follows A once and C once but never follows D or itself.)

Within-Groups Control

If presenting each condition enough times to randomize the order is not possible, or if counterbalancing within subjects does not seem appropriate, then you must leave order and sequence confounded with condition *within subjects* and you must control for order and sequence *within groups*. For example, suppose you have three conditions and each one is to be presented only once to each subject. Then if you have six subjects, or 6N subjects, you can control for order and sequence in the following way:

Subject	*Order*
1	ABC
2	ACB
3	BAC
4	BCA
5	CAB
6	CBA

Both order and sequence are completely counterbalanced within the group because each condition occurs an equal number of times in each rank-order position and follows every other condition an equal number of times. So you have controlled for order and sequence within a group of subjects even though every subject experiences a biased sequence. The disadvantage of this method of counterbalancing is that as the number of conditions increases, the number of orders required increases geometrically. You have 2 possible orders of 2 conditions (AB and BA), 6 orders of 3 conditions (as in the above example), 24 orders of 4 conditions, and 120 orders of 5 conditions! Even for only 4 conditions you would need 24 subjects to control for order and sequence.

It is possible to control for the order in which each condition occurs with fewer subjects than required by complete counterbalancing if you give up the requirement that each condition follow every other condition an equal number of times. You would be controlling for order but not for sequence of conditions. This type of incomplete counterbalancing is called the **Latin square** technique after the ancient puzzle of finding ways to arrange a number of letters in a matrix such that each letter occurs once and only once in each row and column, as illustrated below.

Latin square
control procedure in which each subject experiences each condition in a different order from other subjects

Subject	*Rank order* 1	2	3	4
1	A	B	C	D
2	B	C	D	A
3	C	D	A	B
4	D	A	B	C

If the letters represent conditions, the columns order, and the rows subjects, then you are controlling for order effects with the Latin square counterbalancing technique.

A disadvantage of the Latin square technique is that sequence is not controlled for. Notice in the example above that B always follows A, C always follows B, and so forth. Thus sequence is always perfectly confounded with order in this particular Latin square. If there were a contrast effect between conditions, then this design would not control for it. However, you can control for sequence effects of the *immediately* preceding condition by particular sets of Latin squares known as *balanced squares*. In the balanced Latin square each condition is immediately preceded once by every other condition (Wagenaar, 1969). The following is an example:

Subject	*Rank order* 1	2	3	4
1	A	B	C	D
2	B	D	A	C
3	C	A	D	B
4	D	C	B	A

When you can assume that the contrast effects are primarily between *pairs* of conditions, then the balanced Latin square is effective.

The Latin square technique has the advantage over complete counterbalancing of permitting greater flexibility in choosing the number of subjects to be tested. Instead of needing 24, 48, etc., subjects in a four-condition experiment, you may use 4, 8, etc. This advantage is great enough to outweigh the disadvantage of leaving small sequence effects uncontrolled.

Control in Experiments with Two Independent Variables

What we have said so far assumes one independent variable with several levels, or conditions. Experiments in which there are two independent variables—factorial experiments—require ingenuity in order to counterbalance over both variables. In a factorial experiment one of the variables may permit, or even require, that all of the conditions of Variable *B* be tested first under one condition of Variable *A* and then once more under the other condition of Variable *A*.

Take, for example, an experiment on the effect of light adaptation on visual acuity. Suppose you wanted to measure the visibility of four targets (B_1, B_2, B_3, B_4) under both dark adaptation (A_1) and light adaptation (A_2). Varying the adaptation state between each target would be clumsy because 30 minutes is needed to achieve a state of complete dark adaptation. Following is a sample design of such an experiment. The four targets are abbreviated 1234, and so forth.

	Dark adapted	*Light adapted*	*Dark adapted*
S_{1-5}	2143, 4312,...	1342, 1243,...	
S_{6-10}		4123, 3214,...	3241, 1243,...

The order of stimuli (conditions of Variable *B*) has been block-randomized for all subjects, and the state of adaptation (conditions of Variable *A*) is reversed for half of the subjects.

Often this type of control for order and sequence is only partially successful. We said above that order effects can be controlled for by reverse counterbalancing only if the effects are linear. We also noted that sequence effects can be controlled for by a balanced Latin square only if the effects are caused by the immediately preceding condition alone and not by any other previous conditions. There is a type of sequential interaction, however, that never can be removed from a within-subjects design.

Take the example we gave earlier of an experiment on lifted weights. Suppose that you have two weights and each is lifted only once. You may think that you have controlled for order and sequence effects if half of the subjects experience the order [light, heavy] and the other half the opposite order [heavy, light]. Let us suppose, though, that there is a "true" response of six to the light stimulus and eight to the heavy one. We could determine this in a between-subjects experiment where each subject lifted only one weight. Now, if there were a contrast effect between the two weights that

TABLE 5–6 Illustration of how it may be impossible to control for sequence effects in within-subjects experiments.

Within subjects		
	Stimulus	
Order	*Light*	*Heavy*
Light, heavy	6	10
Heavy, light	4	8
Average effect	5	9
Between subjects		
	Stimulus	
	Light	*Heavy*
"True" effect	6	8

resulted in a doubling of the true difference in the responses when the weights were presented sequentially, then the subjects who experience [light, heavy] would say [six, ten] to the two stimuli instead of [six, eight]. Those who experience [heavy, light] would say [eight, four]. The average responses for the two different orders would be five and nine instead of six and eight. The difference between the stimuli would appear to be four instead of the true difference of two.

The type of effect we have just described is summarized in Table 5–6. Sometimes these effects can simply exaggerate an outcome that would occur between subjects, as in this example. Other times they produce outcomes that would not otherwise be found. The difference between using a within-subjects design and a between-subjects design can cause puzzling discrepancies between the results of experiments.

Returning to the lifted-weights example, we note that Harry Helson and his students (Helson, 1964), in their study of sequence effects in perceptual judgments, gave us the area known as adaptation level theory. They found that a given weight would be called light or heavy depending on what other weights were presented along with it. Effects such as these can be studied only by using designs that permit sequence effects.

REPLICATION, REPLICATION

Replication repeating an experiment to see if the results will be the same as originally

A method of control seldom described as such is **replication**, the repeating of an experiment to see if the same results are found the second time. Laypersons sometimes assume that once a result has been found by a scientific experiment that the conclusions are fixed permanently. The truth is that an experiment seldom stands by itself, particularly if the results are surprising. In fact, an unusual result remains in a kind of limbo until other experimenters have successfully replicated the experiment. If the same results are obtained by other experimenters, then they become part of our scientific knowledge. If the replication is not successful, the supposed facts found in the original experiment are invalid and are forgotten. Many examples of this process have occurred throughout the history of psychology, as well as in the other sciences.

A particularly good example of how dubious phenomena get weeded out is provided by the history of research on transfer of memory by injecting material from a trained animal into an untrained animal. The line of research began with the finding that feeding trained planaria (flatworms) to untrained planaria resulted in a transfer of memory to the untrained worms (McConnell, 1962). Eventually a similar experiment was tried on rats (Babich, Jacobson, Bubash, & Jacobson, 1965), except that instead of feeding the trained rats to untrained ones, the experimenters injected extracts of their brains. The resultant finding created much interest in the scientific community because of its enormous implications for the mechanisms of memory and for the storage of information in the nervous system in general. A number of positive replications were published (see Byrne, 1970, for a review). However, it soon became clear that all was not well with this supposed phenomenon. Not all investigators could replicate the finding. Within a few years of the original research an article was published by 23 authors from seven laboratories (Byrne et al., 1966) reporting that all of these scientists had failed to replicate the original finding. They stated their conclusions cautiously: "Our consistently negative findings . . . indicate only that results obtained with one method of evaluating this possibility are not uniformly positive" (p. 658).

In the intervening years the phenomenon has not been firmly established in spite of continued work. One textbook (Cotman & McGaugh, 1980) summarizes the situation as follows: "In general the findings are extremely conflicting, and as a consequence no firm conclusions can be drawn. Research has not as yet specified either optimal or reliable procedures for producing a transfer effect. Further, it is not at all clear what type of molecule might be responsible for producing the effect. . . . Should such experiments be reproducible, it should be possible to determine the basis of the effects. At the present time, the memory transfer effect must be regarded as not yet convincingly demonstrated" (p. 313).

The history of the research on the transfer of training by injection followed a typical pattern. The first reports elicited a great deal of interest and many attempts at replication. Some of these attempts were successful and the investigators naturally published their results. Those who did not find the effect were reticent to admit their failures and, additionally, may have had difficulty getting negative results published. Enough negative results eventually accumulated, however, to overcome biases, and the literature began to reveal a preponderance of negative results. Such a scenario has occurred repeatedly in science, with the result that those research effects that are not repeatable are discarded.

Two types of replication commonly are distinguished; *direct* and *systematic*. Direct replication occurs when someone repeats essentially the identical experiment in an attempt to find the same results. Systematic replication occurs when Researcher B says, "If A's theory is correct, then the following should happen." Then B performs an experiment different from A's but based on it. If A's results and theory are correct, B should find a certain result.

Direct replication seldom is carried out because finding exactly the same thing as someone else did brings little glory. More specifically, it is difficult to get grants for replications, journals tend to avoid publishing such research, and professors who spend time replicating other people's work do not get promoted. Direct replication usually is attempted only when systematic replication has failed. Investigators then go back and repeat the original method more exactly in order to see where the source of the difference in results lies.

Systematic replication is the usual way that experiments are replicated. Researcher B will do an experiment *similar* to Researcher A's but with different types of subjects, or with different values of the stimulus, or with different ways of operationally defining the theoretical concepts. All of these approaches are considered systematic replication. As long as results consistent with A's are found, then A's original experiment is supported by B's work. You will notice that systematic replication tests external validity by using different subjects, species, or situations. Construct validity is tested when different ways are used to operationalize the theoretical concepts. Statistical validity is tested in all replications, both direct and systematic.

The need for replication sometimes is downplayed in favor of showing that a given result would be unlikely to occur by chance alone. Believers in ESP point out that particular experiments gave results that would have happened only once in billions of experiments by chance alone. The ESP believers' statistics are usually impeccable, but their understanding of the methods of science is faulty. Innumerable ways exist in which an experiment can fail to be valid by giving results that are due *neither* to chance *nor* to the particular hypothesis. Calculating long odds is impressive, but it is only one of a number of considerations in evaluating the experiment. Generally, experiments in ESP fail to replicate. Although believers in ESP can make up reasons for this failure, scientists will pay little attention to ESP until someone devises an experimental situation that gives consistent results in favor of ESP. R. A. Fisher, who largely invented modern statistical methods, said, "Very long odds . . . are much less relevant to the establishment of the facts of nature than would be a demonstration of the reliability of the phenomena" (quoted by Crumbaugh, 1966, p. 527).

HOW TO USE THE REST OF THIS BOOK

By now we have discussed what science is. We have talked about the basic principles of research design, as well as about the principles of validity and the basic means of controlling for threats to validity. We might stop here and tell you to begin designing your own experiments based on these principles. Obviously we have not done that and for a good reason. Important as the principles are, probably no one could become a successful researcher by reading a book on the principles of research.

One learns to do research by studying examples of research and, better yet, by doing research. Scientific research is one of those activities that is best learned by working with someone who serves as a guide in a hands-on situation. In this respect becoming a scientist parallels the way an apprentice becomes skilled by working under the direction of an experienced person. The importance of this process may be seen in the many famous scientists who were students of other learned scientists. First-hand experience in the laboratory of a good scientist has no substitute for learning how to do science. Myriads of attitudes, skills, and techniques are assimilated in such a situation. No book, including this one, can do more than serve as a pale substitute.

My goal in this book is to present those concepts that I spend the most time explaining when I talk with students about research. Although I cannot anticipate all questions, I have tried to answer those that are commonest and most important. Most readers of this book will be taking a course in experimental methods. The instructor, along with this book, will be guides as you learn to do research.

EXPERIMENTAL DESIGN AS PROBLEM SOLVING

The rest of this book consists largely of examples of good research design. We will not discuss all possible designs, for the simple reason that doing so would be impossible. Rather, we will give a list of designs for you to use as models in designing similar experiments of your own. Experimental designs should be tailor-made to each experimental problem. Sometimes an existing design will fit the problem perfectly. More often, alterations must be made. Therefore, it is better to create the design from the beginning.

Designing an experiment is a matter of solving particular problems of validity by the application of particular methods of control. When each problem is solved, the experiment is designed. Then is the time to look in books on experimental design to see if your design can be analyzed according to accepted statistical procedures. To look in the books first is to get the cart before the horse and to forget that the essence of experimental design is solving threats to validity in the best way possible.

Two of the general strategies listed at the beginning of the chapter—the setting as a preparation and instrumentation—are not usually discussed as such in experimental design books. They are the guiding principles of design, however. Use the specific strategies we have discussed as tactics in applying these general principles.

THE ELEGANT EXPERIMENT

The goal of every scientist is to design the best possible experiment. How is such a concept put into practice though? Do you keep testing more and more subjects until the conclusion is inescapable? Do you keep adding variables until every possible source of confounding is taken into account? I find the concept of the elegant experiment helpful in thinking about such questions. In everyday usage the term *elegance* implies richness combined with tasteful simplicity. In mathematics the term emphasizes simplicity. An elegant proof draws a powerful conclusion in the simplest possible way. This idea is what I mean by the elegant experiment: the simplest experiment that will make a clear and convincing test of a hypothesis.

It is possible to include so many variables in a study that not enough measures are made on any one to draw firm conclusions. It is possible to have such a complicated design that you lose sight of the forest for the trees. Consequently, you must realize that many tradeoffs are made in the course of designing an experiment and that this process requires hard decisions. Do you spend more time and effort at the outset testing pilot subjects and refining your experimental procedure? Or do you decide to test more subjects in the main experiment to make up for the uncontrolled variability? I cannot tell you what to do in any particular case. Paying careful attention to these questions, though, will result in experiments that are convincing tests of hypotheses.

In selecting the word *elegance,* I have deliberately chosen a term that has an aesthetic connotation. Designing experiments is an art that requires creativity and that reflects the tastes of the experimenter. Such activity can be both challenging and rewarding.

SUMMARY

1. The fundamental meaning of the term *control* in psychology is that of providing a standard against which to compare the effect of a particular variable.
2. Experiments in which different groups of subjects experience different conditions are known as between-subjects experiments. Those in which each subject experiences every condition are known as within-subjects experiments.

3. The group in a between-subjects experiment that receives the treatment is called the experimental group, the group that does not receive the treatment is called the control group.
4. In within-subjects experiments the condition that does not contain the experimental manipulation is called the control condition.
5. It is not necessary to have a control group or a control condition in an experiment as long as there is some group or condition that may serve as a comparison for the particular experimental manipulation.
6. A second meaning of the term *control* is that of the ability to restrain or guide sources of variability in research. This meaning is captured in the term *experimental control.*
7. There are three general strategies for achieving control in research: using a laboratory setting, considering the research setting as a preparation, and instrumenting the response.
8. Laboratory research is defined not by a particular kind of room but in being able to control the important sources of variability in the research setting.
9. The concept of a preparation emphasizes choosing the best possible research situation in which to test a hypothesis.
10. Instrumentation of the response refers to the means of measuring the dependent variables. Careful measurement renders responses objective and may even be thought of as creating responses.
11. Specific control strategies include: using subjects as their own controls, randomizing, matching, building nuisance variables into the experiment, and using statistical control.
12. Subjects may be used as their own controls when: doing so is logically possible, serving in all conditions will not destroy their naivete, and there will not be serious contrast effects between conditions.
13. The allocation of subjects to conditions is random when each subject has an equal chance of being assigned to every condition.
14. Matching may be used when there is an important variable on which subjects differ that is correlated with the dependent variable and when it is feasible to present a pretest to the subjects.
15. Nuisance variables that cannot easily be removed from the experiment may be controlled for by making them independent variables of the experiment.
16. Statistical control may be thought of broadly as synonymous with inferential statistics. More narrowly, statistical control involves equating subjects on paper by means of the analysis of covariance.
17. Order effects are those that result from the ordinal position in which the condition appears in an experiment regardless of the specific condition that is experienced. Sequence effects are those that depend on an interaction between the specific conditions of the experiment.
18. Within-subjects control of order and sequence effects may be achieved by randomization, block randomization, and reverse counterbalancing.

19. When it is not possible to control for order and sequence effects within subjects, the Latin square technique may be used.
20. Controlling for order and sequence in factorial experiments may be difficult, and certain kinds of order and sequence effects cannot be controlled for in any within-subjects experiment.
21. One of the most important means of control is the replication of an experiment. Direct replication is repeating essentially the same experiment. Systematic replication is doing a different experiment in which certain results should be found if the original experiment was valid.
22. Controlling the sources of invalidity is essentially a matter of solving problems. When the problems are solved, the experiment is designed. The goal of a researcher is to design the most elegant experiment that will answer the questions of interest and will deal with the problems of validity.

SUGGESTION FOR FURTHER READING

SIDMAN, M. *Tactics of scientific research.* New York: Basic Books, 1960. This book presents a classic discussion of experimental control from the Skinnerian perspective.

READING BETWEEN THE LINES

The following problems are presented for you to solve. See Reading Between the Lines in Chapter 1 for an introduction to them. The answers are provided in Appendix A.

11. BRAIN DAMAGE SOMETIMES PRODUCES OBESITY IN RATS

Lesions in a part of the brain known as the ventromedial hypothalamus have been known to produce obesity in rats. Some investigators, however, were unable to find the effect as reliably as others and proposed that the lesion itself did not produce the obesity. Rather, the scar tissue that resulted from the lesion stimulated a nearby area that actually controlled eating. Experiments were done to produce more or less scar tissue and therefore more or less irritation to the nearby area of the brain. These experiments showed that how the lesion was produced did not matter as much as which laboratory did the experiments. One group of investigators consistently found that the lesions produced obesity, while others tended to find no effect. Eventually, a simple difference in methods between the successful and unsuccessful experiments was found. Can you guess what it was?

12. COGNITIVE AND AROUSAL FACTORS IN EMOTION

One of the most influential experiments in social psychology was conducted by Stanley Schachter and Jerome Singer (1962), who hypothesised that people experience particular emotions as the result of a cognitive interpretation of a physiological arousal. According to this hypothesis, the same arousal could be experienced, for example, as euphoria or anger depending on the person's cognitions. The researchers tested their hypothesis by injecting subjects with a stimulating drug. Subjects then were exposed to a confederate who acted either euphoric or angry. The authors reported that the emotions of the subjects tended to match those of the confederate. Later the experiment was attacked in two separate research papers. Because the flaw in the experiment is not obvious, I will tell you that it has to do with replication.

6

CONDUCTING RESEARCH

Up to now we have talked about principles of research design and have given many examples. At some time we must strike out and actually start doing research. This transition from the principles to the nuts and bolts of research is often difficult. As we emphasized earlier, working with someone who is experienced in the field is helpful. This chapter will provide some of the advice that students beginning to do research will need.

CHOICE OF A PROBLEM

You would be surprised to learn how many scientists have chosen by accident the problem they make their life's work. Perhaps they enrolled in psychology so they would not have to walk too far between classes. They liked the course and subsequently majored in psychology, then went to the graduate school recommended by their instructor, were assigned to an adviser, and began working on whatever that person was doing. Their interest in the area grew until it consumed their working hours. Because this process is little appreciated, students become anxious when they must choose a problem for an experimental psychology class. How do they find the right project on which to spend a whole term?

Ideas will be found in several likely places. Previous psychology courses may have covered topics that especially interested you. Most psychology textbooks and lectures contain statements of unsolved problems and suggestions for future research. Everyday observation is another source of research problems. For instance, you may have wondered what caused a certain type of behavior. The list of sources is perhaps endless, including such possibilities as dormitory bull sessions and newspaper articles.

A valuable source is your instructor or adviser. He or she has been thinking about research for a number of years and often can respond to an idea with a key reference or a suggestion. You would be wise to ask what problems your instructor is interested in and pick one that appeals to you. The advantage in this procedure is that, by virtue of background knowledge in the area, your instructor can give you sound advice and will be more motivated to do so than if you chose an unfamiliar problem.

THE LITERATURE REVIEW

If you pick a problem suggested by your adviser, that person no doubt will suggest a few references with which to begin your search of the literature. If you select a problem of your own, you may be able to start with a reference from a textbook you have studied. Otherwise, you may have to start from scratch in the library. The first source to check for books in the area is the card catalogue. If you do not find any books on your topic, consult one of the many handbooks that have broad coverage of most areas. These books and handbooks should give you access to the literature you need. Skim as many of these books as are available to you to get an overview of your topic. After you have an initial idea of the scope of what is known in your field, you are ready to dig a little deeper.

An indispensible tool is the *Psychological Abstracts.* This publication contains abstracts of most psychological articles published. The extensive index lists articles by subject areas and gives a short description of each. A careful review of *Psychological Abstracts* will eventually lead you to virtually all of the literature in an area. Two aspects of your search in *Psychological Abstracts* may be frustrating, however. First, the subject headings are broad, so it is necessary to sift through many irrelevant articles to find the ones you want. Second, you have no way of telling which article will be a gold mine of information and which will be a minor note.

Another powerful bibliographic tool exists in the form of the *Science Citation Index* and the similar *Social Science Citation Index*. These publications may not be in your library, but you should know about them because of their great usefulness. They do not contain abstracts of articles, and they are not arranged according to topic. Rather, they contain the references to articles and books that have been cited by any other article or book in a given year and the references for the articles that did the citing. They permit you to do something that is impossible to do with *Psychological Abstracts:* You can move *forward* in time, following the development of a field by tracing the influence of particular articles on later ones. You can start with any article from any date. The *Citation Index* then will tell you whether anyone has referred to that article in a particular year. The process is similar to taking a key article and then looking up the articles in its reference list. Only, using the *Citation Index* you can find any other article (a) that is published *after* the article you started with and (b) that cites your initial article in *its* reference list. By using this method you can trace what has happened to a field after your initial article was written. Thus you follow pertinent articles and are not distracted by the many articles that may sound relevant to your topic but are not. If the *Science Citation Index* is available at your school, by all means use it. If it is not, you may be able to find it at a nearby institution.

Now that you have identified most of the key articles in your field, you should begin to read them. Pay particular attention to the introductions to the articles: What was known at the time the authors began their work, what are the major theories, what are the major unsolved problems? At this point do not worry about the details of the methods and results. Read the abstract and the conclusion, if there is one, to learn the basic results. Skim the rest. Check the reference list for articles you may have missed. By this time you will begin to get a grasp of the subject area. You will find that certain experiments are the key ones in the field.

After this initial review, you can begin to focus on the methods of these key experiments. What are their strengths and weaknesses? Remember that well-trained scientists can make mistakes and sometimes overlook important problems of design. Some of these problems will be pointed out by other authors; some you may think of yourself. All experiments are not created equal. The fact that they are published in major journals does not make them perfect. In addition to the author, as few as three people may have read a particular paper—the editor and two reviewers. In any case you will find that there are some unsolved problems, some theories to be tested, some conflicting results to be resolved. These may give you an idea for your own study.

THE RESEARCH QUESTION

Up to now you have been working on a general research problem. For example, why do people in large cities fail to help the victim of a crime? You have developed some ideas and you feel ready to test them. You must narrow down the larger research problem to a specific testable question. You may want to test the idea that people in large groups feel less responsible for other individuals. This would be your hypothesis, which is a specific prediction of a relationship between variables. You may hypothesize that as group size increases, the members feel less responsibility for the other people in the group.

The rest of the experimental process will be an empirical test of your hypothesis. It is essential that your hypothesis be as specific as possible. In the hypothesis about group size and responsibility, do you mean that the subjects will feel less concern for other persons, or do you mean that they feel just as concerned but they believe that someone else will do something? (See Darley and Latane, 1968.) The more precise you can be in stating the hypothesis, the better you can design a cogent and straightforward test of it. If the hypothesis is vague, the experiment is likely to be difficult to interpret. When the hypothesis is stated in vague terms, the temptation arises to develop a kitchen-sink design—to throw in every variable that might bear on the phenomenon. As you develop the hypothesis and then design the experiment, you must keep asking yourself, "Exactly what am I trying to find out?" All efforts should be bent toward that question, and care should be taken to pare ancillary questions from the experiment unless the added cost of answering them is negligible.

CHOICE OF METHOD

Now that you have a question that you wish to investigate, you are faced with many decisions: what kind of subjects, what task, what apparatus, what kinds and values of independent variables? By the nature of this book, we must deal with these questions in a rather general fashion. Nevertheless, certain principles can be stated. Your review of the literature will reveal standard tasks, apparatus, subjects, and so forth that generally are used in studying a certain problem. For practical and theoretical reasons it makes sense to follow the standard practice as much as possible and deviate only where there is good reason to do so.

On the other hand, you may feel that a different task, for instance, might be more appropriate. What you want to find out will dictate many of these choices. Recall our earlier discussion of the research setting as a preparation. You will make your choices of subjects, apparatus, and so forth with the following question foremost in mind: Which alternative will permit the most sensitive test of the hypothesis? Above all, you must chose a design that will yield data that you can analyze statistically.

CHOOSING THE STIMULUS VALUES

Many experiments involve only two conditions, such as presence or absence of a variable. In other experiments the number of conditions is strictly limited by practical or theoretical considerations. This section concerns experiments that call for several stimulus conditions. Many will be perceptual experiments and many will be run as within-subjects designs. For such experiments we can state four principles.

First, the stimuli should cover as much of the range as practicable. Relationships between the variables will be better understood if the limits

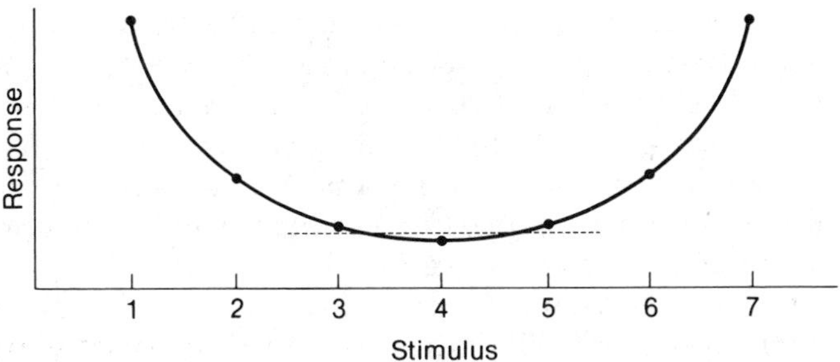

FIGURE 6–1. Illustration of the need to test a wide range of stimulus values.

of the system are explored. Figure 6–1 shows how too short a stimulus range can be misleading. If the middle three stimuli were chosen, the experimenter probably would conclude that no relationship is present between the stimulus and the response. Adding more stimuli above and below the middle three, however, shows clearly that there is a U-shaped function relating stimulus and response. The middle three stimuli are not sufficient to provide an accurate picture of the functional relationship between stimulus and response.

The second principle is that the stimuli should be close enough together that overlooking any interesting effects between the stimuli is unlikely. See Figure 6–2. Here the range of stimuli is wide enough, but the wrong conclusion could be drawn if the middle stimuli were not included.

The third principle is that when a subject is to experience all stimuli in a single session, at least seven stimuli should be presented if possible. If fewer than seven are experienced, subjects can identify and remember each stimulus. Then responses may not be based on the stimulus itself but may be related to the memory of stimuli from previous trials. With seven or more stimuli, subjects respond to the stimulus itself because they are not able to identify it (Miller, 1956). Of course, using seven stimuli may not be possible because doing so may make the experiment too long.

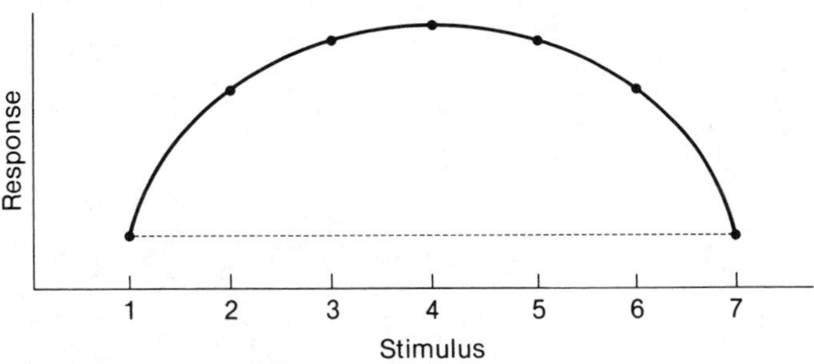

FIGURE 6–2. Illustration of the need to test a sufficient number of stimulus values.

The fourth principle of choosing stimuli concerns the spacing of quantitative variables, those that vary in amount along some continuum. If you plan to use only two stimuli, you simply pick the ones that seem the most appropriate. If you have more than two, you are faced with a choice of spacings. Should you make equal intervals between stimuli or should you use some other intervals? You might wonder why you would ever use anything but equal intervals.

Suppose your experiment involves the effect of number of rat pellets on the speed a rat will run a maze. You want to use 1 pellet as the fewest and 81 as the most. You are going to have five groups of rats, each of which receives a different number of pellets. If you wanted to space the stimuli evenly, you would use 1, 21, 41, 61, 81 for the various groups. However, you suspect that the difference between 61 and 81 pellets on the rat's running speed may not be as great as the difference between 1 and 21. An alternative would be to space pellets evenly according to *ratios* between number of pellets, which would work out to 1, 3, 9, 27, 81. Here each condition has three times as many pellets as the one before.

The difference in spacing is illustrated in Figure 6–3. Running speed is plotted as a function of number of pellets of reinforcement. Notice that the difference in running speed between 1 pellet and 21 pellets is 2.75 units, whereas the difference between 61 and 81 is only about .25 units. If you had used the equal-difference spacing, you would have missed most of the "action," which occurs between conditions that present 1 or 21 pellets. On the other hand, by spacing pellets according to equal ratios, you have found equal effects on the running speed between each number of pellets used. Of course, this example was created so that such would be the case. Notwithstanding, a great many stimulus dimensions—perhaps most—are such that most action takes place at the lower end of the scale. In these cases stimuli should be spaced so that equal ratios fall between stimuli. This kind of spacing is also known as logarithmic spacing.

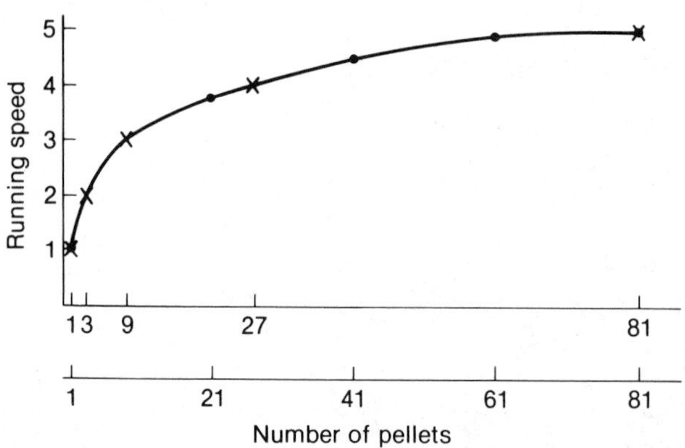

FIGURE 6–3. Illustration of the need to space the stimuli carefully.

CHOICE OF SUBJECTS

We will make only general statements about choice of subjects because many considerations are specific to particular experiments.

The allegation that the college sophomore and the white rat have been studied too often is true. The reasons become obvious when you start to consider your own alternatives. If the problem lends itself to study with animals and other experimenters have used the rat, those facts become good reasons for you to do so. Changing strains of rat or even the supplier of the rats can make comparing results between experiments difficult. In addition, using another species of animal may require you to solve new housekeeping problems. For example, can you keep another species of animal healthy in a laboratory?

If you are studying humans and you wish to use a population other than the college student, what problems will you face with recruitment and payment of volunteers, standardization of technique on the population, and so forth? Such considerations help to explain the extensive reliance on these two classes of subjects. Of course, if you have good reason to use a different population, a little care and effort in designing the study around other subjects often pays big dividends.

SELECTION OF SUBJECTS

Ethical and practical considerations enter into the selection process. With the exception of naturalistic observation and certain other types of research, the consent of the subjects must be obtained before they participate. We will discuss ethics of research later in this chapter, but meanwhile let us note that subjects in psychological research ordinarily should participate voluntarily.

Ideally, subjects should be a random sample of the population to which you wish to generalize the results of your study. For example, in order to generalize the results of an experiment on college students to the entire adult population of the United States, the students ought to be a random sample of that population. Obviously they cannot be, but they should be at least a random sample of college students.

In actuality most experiments on humans draw subjects from introductory psychology classes. Furthermore, subjects usually volunteer because of coercion, such as course credit or requirement. For this reason you can see that the students who sign up for experiments early in the term may be different from those who wait until the last week of class to "volunteer." Even going into a class and asking for volunteers will produce a biased sample. For example, women are more likely to volunteer for an experiment when they are in the ovulatory phase of their menstrual cycle and less likely to volunteer when they are menstruating (Doty, 1975). If this variable were important in an experiment, atypical results would be found using women who volunteer spontaneously. The problem can be minimized by calling women randomly from a list of potential volunteers and asking them to come in at a particular time. In this situation they are less apt to participate differentially than when spontaneously volunteering.

Your college likely will have standard procedures for recruiting subjects. In fact, as we will discuss below, *all details of the experiment must be approved by the appropriate authorities.* You should follow these procedures carefully. For example, if all introductory psychology students must participate in a certain number of hours of experimentation as a course requirement, and they are supposed to sign up through a central office, then going directly to the classroom to seek volunteers is not fair to other experimenters.

However subjects are to be recruited—either in class, by poster, or by ads in a newspaper—make sure they know the exact building, room, time, and date of the experiment. You should give them a telephone number to call if they must cancel, and you should have their number in case you must cancel.

Random assignment of subjects to conditions is essential. You must decide in advance your procedure for achieving this. If the experiment is a between-subjects design, you should have a random order made up before the subjects arrive. Then you will follow the assignment as the subjects show up; the first one will receive the condition that is scheduled first, and so forth. Leave no room for subjectivity when you assign subjects to conditions. If subjects are to be tested in pairs, flip a coin to determine which one is assigned to which condition.

How many subjects should you test? There is a rational way of deciding how many subjects to use in an experiment, provided you know how much variability to expect in your data. In ordinary laboratory experiments, however, almost nobody uses this basis for deciding number of subjects. The reason is simple and practical. Suppose that you wish to achieve a particular degree of precision in your results. Of course, the more subjects you have, the less the means of your data will deviate from their true values. The usual way of representing this error of measurement is called the *standard error of the mean.* The following equation shows how the standard error of the mean decreases with the number of subjects:

$$\sigma_{\overline{X}} = \frac{\sigma_{X}}{\sqrt{N}}$$

In the equation, sigma represents the standard deviation of the scores, and N is the number of subjects. You can see from the equation that in order to cut the standard error of the mean in half, you must double the square root of N. In order to double the square root of N, you must quadruple N.

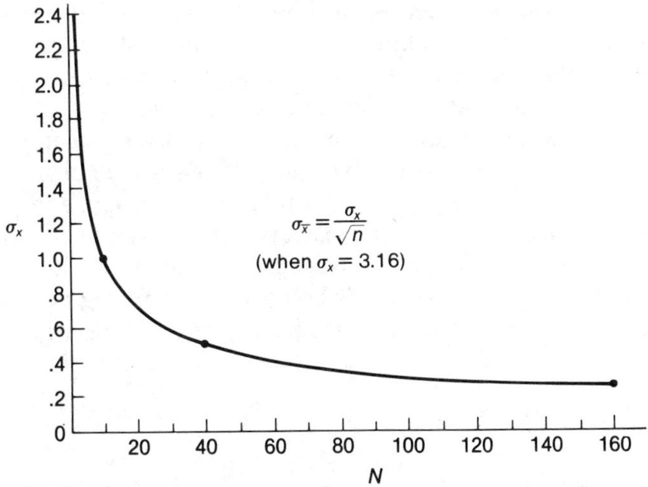

FIGURE 6–4. Relationship between the standard error of the mean and the number of subjects in an experiment.

How the number of subjects affects the precision of an experiment is illustrated in Figure 6–4, which shows how the standard error of the mean decreases with N. In this figure we assume that the standard error of the mean is 1 unit when there are 10 subjects. In order to reduce the standard error of the mean to .5 units, we must increase the number of subjects to 40. If we wish to reduce the standard error of the mean again by a factor of 2, to .25, we must use 160 subjects!

Thus you can see that increasing the number of subjects does not decrease the error of measurement in a linear way. Doubling the number of subjects only reduces the standard error of the mean by 30 percent. (Not all experiments will use the standard error of the mean in data analysis, but the effect is the same for other statistics.) The law of diminishing returns operates. For this reason most experiments will use about 10 subjects or, if they have more than one condition, 10 subjects per condition. Observe how many subjects have been used in experiments similar to yours and how such precision was obtained. If you want more precision, ask yourself if using more subjects will make a significant improvement. If not, try to increase the precision of measurement experimentally.

PROCEDURE

Procedure is different from method. Method is a broader term that encompasses all aspects of the experiment, including the logic of the design and the steps for carrying it out. Procedure refers only to the latter, what the experimenter does in translating the design into action. The design may be a within-subjects, two-by-two factorial. Procedural concerns include whether each condition in the factorial is tested on the same day or on different days. Procedure also involves instructions and how they are given, the debriefing, and so forth. Many details must be worked out in the course of translating a design into practice.

The step of going from design to procedure can be a difficult one for students because it involves going from a logical plan in the mind to a practical plan of action in the lab. After the design is completed, you should develop a clear idea of the exact procedure—or **protocol**—you will follow. A protocol is a list of the exact steps needed to test a subject from start to finish. A written protocol is helpful for beginning experimenters, especially so when more than one experimenter will help run a given experiment.

Protocol
list of all the steps that a subject goes through in an experiment

THE PILOT STUDY

Pilot study
tentative, small-scale experiment done to pretest and modify experiment design and procedures

Once a protocol is developed, you should do a **pilot study** to find the bugs in the procedure. Almost always there are some problems to be smoothed out. One of the experimenters, your adviser, or a friend should be run through all steps of the experiment exactly as it will be carried out. Although the temptation to skip the pilot phase may be great, you should resist it. Nearly every experiment I have performed without testing some pilot subjects has been disappointing. Here is where a little effort can greatly increase the precision of an experiment.

Experimenters with reputations for excellent design often are those who do extensive pilot experimentation. Some experimenters will not proceed to the main experiment until they have a good idea what they will find based on pilot work. This preliminary step is not always possible, but it is an aid to careful experimentation. It also emphasizes that experimentation is not a one-step process. When a pilot study has been done, followed by a main experiment that has been run once and replicated one or twice, the credibility of the finding is increased tremendously over a single experiment that was not preceded by pilot work.

The phase in which the design is translated into procedure and then to a pilot study often takes longer than the experiment proper. You may have difficulty understanding what took all the time and effort. It is not unusual for the literature search and design phase of an undergraduate project to require three-fourths of the term. Running the subjects may take only a week.

THE PROPOSAL

Your instructor may ask you to prepare a proposal before you proceed with your research project. This proposal is often called a *prospectus*. Proposals are required in various situations. Graduate students usually prepare proposals that are presented to the committee that oversees master's theses or dissertation research. Proposals are also required by some agencies, including universities, before research is permitted in their institution. Thus, although the proposal is not logically necessary in designing research, it is often a practical necessity, and it has the advantage of getting the researcher to sit down and think through the issues before proceeding.

Proposal preliminary statement outlining the literature review, statement of problem, research design, and expected results and their significance

The **proposal** is a statement of everything necessary to evaluate the adequacy of the research before the research is conducted. As such the proposal serves some of the same functions as does the published report that will result from the research. For this reason you will find it convenient to follow the same outline and style in the proposal as in the final report (see Chapter 11). In this way you may be able to take much of the final report from the proposal, especially the introduction and the methods section.

The results section of the proposal indicates the expected results and the ways in which you intend to analyze and display them graphically. This function of the proposal is particularly useful. It is embarrassing to conduct an experiment and then find that you have to use some unconventional statistic to analyze the data simply because you overlooked an elementary design consideration. You can usually avoid this problem by deciding in advance what statistics you will use, obtaining advice when necessary.

The discussion section of the proposal is short and indicates the significance of your expected results. Both the results and discussion sections will need to be completely rewritten for the final report!

Although the proposal, when it is approved, serves as a sort of contract between the student and the adviser or committee, this does not mean that it must be adhered to slavishly. When a problem arises, as often happens, the researcher should solve it the best way possible, with the approval of the adviser or committee.

ETHICS OF RESEARCH AND TREATMENT OF HUMAN SUBJECTS

The concern for ethics in psychological research may be seen as part of the historical trend in civil and human rights. Before World War II research ethics were considered a matter for the individual researcher to worry about. However, the Nuremberg trials of the Nazi war criminals led to a consciousness of the need for ethical controls in scientific research. In addition, the growth of all types of human research, fueled by increasing government funding, prompted concern with research ethics. As a result research ethics are in a state of rapid evolution. Some practices that were considered acceptable and routine ten years ago are considered unethical today. For this reason we must present our discussion of research ethics as tentative, rather than chiseled in stone. What will be acceptable practice ten or twenty years from now cannot be predicted.

The APA Ethics Code

As part of its ethics code, the American Psychological Association has developed a statement of research ethics. We will quote part of the *Ethics Code on Research Activities* (American Psychological Association, 1979) and make some comments about it.* The APA ethics code represents the consensus of the psychology profession as to what is considered acceptable practice. Certain states, however, have passed laws governing the conduct of research, and the federal government requires institutions that receive research funds from the Department of Health and Human Services (HHS) to establish internal mechanisms for reviewing the ethics of research funded by HHS. In addition, HHS encourages that institutions develop procedures to protect subjects involved in research not funded by HHS. As a student, you should consult your instructor, department chairman, or school's review board before you initiate any research.

General Considerations

> The decision to undertake research should rest upon a considered judgment by the individual psychologist to contribute to psychological science and to human welfare. Psychologists carry out their investigations with respect for the people who participate and with concern for their dignity and welfare (p. 17).

The conducting of research often presents a conflict between two sets of values. In general the conflict is between the commitment of the psychologist to expanding our knowledge of behavior and the potential benefit the research may have for society on the one hand, and the cost of the research to the participants on the other. It is not possible to resolve this conflict in terms of moral absolutes or by a set of prescriptions that will cover all cases. The conflict must be faced continually by researchers, who must consider themselves responsible for deciding to conduct their research. Researchers who do not review ethical problems carefully are negligent toward society. From another viewpoint, a researcher who refrains from doing an important study because of an excessively tender conscience is also failing to keep a commitment to the same society that supports behavioral research with the hope that it will provide important social benefits.

---

*From "APA ethics code," *APA Monitor*, November 1979, p. 17. Copyright 1979 by the American Psychological Association. Reprinted by permission of the publisher.

Deciding Whether to Conduct a Particular Investigation

> 1. In planning a study, the investigator has the responsibility to make a careful evaluation of its ethical acceptability. To the extent that this weighing of scientific and human values suggests a compromise of any scientific principle, the investigator incurs an increasingly serious obligation to seek ethical advice and to observe stringent safeguards to protect the rights of the human research participants.
>
> 2. Responsibility for acceptable ethical practice in research always remains with the individual investigator. The investigator is also responsible for the ethical treatment of research participants by collaborators, assistants, students, and employees (p. 17).

The investigator is the person who is in overall charge of the research. In most cases students work in the capacity of experimenters or assistants under the supervision of the investigator. All persons working on a research project, however, should consider themselves bound by the APA ethics code, even if they are not professional psychologists or members of APA.

Investigators should discuss their research with colleagues and seek advice on the ethics of the research procedures. This carefulness helps to curb the bias we all have of thinking that our research is more important than it really is and that we are morally superior and therefore will act ethically. Most institutions have committees that review all research on human subjects. Before investigators begin any research, they should be certain that they are complying with institutional procedures. Students should initiate research only under the sponsorship of a faculty member, who is in turn subject to professional sanctions.

Informed Consent and Deception

> 3. The investigator informs the participant of all aspects of the research that might reasonably be expected to influence willingness to participate, and explains all other aspects of the research about which the participant inquires. Failure to make full disclosure imposes additional force to the investigator's abiding responsibility to protect the welfare and dignity of the research participant.
>
> 4. When the methodological requirements of a study necessitate concealment or deception, the investigator promptly provides the participant with a sufficient explanation of this action (p.17).

Subjects should be given a true picture of what the research is about and what is expected of them. Of course situations exist in which such an explanation would substantially weaken the validity of the experiment. The common practice in such situations is to conceal the true purpose of the experiment by means of a cover story. The deceit must be revealed afterward in the debriefing, which we will discuss shortly. Research on children or others who cannot be expected to give informed consent must be done with consent from the parents or guardians of the subjects.

Medical researchers have developed a concept of informed consent, according to which patients have the right to know exactly what is being done to them and for what reasons. The APA ethics code differs from this medical view of informed consent by saying that subjects need be informed only of aspects of the research that would influence their decision to participate. This view assumes that subjects in psychological experiments ordinarily do not care what the hypothesis or purpose of the experiment is.

So many experiments require subjects to be naive about the hypothesis that deceiving subjects about the true purpose has almost become standard practice. The APA ethics code requires that a subject who has been deceived be promptly provided with a sufficient explanation of the action. On the other hand, some researchers feel that deception is always objectionable. They note that the prevalence of deception in psychological experiments is common knowledge among college students and that most subjects routinely assume that the story they are given at the beginning of an experiment is false. The effects of this pollution of the subject pool are not known.

On the other hand, to forswear deception would rule out the study of many important problems. In order to handle this problem, some departments inform people at the time they join the subject pool that certain experiments in which they participate may use deception. Other experimenters have used role playing instead of deception to induce behaviors of interest. The subjects are asked to act as if they were in a certain situation or to tell what they would do in such a situation. The disadvantage of role playing is that it assumes that subjects can tell what they would do in a situation by just adopting a role.

The simple term *deception* covers a wide range of actions on the part of experimenters. Relatively innocuous deceptions routinely involve setting up false expectations of the processes under investigation. More serious deceptions include giving subjects false information about their performance on a task. Some research has shown that the initial false feedback may be believed even after debriefing (Ross, Lepper, & Hubbard, 1975). Deception that presents subjects with a negative evaluation of themselves should be avoided.

Freedom from Coercion

> 5. Ethical practice requires the investigator to respect the individual's freedom to decline to participate in or withdraw from research. The obligation to protect this freedom requires special vigilance when the investigator is in a position of power over the participant, as for example,

when the participant is a student, client, employee, or otherwise is in a dual relationship with the investigator (p. 17).

The idea of freedom from coercion is part of the larger question of civil rights and the right to privacy in particular. The legal concept of a right to privacy is a development of the last hundred years or so. It is agreed that people have the right not to be disturbed, as well as the right not to reveal certain information about themselves. Although psychologists respect this right to privacy, it must be balanced against the welfare of society as a whole. The solution to many thorny social problems may require information that people are reluctant to reveal. How does one weigh the value to society of understanding and controlling the behavior of criminals and tax evaders against the rights of law-abiding citizens to be left alone? The reluctance of many people, particularly illegal aliens, to respond to the 1980 U.S. census is an indication of this tension. Although the census bureau stated that its information would not be made available to other government agencies, the Internal Revenue Service in particular, many people refused to answer the questions.

The experimenter must remember at all times that the subject is doing a favor by participating. The freedom to refuse to participate or to withdraw at any time without penalty should be made clear to the subject at the beginning of the experiment if it has not already been explained during the recruitment of subjects. The experimenter should realize that many subjects are apprehensive about participating and will tend to tolerate considerable discomfort without complaint. This response increases the researcher's obligation not to exploit the subject.

The most likely problem of coercion that you as a reader of this book will face is the decision to use introductory psychology students as "volunteers." In many colleges introductory psychology students are commonly asked to serve as research subjects as part of the course requirements. Some departments avoid the problem of coercion by allowing students extra credit for participation or by providing alternative means of satisfying the requirement. In favor of such a requirement is the educational value of serving in an experiment. Coercion, however, may be subtle if a student feels that participation may lead to a chance for a better grade. Most students do not seem especially concerned over this degree of coercion. In my experience few students have ever requested alternative service in contrast to the several thousand who have complied. Serving as subjects appears to be as acceptable to them as other course requirements.

Issues of coercion become more serious if substantial sums of money are offered for service or if subjects are induced to participate with promises to "improve your relations with the opposite sex" or "gain valuable insights into your personality." The APA ethical principles (1973) contain a list of guidelines for departments that wish to set up experimental participation requirements for students.

Fairness

> 6. Prior to conducting research, the investigator establishes a clear and fair agreement with the research participant that clarifies the responsibilities of each. The investigator has the obligation to honor all promises and commitments included in that agreement (p. 17).

This principle in reality is an extension of principles three through five. It is met when each party has a clear understanding of what is expected. Investigators will do well to keep the golden rule in mind and remember that the subjects are doing them a favor by participating.

Protection from Harm

> 7. The investigator protects participants from physical and mental discomfort, harm, and danger. If a risk of such consequences exists, the investigator informs the participant of that fact, secures consent before proceeding, and takes all possible measures to minimize distress. Research procedures likely to cause serious or lasting harm to a participant are not used (p. 17).

Clearly it is impossible to entirely avoid risk of harm in behavioral research, because any new situation by definition is stressful and conceivably could be harmful. Some experiments, though, have subjected people to the threat of shock, to being told that they have latent homosexual tendencies, or to being locked in a room that appears to be on fire. Today these situations are considered unduly stressful. Stress in an experiment may be either physical or psychological. In judging the acceptability of stress, the researcher must assess how stressful the situation is likely to be compared with activities of everyday life. Would people willingly put themselves into this situation? What special groups must be considered, such as heart patients, epileptics, or borderline schizophrenics?

Debriefing

> 8. After the data are collected, the investigator provides the participant with information about the nature of the study and removes any misconceptions that may have arisen. Where scientific or human values justify delaying or withholding information, the investigator acquires a special responsibility to assure that there are no damaging consequences for the participant (p. 17).

Debriefing
after the session the process of informing subjects of the experiment's true purpose in order to increase their understanding and to remove possible harmful effects of deception

Debriefing is an extremely important part of the experiment. Subjects must be told the purpose and expected results of the experiment so that their experience has as much educational and personal value for them as possible.

When deception has been employed, the experimenter has a touchy situation. A blunt admission of deception can make subjects feel foolish, stupid, or abused. Because many investigators additionally use the debriefing to ascertain whether the deception was effective, their explanation requires great subtlety. In the first place subjects, in an effort not to embarrass the experimenter, may be reluctant to admit that they saw through the deception. This response is part of the good-subject role that they tend to adopt. Second, the degree of awareness of deception varies greatly with the phrasing of the question. A simple "Any questions about the experiment?" may elicit no response, whereas "Was there anything that might lead you to suspect that the experiment was not exactly what it seemed on the surface?" is more likely to yield a statement indicating awareness of the deception. For this reason any estimate of the effectiveness of the deception is highly uncertain.

Some investigators delay the debriefing so that other potential subjects will not learn the purpose of the study. In this case the investigator may wish to take subjects' addresses and send them an explanation when the experiment is completed. This delayed debriefing is less effective because subjects may move away or may lose interest in the study over time.

Removing Undesirable Consequences

> 9. When research procedures may result in undesirable consequences for the individual participant, the investigator has the responsibility to detect and remove or correct these consequences including, where relevant, long-term after effects (p. 17).

In clinical research a problem occurs when subjects who anticipated receiving help feel cheated when they learn that they were put into a control group or into a condition that turned out to be less effective than another condition. In these cases some investigators offer the subjects experience with the other condition after the experiment is completed. Others argue that the participants in the control condition were not any more deprived of benefit than all other persons who did not participate in the study. Nevertheless, most researchers would feel conflict over placing a suicide-prone person in a control group if they believed that the experimental procedure was likely to be effective in preventing suicide.

Confidentiality

> 10. Information obtained about the individual research participants during the course of an investigation is confidential unless otherwise agreed in advance. When the possibility exists that others may obtain access to such information, this possibility, together with the plans for protecting confidentiality, is explained to the participants as part of the procedure for obtaining informed consent (p. 17).

People who participate in psychological studies have the right to expect that their data will never be made public in a way that would permit their identification, unless they agree to such publication. Problems have arisen when researchers have written up actual cases in a thinly disguised fashion. In other instances courts have subpoenaed information from social scientists about their clients or subjects who are involved in cases of alleged criminal activities. This situation is particularly problematic when a scientist has studied members of deviant groups or those involved in illegal activity and has promised them confidentiality. Social scientists do not enjoy the legal protection that lawyers and physicians have against being forced to reveal information about their clients. In one case a rape counselor was ordered to reveal information that the victim had given as part of the counseling process following the rape.

When data are coded, cases that involve sensitive material should be coded so that all information is destroyed that would permit identification of the individual. This process may not be possible in some types of case study work because of the continuing nature of the data collection. In some instances researchers send data out of the country for safekeeping, outside the jurisdiction of the courts.

Drugs

> 11. Investigations of human participants using drugs are conducted only in such settings as clinics, hospitals, or research facilities maintaining appropriate safeguards for the participant (p. 17).

The greatest of care must be exercised in research involving drugs. Ordinarily students will not use drugs in research. This caution includes legal drugs such as alcohol, widely available illegal drugs such as marijuana, as well as prescription drugs.

Role of the Research Participant

The debate on research ethics has raised questions about the role that the subject plays in psychological research. According to the traditional view, the subject contributes behavior to the experiment in much the same way that a subject in a medical experiment might contribute a urine specimen.

The very term *subject* is believed by some to imply that the participant is made an object of study and, necessarily, is dehumanized. This objectification is held to be a consequence of the traditional view of science that requires a separation between the observer/scientist and the observed/subject.

Another view of the research participant is one popular with humanistic psychologists, which holds that the participant is a colleague who cooperates in providing the data. In some examples of this process the participants take a role in designing the experiment and may have a degree of control over the conditions in which they are tested. Similarly, some psychologists have argued in the Marxist tradition that the participant should be considered part owner of the data by virtue of having helped to create them. Although this view of research may increase cooperation on the part of the participant, it increases the risk of sloppy experiments.

The humanistic view of research is popular among parapsychologists and has led to many poorly conducted and uninterpretable experiments. In order to assure valid results, the experimenter must assume responsibility for the experimental situation. Certain types of research may lend themselves to informality between experimenter and subject, but the scientist must have ultimate control. One thing that can be learned from the humanistic viewpoint, however, is to treat the subjects with dignity and respect and to make them know that they are doing the experimenter a favor. Another advantage of looking at the subject as a cooperator in the research effort is that the researcher becomes more sympathetic with the viewpoint of the participant. Minority groups in particular have become resentful of being endlessly studied when they perceive that the only apparent result is to promote the careers of the already advantaged scientists.

ETHICS OF ANIMAL EXPERIMENTATION

Experimenting on animals is considered permissible as long as humane considerations are satisfied. This attitude follows from the dominance of the Judeo-Christian tradition and, in particular, its teaching that people are intended to rule over the animals and use them for human benefit. Nevertheless, the point of view that animals have rights of their own and that they should not be exploited for human benefit has become increasingly accepted. One controversial practice is the testing of hair spray by dripping it into the eyes of rabbits. Researchers are looking for other ways of testing that will reduce the need for animals to suffer in research projects, including the use of tissue cultures in the place of whole animals. In the meantime, however, there is no substitute for the use of animals in certain types of research, particularly psychology. Most behavioral research requires the use of intact animals.

Pressure from animal welfare groups and pet owners has led to a tightening of practices in animal experimentation and to the promulgation of federal standards for the care of experimental animals. The days when researchers obtain their experimental cats and dogs by prowling the streets dragging a piece of meat are over. In general acceptable practice in animal experimentation consists of assuring that the scientific benefit of the study warrants whatever discomfort is caused and that the animals are kept in comfortable and sanitary conditions. Furthermore, the decision to use animals in an experiment involves a commitment to their care. Many species cannot tolerate the extremes of temperature common in academic buildings. Nor can animals be left uncared for during weekends or holidays. A researcher cannot initiate an experiment using animals without considering a host of logistical problems. For example, many people are allergic to rats. If a special facility with separate ventilation is not available, a number of people who share the building likely will suffer allergic reactions.

Ordinarily, a student who uses animals in research will be joining an ongoing laboratory with well-established animal care procedures. Most institutions have an animal care committee that oversees the operation of the animal facility. Such a committee is required for nearly all institutions that receive federal research grants. The Department of Health and Human Services (formerly HEW) has prepared a publication, *Guide for the Care and Use of Laboratory Animals* (1978), that summarizes guidelines for animal research. This document lists standards for food, sanitation, and health, including size of cage and recommended institutional policies on veterinary care and personnel. In addition the document has a valuable bibliography on animal care and lists federal laws that relate to animal experimentation. Among recommended practices is the responsibility to make sure that the animals are kept in adequate-size cages and that they are warm, dry, and well fed and watered at all times, unless the experiment legitimately requires other conditions. Their health must be maintained and they must be disposed of properly after the experiment. Any experiment that causes pain should employ anesthetics if possible. The animals should be as well cared for as would a pet. These provisions are not just idealistic notions. Much of the impetus for the restriction of animal research has come from pet owners.

THE SOCIAL PSYCHOLOGY OF THE PSYCHOLOGY EXPERIMENT

Over the last two decades much attention has been paid to the biases that can enter into an experiment as a result of the interaction between the subject and the experimenter. This concern comes from the realization that an experiment is a social situation with its own set of rules. Both the subject and the experimenter have expectations about how they should behave in an experiment. We talked in Chapter 4 about two problems resulting from the subjects' expectations, the good-subject tendency and evaluation apprehension. In this section we will further discuss the biases resulting from the interactions between subject and experimenter, and we will suggest ways of overcoming them.

Role Demands

The subjects' knowledge that they are participating in an experiment constitutes a set of expectations about how they are to behave. These expectations are called *role demands* or *demand characteristics* of the experiment. In one experiment I had subjects smell dirty T-shirts and judge them for unpleasantness and other attributes (McBurney, Levine, & Cavanaugh, 1977). Halfway through the series of shirts, one subject looked up and said, "You know, I don't believe I am doing this." Nevertheless, she continued. This illustration is just one of the apparently pointless and/or socially unacceptable behaviors that people will engage in when they believe that they are in a psychological experiment.

The role demands of an experiment can cause serious problems with interpreting the results. In hypnosis, for example, people have been concerned that they or others might be induced to perform antisocial acts while hypnotized. In one experiment hypnotized subjects threw a concentrated acid at someone's face on the experimenter's request. (The person was protected by an invisible glass pane.) Interpretation of the results has been controversial. Did the hypnosis cause the compliance or would nonhypnotized subjects do the same thing? Martin Orne and Frederick Evans (1965) replicated the study using several new control groups. The experimental group was hypnotized and asked to throw "acid" at the assistant, which they did. One control group was instructed to pretend to be hypnotized. Five out of six of these faking subjects complied with the request to throw "acid." The subjects later said that they had thought that some safety precaution had been taken to prevent injury to the other person. Orne and Evans decided that no conclusions could be drawn about the likelihood of people doing antisocial acts under hypnosis because subjects could so easily be induced to perform the same acts without hypnosis.

One of the most extreme examples of the effects of role demands is the well-known Milgram study (1963), in which subjects were led to believe that they were delivering electric shocks to others over their vigorous protests. The subjects later said they did believe that the other person was being shocked. The fact that they were subjects in an experiment led them to engage in behavior that people have since found surprising and disturbing.

These role demands, together with the good-subject tendency, may cause subjects to play dumb about the purpose of the experiment even if they can figure out the hypothesis or see through a deception. Getting subjects to admit that they have learned the purpose of the experiment from someone else is difficult, because they don't want to make the experimenter feel badly.

Preventing Role Demands from Biasing the Results

Role demands behavior that results from subjects' expectations of what an experiment requires them to do

Much ingenuity has been devoted to keeping the influence of **role demands** from undermining the validity of experiments. The most obvious and seemingly simplest solution is to deceive the subject about the experiment's purpose. A cover story is devised that provides a plausible rationale, and the true hypothesis is not revealed. This ploy often works but has several drawbacks, not the least of which involves ethics. In addition, developing a satisfactory cover story that will not affect the behavior being studied often is difficult. The story may cause subjects to behave in a way that interacts with the true hypothesis. Inevitably, too, subjects hear that many psychological experiments are not what they seem to be on the surface. This occurrence increases the difficulty of devising a believable cover story, and it may also influence the results of experiments that do not use deception.

Another approach is to divide the experiment in such a way that part of the data are obtained in another setting. In this way subjects are unlikely to put two and two together and surmise the hypothesis. For example, subjects first may be given a test of anxiety. Later, those who scored either high or low on the test may be requested to take part in an experiment without knowing the basis for their selection.

An additional method of counteracting bias is to use a measure that is unlikely to be influenced by subjects' guesses about the hypothesis. Some examples might be such nonverbal behavior as how close people sit to one another or whether they look a person in the eye. Finally, we will mention the tactic of keeping the subject unaware that an experiment is being conducted. Chairs may be rearranged in a public room to study the influence of seating arrangement on social interaction, for example. These and other methods of avoiding bias from role demands are discussed by Aronson and Carlsmith (1968).

Experimenter Bias

A large number of studies indicate that the experimenter unintentionally can bias the results of an experiment (Rosenthal, 1976). In one study experimenters were given rats to train. Some were told that their rats had been specially bred for intelligence; others were told their rats were particularly dull. Those experimenters who had the "bright" rats found faster learning than the others (Rosenthal & Fode, 1963). The mechanism of the bias in this case was that the experimenters who had the "bright" rats handled them more than did those who had the "dull" rats. Some of these studies of bias have become controversial (Barber, 1976). Experiments often were designed to allow bias to operate freely. In some studies evidence exists that the experimenters simply may have fudged the data, rather than biasing them. Nevertheless, there is widespread agreement that an experimenter's biases can subtly influence experiments.

Reducing Experimenter Bias

The effects of experimenter bias are so ubiquitous that a standard procedure in many disciplines is for the experimenter to be "blind" to the condition a subject experiences. This method of preventing experimenter bias is excellent and foolproof but not always possible in a psychological experiment. In one experiment in my laboratory we were interested in whether smokers had lower taste sensitivity than nonsmokers. Subjects were met by someone who asked them to empty their shirt pockets (to remove cigarettes or lighters) and who sent them on to the experimenter. Only after the experiment did we inquire about smoking habits. This technique probably was effective in most cases, but it could not make the experimenter blind to obvious tobacco stains or tobacco odor. Too, blind experimenters may devise their own hypotheses about experiments and thus unintentionally bias the subjects in the direction of their concocted hypotheses.

Another basic strategy for reducing experimenter bias is to standardize experiments as much as possible. In some experiments testing subjects in all conditions at the same time may be possible. The various conditions can be induced by written instructions given to each subject. Or, if subjects must be tested individually, instructions can be tape-recorded so that each subject receives the same experience.

Variations on these basic strategies can be used in particular situations. Further discussions may be found in Aronson and Carlsmith (1968) and Carlsmith, Ellsworth, and Aronson (1976).

GUARDING THE INTEGRITY OF THE DATA

All of the care expended on designing and conducting an experiment is wasted if the data are compromised by carelessness in recording and handling. Before the experiment begins, the researcher must have a plan for recording and handling the data. A good procedure is to keep all data and other experiment details such as dosages, stimulus settings, and the like in a notebook. If loose sheets are used, they must be dated and identified in such a way that they can be replaced if any sheets become misfiled. Often it is convenient to reproduce a blank set of data sheets with spaces for all necessary information so that nothing will be overlooked. Data should be placed in a file and kept in a secure place. They should never be carried around in a briefcase from which they can be lost. Too often data have been eaten by the dog, scribbled on by the baby, or left on the bus. Making photocopies of any data that must be taken out of the laboratory is a good practice.

Later the raw data will be transferred from the data sheets to a summary form. Preparing the format of the summary data sheet ahead of time is a good idea. The summary sheet should allow space for doing simple manipulations of the data, such as taking the logarithm and/or means, before the statistical analysis is performed. Any information necessary to recreate the summary data from the data sheets should be carefully recorded, such as the random order of stimuli that was used for each subject. Records of the experiment should be set up in such a way that another person could decipher the experiment from the records alone. Essential features of experiments can be forgotten, especially if the researcher has conducted a number of experiments.

The data sheets should be kept for as long as anyone is likely to want to reanalyze the data. Although fraud in research is not a welcome topic, it does happen. The existence of original data sheets may be the only proof that the data were collected as claimed. The original data sheets should be delivered to an adviser or locked up after the data have been transferred to a tabular form before data analysis is begun. This procedure protects from the temptation to fudge data to make them fit the hypothesis (the raw data often do not permit ascertaining whether the hypothesis was confirmed). Recording the original data in ink is advisable. A modicum of compulsiveness in guarding data is a good idea.

SUMMARY

1. Sources for the literature review include textbooks, handbooks, *Psychological Abstracts*, and the *Science Citation Index*.
2. The research problem is narrowed down to one or more specific hypotheses that the research is designed to answer.
3. The choice of method is dictated by factors such as the exact hypothesis to be tested, the methods that are standard in the particular field, and practical considerations.
4. The choice of the stimulus values is guided by four principles: The stimuli should cover as much of the range as possible; they should be close enough together to prevent overlooking interesting effects between stimuli; in within-subjects experiments about seven stimuli should be presented if possible; and the stimuli should be logarithmically spaced if the continuum is quantitative.
5. Selection of subjects involves many practical and ethical considerations. Procedures of the institution should be followed.

6. The number of subjects to be used depends on the size of the effect and the anticipated variability of the data. The power of the experiment increases proportionately with the square root of the number of subjects.
7. The procedure involves the steps taken by the experimenter to carry out the experiment design. These steps are sometimes written out in the form of a protocol.
8. It is common to prepare a proposal or prospectus, which is a complete statement of everything necessary to evaluate the adequacy of the research before it is conducted.
9. All psychological research should be guided by the APA ethics code, which deals with the following areas: deciding whether to undertake a particular investigation, informed consent and deception, freedom from coercion, fairness, protection from harm, debriefing, removing undesirable consequences, confidentiality, and drugs.
10. Although the traditional and dominant view is that the researcher maintains control over the experiment situation and the subject in the interest of objectivity, humanistic psychologists consider the participant to be a colleague who cooperates in providing the data.
11. Acceptable practice in animal experimentation consists in assuring that the scientific benefit of the study warrants whatever discomfort is caused to the animals and that they are kept in comfortable and sanitary conditions.
12. Most institutions doing animal research have animal care committees that oversee the operation of animal facilities.
13. Psychology experiments may be considered social situations with their own role demands that may interfere with the purpose of the study.
14. Ways of preventing role demands from biasing experiment results include: inventing a cover story that deceives the subject about the purpose of the experiment, dividing the experiment in such a way that part of the data are collected in another setting, using measures that are unlikely to be influenced by the subject's expectations, and keeping the subject unaware that an experiment is being conducted.
15. Experimenter bias may be reduced by keeping the experimenter blind as to the conditions in the experiment or its purpose and by standardizing the procedure as much as possible.
16. Data must be recorded and kept in such a way that there is minimum possibility of their being lost or their integrity being compromised.

SUGGESTIONS FOR FURTHER READING

AMERICAN PSYCHOLOGICAL ASSOCIATION. *Ethical principles in the conduct of research with human participants*. Washington, D.C.: American Psychological Association, 1973. Ethical principles of research are presented, along with case studies and discussion of issues. This book is basic reading on the topic of ethics. (The version of the principles presented in this chapter is the 1979 revision published in the *APA Monitor* of November 1979, p. 17.)

COOK, S. W. Ethical issues in the conduct of research in social relations. In C. Selltiz, L. S. Wrightsman, & S. W. Cook (Eds.), *Research methods in social relations.* New York: Holt, Rinehart & Winston, 1976. This excellent discussion is somewhat broader than the issues covered in the APA principles.

STOLZ, S. B., et al. *Ethical issues in behavior modification.* San Francisco: Jossey-Bass, 1978. This book is the report of the Commission on Behavior Modification of the American Psychological Association. It considers ethical and legal issues dealing with behavior modification in out-patient settings, institutions, schools, prisons, and society at large. The presentation is balanced and well reasoned.

READING BETWEEN THE LINES

The following problems are presented for you to solve. See Reading Between the Lines in Chapter 1 for an introduction to them. The answers are given in Appendix A.

13. ULCERS IN EXECUTIVE MONKEYS

In a famous study (Brady, Porter, Conrad, & Mason, 1958) pairs of monkeys received electric shocks. One of the monkeys in a pair received a shock when it failed to press a lever at least once every 20 seconds. The other monkey received shock according to the behavior of the first monkey; its own behavior had nothing to do with the shock it received. The monkey whose behavior determined the shock was called the executive monkey. Before the experimenters placed the monkeys in the experiment, they gave them a pretest on their ability to learn the avoidance response. Those monkeys in each pair that learned more quickly were made the executive monkeys, and the ones that learned more slowly became the control monkeys. Brady et al. found that the executive monkeys tended to develop ulcers, whereas the control monkeys did not. Although this experiment became well known, other researchers were unable to replicate it. Can you think of any fault in the procedure?

14. SIZE OF REWARD AND COGNITIVE DISSONANCE

Festinger and Carlsmith (1959) had subjects perform a boring task for an hour. They were then offered either $1 or $20 to tell the next subject and others that the experiment was interesting. Afterward, the subjects were asked to rate how much they enjoyed the first task. The $1 group said it was somewhat enjoyable, but the $20 group rated the task as neutral.

Festinger and Carlsmith interpreted the experiment as evidence that doing something for which one does not have a good reason causes an unpleasant state known as cognitive dissonance. In this experiment $1 was supposed to be an insufficient reason to tell someone that the task was interesting. These subjects, therefore, should feel cognitive dissonance between the belief that the task was boring and the knowledge that they had accepted $1 for telling others that it was interesting.

The dissonance can be reduced by changing one of the opinions that caused the dissonance. For example, subjects could reduce the dissonance by deciding that the original task had been interesting after all. The subjects who received $20 to tell the others that the task was interesting had a sufficient reason to do so and consequently would not feel the cognitive dissonance. Do you think Festinger and Carlsmith were justified in their conclusion?

TRUE EXPERIMENTS

As we saw in Chapter 5, a key concept in designing experiments is that of control. The experimenter seeks to control as many of the potential threats to validity as possible. When a sufficient number of these are under control, the study is a true experiment. A true experiment is an experiment in which the experimenter has reason to believe that he or she has both control over the assignment of subjects to conditions and control over the presentation of conditions to subjects. When a study does not meet the requirements of a true experiment, it is called a quasi experiment. The word *quasi* means *as if* or *to a degree*. Therefore a quasi experiment is one that resembles an experiment but lacks at least one of its defining characteristics.

In the first section of this chapter we will define true experiments and quasi experiments and will discuss their differences. Then we will define the basic elements of a valid experimental design, mention some designs that should be avoided, and finally, describe some representative experimental designs.

Scattered throughout the chapter are four boxes; each illustrates the statistical analysis of an experiment we've discussed.* For more information you may refer to any standard statistics book.

*Statistics boxes drafted by J. F. Gent, 1982.

TRUE EXPERIMENTS, QUASI EXPERIMENTS, AND THEIR DIFFERENCES

True experiment research procedure over which the scientist has complete control of all aspects

In a **true experiment** the experimenter has complete control over the experiment: the who, what, when, where, and how. Control over the who of the experiment means that the experimenter may randomly assign subjects to conditions. Recall that random assignment is preferred because it allows one to conclude that any other variable could be confounded with the independent variable only by chance. No other method of assignment of subjects to conditions permits such a conclusion. Control over the what, when, where, and how of the experiment means that the experimenter has complete control over the way that the experiment is to be conducted.

Quasi experiment research procedure in which the scientist must select subjects for different conditions from preexisting groups

A **quasi experiment,** on the other hand, is an experiment in which the investigator lacks the degree of control over the conditions that is possible in a true experiment. The most important difference is that whereas it is possible to *assign* subjects to conditions in a true experiment, in a quasi experiment it is necessary to *select* subjects for the different conditions from previously existing groups.

For example, you may wish to study the effect of number of food pellets on the rate at which rats learn a maze. This situation would permit the design of a true experiment because you could arbitrarily assign some rats to the large-reward condition and others to the small-reward condition. Assume that before the experiment the rats belonged to a homogeneous population of rats. For experiment purposes you assign the rats to groups that you *create* according to your needs.

On the other hand, if you were interested in sex differences in detecting hidden figures, you would have to conduct a quasi experiment because you cannot assign subjects to the two conditions, male and female. Here the researcher cannot create groups of males and females but instead selects members from *preexisting* groups.

Quasi experiments are sometimes called ex post facto, or after the fact, experiments because the experiment is conducted after the groups have been formed. In the case of a quasi experiment with sex as the independent variable, the experiment takes place long after the subjects become males or females. If you performed an experiment using preexisting classes of students, the two classes would be an ex post facto variable because the classes were formed before you did the experiment.

Another way to look at the difference between true experiments and quasi experiments is to note that in true experiments we *manipulate variables,* whereas in quasi experiments we *observe categories* of subjects. When we take two preexisting groups and consider a difference between them to be the independent variable, we are not manipulating a variable but simply labeling groups according to what we think is the important difference between them. The true difference between them for our experiment may be quite different from what we think it is. If we find that two different socioeconomic groups differ on some measure, the difference may not be caused by the socioeconomic difference itself but by cultural differences between the two socioeconomic groups. By calling the difference socioeconomic, we may obscure the fact that the difference is actually a difference in need achievement or perceived helplessness or religion.

When we present some independent variable to two preexisting groups, more is involved than measuring their behavior. We have the additional problem of not knowing whether the difference in behavior was caused by differences between the groups or by the independent variable. If we studied the effects of two different teaching methods on learning in two preexisting classes, we would not be sure whether any differences in learning resulted from the teaching methods or from preexisting differences between the classes.

It is possible to have one experimental variable and one quasi-experimental variable in an experiment. Thus in studying the effects of two different teaching methods on classroom learning, we might be interested in whether slow learners differ from fast learners in their response to the teaching methods. The two teaching methods would constitute a true experimental variable, and the classification into slow and fast learners would constitute a quasi-experimental variable.

The degree of control that is possible varies from one type of investigation to another. The fact that we are discussing true experiments first does not reflect a bias that true experiments necessarily are better than other types of investigations. Rather, it reflects the fact that as the degree of control that the researcher can exercise decreases, the threats to the validity of the conclusions increase. Other things being equal, one would choose a true experiment over a quasi experiment and a quasi experiment over a nonexperimental method. Things are seldom equal, though. Many social-psychological phenomena are difficult to bring into the laboratory in a realistic fashion. Therefore a field study may be preferable to an experiment, because the advantage of realism outweighs the loss of control. Nevertheless, you should try first to design a true experimental study and use the other designs only when you believe that the gain in validity will be worth the loss of control.

THE BASIC ELEMENTS OF A VALID EXPERIMENTAL DESIGN

Chapter 4 discussed types of validity and the many threats to validity that exist, and Chapter 5 discussed methods of control that are available to improve the validity of an experiment. In this chapter we begin the consideration of some particular experimental designs as examples of ways of achieving control over threats to validity. You should keep in mind a point made previously, that designing an experiment is an exercise in problem solving. When threats to validity are adequately controlled for, the experiment has been designed. At the same time you should realize that no design can rule out all threats to validity for all time. For example, as we said in Chapter 4, societal changes since the "dirty word" study was conducted have reduced the external validity of that experiment.

Even though there can be no perfect experiment, two particular elements of design provide control over so many different threats to validity that they are basic to all good experimental designs. They are: (1) the existence of a control group or a control condition and (2) the random allocation of subjects to the various conditions (for between-subjects experiments). These two elements are illustrated in Table 7–1, which represents a simple experiment with two conditions. If this is taken to represent a between-subjects experiment, then different subjects would be randomly allocated to the two conditions. This allocation assures that the groups will be equal in all respects, except as they may differ by chance. On the other hand, if this is a within-subjects experiment, then all subjects experience both conditions. A subject's behavior in one condition is compared with his behavior in another condition. Either way, we have reason to believe that the subjects in both conditions were equal to begin with, which enables us to compare their performance between experimental and control conditions. Any difference in behavior can be attributed to differences between the two conditions.

SOME DESIGNS TO AVOID

The experiment outlined in Table 7–1 is a simple one, but it embodies the two basic elements of design. In this chapter we will consider a number of examples of designs that are appropriate to the particular problem they address. However, before we consider good designs, let us look at some designs that should be avoided. These undesirable designs are weak in that they do not control for various alternative explanations of the results. They all fail to control for certain threats to validity discussed in Chapter 4.

TABLE 7–1 Basic elements of good experimental design.

	Allocation	Treatment	Test
Condition 1	*Either* random allocation of subjects to conditions	yes (or A_1)	yes
Condition 2	*or* all subjects experience both conditions	no (or A_2)	yes

TABLE 7–2 One-group posttest only design.

	Treatment	Test
Single group	yes	yes

The One-Group Posttest Only Design

One-group posttest only design research design that measures the behavior of a single group of subjects after the treatment only

The **one-group posttest only design** is a simple one in which a group of subjects is given a treatment and then tested on some dependent variable (see Table 7–2). Suppose you wanted to test the effectiveness of est (Erhard Seminars Training), a program in which people attend a series of lectures and group activities, some of which are humiliating and exhausting. In order to evaluate the effect of the training, you decide to survey the participants. You find that most of them say that the experience was worthwhile and that they feel better about themselves than they did before the training. After a little reflection you realize that the results of your survey are nearly worthless. Although the people report that they feel better than they did before the training, you have no measures of how they felt before. Therefore you cannot determine if they changed. Furthermore, even if they did change, you have no assurance that the training itself caused this change. Perhaps the interruption in their routine caused the change. Or perhaps they would have felt better if they had gone to the movies for several evenings and then gone camping for a weekend.

Such a one-group posttest only design leaves so many threats to validity uncontrolled that it is nearly worthless. Nevertheless, you can certainly recall people who have recommended a product or practice to you on the basis of their experience. Many people in everyday life, as well as some scientists, have used this design.

The Posttest Only Design with Nonequivalent Control Groups

Suppose that you wanted to improve on the study of the effectiveness of est by comparing people who had taken the training with a control group who had not. You might try to find a group of people who matched the est group on as many variables as possible: age, income, education, and so forth. Table 7–3 illustrates this design. Although the design is an improvement

TABLE 7–3 Posttest only design with nonequivalent control groups.

	Allocation of subjects and groups	Treatment	Test
Group 1	Any method that is *not* random	yes (or A_1)	yes
Group 2		no (or A_2)	yes

over the one-group posttest only design, it still has a serious flaw. The flaw is that the control group is not equivalent in every way to those who took the training. The most important difference is that the est persons had selected themselves for the training and the control groups had not. Thus we have a **nonequivalent control group** because the two groups were not randomly constituted from the same population.

Nonequivalent control group group of subjects that is not randomly selected from the same population as the experimental group

A nonequivalent control group is better than no control group, but you would have to consider this study a quasi experiment at best because the subjects were not randomly assigned to groups. The only way you could construct a control group that was equivalent to the est group would be to ask the est organization to provide a list of all people who applied for the training. Then you would randomly place half of them into a control group that would not be allowed to take the training.

The One-Group Pretest-Posttest Design

Another way of improving on the one-group posttest only design is to take a measure of behavior before the treatment that may be compared with behavior after the treatment. This approach is called the **one-group pretest-posttest design.** In the example of the est study, you might obtain responses of the participants before they took the training to compare with responses after training. Such a design is illustrated in Table 7–4. If you were to use this design in the est study, you would probably find a change in the subjects' reports of their moods, feelings of self-worth, and so forth. You would still have the problem of determining what caused the changes, the est training or some unrelated event. Even if the est procedure did cause the changes, you wouldn't know what aspect of it was responsible. You still wouldn't know if going to the movies for several nights followed by a camping trip might have been equally beneficial. The following example discusses these problems in the context of a different situation.

One-group pretest-posttest design research design that measures the behavior of a single group of subjects both before and after treatment

A company may introduce a new work schedule whereby its employees put in four 10-hour days instead of five 8-hour days. If output increased, the management probably would credit the new schedule. This conclusion represents an improvement over the one-group posttest only design because you know that a behavior change did follow the treatment. However, you have not considered other potential causes of the increase in output and hence other threats to validity. Workers may have responded to the attention paid them by management when the change was initiated. Or

TABLE 7–4 One-group pretest-posttest design.

Pretest	Treatment	Posttest
yes	yes	yes

any number of events may have led to increased productivity: favorable weather conditions that allowed the workers to get to work on time, a change in seasons that may have made the plant more confortable, or a favorable response to a new supervisor. These occurrences represent threats to internal validity: The change was caused by a variable other than the one management thought to be responsible. Threats to external validity could come from the possibility that the workers may be young and may like long hours, whereas older workers may have preferred shorter days.

This study would have been better designed by forming two groups via random allocation of workers to different schedules so that one group would remain on the old schedule as a control group. This control would have eliminated the threats to internal validity that we listed above. Random allocation of workers to two groups may not be possible, however. In that event if the company had two plants, one could be switched to the four-day week, while the other is kept on the five-day week. Productivity in the two plants could be compared. This example is a nonequivalent control group design. Differences between the workers at the two plants or in the plants themselves may account for the results instead of the work schedule itself. The addition of a nonequivalent control group to a pretest-posttest design improves the control sufficiently that the design may be considered a quasi experiment. Chapter 8 will discuss a number of quasi-experimental designs.

SOME REPRESENTATIVE EXPERIMENTAL DESIGNS

The following section discusses designs that represent typical solutions to problems of validity and control discussed in Chapters 4 and 5. The designs presented do not constitute all that are possible, because an indefinite number of designs exists. These simply are designs that are the most common solutions to common experimental problems.

Two Conditions, Tested within Subjects

Two-conditions design the simplest research design; involves only two conditions; can be tested within or between subjects

This **two-conditions design** is the simplest possible true experiment design because it has only two conditions and each subject serves as own control. The design is illustrated in Table 7–5. The two conditions are indicated as Condition 1 and Condition 2, although one of them may be considered the experimental condition and the other the control condition. All subjects experience both conditions in counterbalanced order. In spite of its simplicity, this design is not used as often as one might expect, for two reasons. First, many experiments involve more than two conditions. Second, there is the possibility of carry-over effects from one condition to the other.

An experiment that serves as an example of this design is one by John Marshall and Philip Teitelbaum (1974) on the phenomenon of sensory

TABLE 7–5 Two-condition design, tested within subjects.

	Allocation	Treatment	Test
Condition 1 (or experimental)	All subjects experience both conditions in counterbalanced order	Condition 1 (or experimental treatment)	yes
Condition 2 (or control)		Condition 2 (or control treatment)	yes

neglect. Research has shown that damage to both sides of a small part of the brain known as the lateral hypothalamus produces a severe impairment of feeding and drinking. In addition to these motivational effects was interference with the ability to respond to sensory stimulation after this damage. Marshall and Teitelbaum were interested in the contribution of the sensory neglect to the motivational deficit.

Recall that the brain is approximately bilaterally symmetrical; that is, the left half is the mirror image of the right. Marshall and Teitelbaum destroyed the lateral hypothalamus on one side of the brains of 12 rats. When the rats had recovered from the operation, they were tested for their responsiveness to stimuli that were presented to one side or the other of their bodies. Visual, tactile, and olfactory stimuli were used. In all cases the rats responded only when the stimuli were presented to the same side that had received brain damage. (Each side of the brain controls the opposite side of the body.) When the rats were stimulated on the opposite side, they did not respond.

Thus, from the design point of view, the unilateral damage allowed each animal to be used as its own control. One side of the brain was a control for the other, ruling out differences between subjects as a possible source of error. For example, one of the tests used was whether the rat would attack a mouse presented to the brain-damaged side. (Some rats will kill mice and others will not.) By using each rat as its own control, the experimenters were able to say that all rats that were mouse killers attacked mice presented to the undamaged side of the brain but did not react to those presented to the damaged side.

Two Conditions, Tested between Subjects

The experiment by Marshall and Teitelbaum was a within-subjects experiment because each rat served as its own control. This design may not be desirable when the possibility of large order or sequence effects is present. Such was the case in an experiment on the effect of anxiety on affiliation conducted by Stanley Schachter (1959). He hypothesized that inducing anxiety in people would cause an increase in their tendency to seek the

BOX 7–1 Example of the Analysis of the Results of a Two-Condition, Between-Subjects Experiment by Chi-Square

The following is the analysis of the data of the Schachter (1959) experiment on the choice of waiting either alone or together by subjects who were expecting either high or low level of shock. The following shows the data of the experiment. Because each subject fell into one and only one cell of the table, analyzing these data by chi-square (χ^2) is appropriate.

Data from the Schachter study.

Induced anxiety	Number choosing to wait		
	With others	Alone	Don't care
High	20	12	32
Low	10	20	30
	30	32	62

Following is the 8-step procedure:

1. Assumptions
   a. Every sample observation falls into one and only one category. (In this example no subject served twice.)
   b. The sample observations are independent. (Although the subjects were run in groups, the author felt that the interaction among them was minimal.)
   c. N is large ($N = 62$).
2. Hypotheses
   a. H_0: Our null hypothesis is that there is no difference in companionship-seeking behavior between the high- and low-anxiety groups.
   b. H_1: Our alternative hypothesis is that there is a difference.
3. $\alpha = .05$
4. $\chi^2 = \sum_{ij}(E_{ij} - O_{ij})^2/E_{ij}$
5. Sampling distribution: $\chi^2(1)$
   $df = (R - 1)(C - 1)$
   $= (2 - 1)\ (2 - 1)$
   $= 1$

6. Look in a χ^2 table under $\alpha = .05$ and $df = 1$.
   $\text{Chi}^2_{.05} = 3.841$. If χ^2 calculated in step 7
   is greater than 3.841, reject H_0.
7. Calculation of test statistic.

$$\chi^2 = (15.48 - 20)^2 / 15.48 + (16.52 - 12)^2 / 16.52 + (14.52 - 10)^2 / 14.52 + (15.48 - 20)^2 / 15.48$$
$$= 1.32 + 1.24 + 1.41 + 1.32$$
$$= 5.29$$

8. Since $5.29 > 3.841$, reject H_0. There is a significant difference between high- and low-induced-anxiety subjects in their companionship-seeking behavior.

company of others. He induced anxiety by telling subjects that they were to be connected to an apparatus that would deliver painful electric shock. After a lecture on the purpose of the research, subjects were instructed that they were to wait ten minutes before receiving the shock. They filled out a questionnaire that asked whether they wished to wait alone or with other subjects. Subjects in the control condition were told they would receive mild nonpainful shock. Otherwise, they were treated the same as the experimental subjects. Of the low-stress subjects 33 percent indicated they wished to wait with others, while 63 percent of the high-stress subjects wished to wait with other subjects.

You can see that this experiment had to be conducted as a between-subjects experiment. Once subjects had experienced one of the conditions, they would no longer be naive about the situations. In actuality none of the subjects in either condition received shock. If they had been asked to serve again in the other condition, the instructions would not have had the same effect. Even if they had been shocked and then asked to participate again, they would have noticed the difference in instructions between conditions and would have begun to suspect the experiment's purpose. Only by having a separate group in each condition could Schachter test the effect of anxiety on the dependent variable.

Multiple-Conditions Experiments

Multiple-conditions design research design that involves more than two conditions; can be tested within or between subjects

Psychology experiments generally employ more than two conditions. The first reason researchers choose **multiple-conditions experiments** is that seldom do they wish to ask a simple yes-or-no question. Usually they want to compare several variables or treatments for effectiveness. For example, the question may be which of three different types of psychotherapies is most effective.

A second reason for conducting multiple-conditions experiments is to determine the shape of the function that relates the independent and dependent variables. When experimenters want to know how brightness increases with intensity of a light, they present each of several intensities of the light to a group of subjects. From the responses to the various intensities they can plot the relation between intensity and brightness. Each intensity is a condition of the experiment.

A third reason for doing multiple-conditions experiments is the presence of more than one rival hypothesis that must be ruled out. Suppose a child has a favorite toy that is fuzzy, colorful, and noisy. If you want to find out which of the three characteristics is responsible for the child's attachment to the toy, you could make up three versions of the same toy:

A: *fuzzy*, not colorful, not noisy

B: not fuzzy, *colorful*, not noisy

C: not fuzzy, not colorful, *noisy*

Toy A tests for fuzziness, B for colorfulness, and C for noisiness, as the independent variable causing attachment. Because toys A and B are not noisy, they control for noisiness. Similarly, A and C control for colorfulness, B and C control for fuzziness. To accommodate the three hypotheses, you would need three conditions (toys). Each toy serves as a partial control (condition) for the other hypotheses. In this example we varied three independent variables in a single experiment.

Multiple-Conditions Experiments, within Subjects. The example of scaling the brightness of lights would be a multiple-conditions, within-subjects experiment. Such an experiment, indicated schematically in Table 7–6, is common in perceptual research.

Multiple-Conditions Experiments, between Subjects. The design of a multiple-conditions, between-subjects experiment is indicated in Table 7–7. An interesting example of such an experiment was conducted by Andrew Baum and Glenn Davis (1980). Their experiment is unusual in that it was a true experiment, with the experimenters having complete control over the independent variables even though it was conducted partly as a field experiment and partly as a laboratory experiment. (Often field experi-

TABLE 7–6 Multiple-condition design, tested within subjects.

	Allocation	Treatment	Test
Condition 1	All subjects experience all conditions, either in random or counterbalanced order	1	yes
Condition 2		2	yes
Condition 3		3	yes

TABLE 7–7 Multiple-condition design, tested between subjects.

	Allocation	Treatment	Test
Group 1	Random allocation of subjects to groups	1	yes
Group 2		2	yes
Group 3		3	yes

ments must be run as quasi experiments due to practical complications.)

Baum and Davis wanted to study the effect of residential crowding on stress and social behavior. Through the cooperation of a college administration, they were able to conduct the experiment in a women's dormitory. The dormitory had long corridors that subjected residents to frequent interaction, which was believed to cause stress. One dormitory floor was modified by converting three rooms in the middle of the floor into lounges that were separated from the rest of the floor by unlocked doors. Thus two shorter hallways were created, divided by this lounge area. Another floor was not modified. A third floor was shorter than the other two and had the same number of residents as had either half of the divided floor. This arrangement allowed three floors to be studied: a long divided floor, a long undivided floor, and a short floor. Women were randomly assigned to the three floors. During the term the experimenters made a number of observations of hallway activity on the floors. An observer, who was not aware of the hypothesis of the study, spent a predetermined amount of time on each floor throughout the term. The observer's presence in the hallways was sufficiently unobtrusive that at the end of the term none of the women could identify him.

Although each hallway had equal activity, by the end of the term approximately twice the activity could be classified as social in the two short-hallway floors as in the long-hallway floor (See Figure 7–1). Whether

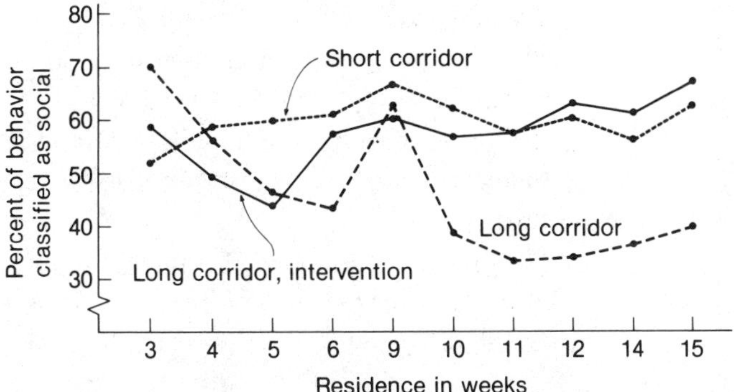

FIGURE 7–1. Percentage of hallway activity on dormitory floors rated as social.

Note. From "Reducing the stress of high-density living: An architectural intervention" by A. Baum & G. E. Davis, *Journal of Personality and Social Psychology,* 1980, *38,* 471–481. Copyright 1980 by the American Psychological Association. Reprinted by permission of the publisher and authors.

BOX 7–2 Example of a One-Way (Multiple-Condition), Repeated-Measures Analysis of Variance (ANOVA)

The following example analyzes fake data that might have been obtained in the experiment on the effect of long and short hallways on amount of social activity in the hallways (Baum & Davis, 1980). The following table shows the fake data.

Hypothetical data on amount of social activity.

	Corridor type		
	Long	Long, interrupted	Short
	70	60	52
	55	50	58
	45	50	58
	40	55	61
	60	60	65
	35	55	60
	30	55	55
	30	60	58
	35	58	53
	37	65	60
$X_{i\cdot}$*	437	568	580

Hypothetical data on amount of social activity for ANOVA, 3 groups, repeated measures (I = 3 corridor types, J = 10 observations per corridor, N = 30 observations)

Following is the 8-step procedure:

1. Assumptions
   a. The population from which each sample is drawn is normally distributed.
   b. The variances of the three treatment populations are equal. (They have homogeneous variance.)
   c. The three samples and ten observations in each sample are randomly and independently drawn.
2. Hypotheses
   a. H_0: Our null hypothesis is that there is no difference in the activity observed in the three corridors.
   b. H_1: The alternative is that there is a difference.
3. $\alpha = .01$.

*See note on dot notation, p. 152.

4. Refer to the following table.

ANOVA: Sums of squares calculation formulas.

Source	df	SS	MS	F
Between I	$I-1$	$\dfrac{\sum_j X_{i.}^2}{J} - \dfrac{X_{..}^2}{IJ}$	$\dfrac{SS_{bet}}{df_{bet}}$	$\dfrac{MS_{bet}}{MS_{err}}$
Error (between J within I)	$I(J-1)$	$\sum_{ij} X_{ij}^2 - \dfrac{\sum_j X_{i.}^2}{J}$	$\dfrac{SS_{err}}{df_{err}}$	
Total	$IJ-1 = N-1$			

5. Sampling distribution, $F(2, 27)$. (F distribution with $V_1 = 2$ and $V_2 = 27$ degrees of freedom.)
6. Look in an F table under $\alpha = .01$.

   $F_{.01}(2, 27) = 5.49$. If the F calculated in step 7 is > 5.49, reject H_0.
7. Refer to the following table.

ANOVA: Data summary table.

Source	df	SS	MS	F
Between corridor	$I-1 = 2$	$\dfrac{846662}{10} - \dfrac{(1582)^2}{30} = 1242.1$	$\dfrac{1242.1}{2} = 621.05$	$\dfrac{621.05}{77.92} = 7.97^*$
Error	$I(J-1) = 27$	$86770 - 84666.2 = 2103.8$	$\dfrac{2103.8}{27} = 77.92$	
Totals	29	3345.9		

$^*p < .01$

8. Since $7.97 > 5.49$, reject H_0. The activity level in the three different corridors is significantly different.

doors were open or closed was also counted. About twice as many doors were open in the short-hallway floors as in the long-hallway floor.

Besides these observational results, another phase of the study involved behavior measured in the laboratory. Women were randomly recruited from the three floors to participate in an experiment ostensibly on impression formation. When each subject arrived at the laboratory, she was asked to wait for a few minutes in a room that contained a confederate. Observations were made of how many seats away from the confederate she sat and how many seconds she spent looking at her. After five minutes the

TABLE 7–8 Mean responses to the confederate in the laboratory.

Dormitory design	Seats away from confederate	Facial regard for confederate (in seconds)	Discomfort after waiting
Long corridor	2.6_a	18.2_a	4.3_a
Long corridor, with intervention	1.9_b	50.3_b	2.8_b
Short corridor	2.0_b	52.0_b	2.7_b

Note. Discomfort was assessed on a 7-point scale where higher values represented greater discomfort. Numbers with different subscripts are significantly different from one another ($p < .05$).
Note. From "Reducing the stress of high-density living: An architectural intervention" by A. Baum and G. E. Davis, *Journal of Personality and Social Psychology*, 1980, *38*, 471–481. Copyright 1980 by the American Psychological Association. Reprinted by permission.

experimenter returned and administered a questionnaire that asked the subject, among other things, how comfortable she felt at the moment. Then subjects took part in a dummy task and were debriefed. Table 7–8 shows that residents of the long hallway floor sat farther from the confederate, spent less time looking at her, and felt more discomfort after having waited five minutes for the experimenter. These results are impressive because the only manipulation was a change in the dormitory hallway length.

Note on dot notation.

In general, $X. = \sum_i^n X_i = X_1 + X_2 + \cdots + X_n$

Dot notation is a useful, shorthand way to keep track of the sums and sums of squares in an analysis of variance. For example, suppose we have the following scores for two groups that experienced three different treatment levels:

I groups	J treatment levels 1	2	3	
Group 1	$X_{11} = 22$	$X_{12} = 50$	$X_{13} = 55$	$X_{1.} = 127$
Group 2	$X_{21} = 20$	$X_{22} = 51$	$X_{23} = 60$	$X_{2.} = 131$
	$X_{.1} = 42$	$X_{.2} = 101$	$X_{.3} = 115$	$X_{..} = 258$

In this example:

X_{ij} = the score in the cell in the *i*th row and *j*th column

$X_{1.} = X_{11} + X_{12} + X_{13} = 20 + 50 + 55 = 127$

$X_{2.} = X_{21} + X_{22} + X_{23} = 20 + 51 + 60 = 131$

$\sum_i X_{i.} = X_{1.} + X_{2.} = 127 + 131 = 258$

$\sum_i X_{i.}^2 = X_{1.}^2 + X_{2.}^2 = (127)^2 + (131)^2 = 33290$

$X_{..} = \sum_j \sum_i X_{ij} = 22 + 20 + 50 + 51 + 55 + 60 = 258$

Factorial Designs

Up to now we have primarily discussed experiments in which the researcher was interested in determining the effect of one independent variable. Often, however, you will want to study the joint effect of two or more variables. As long as you are designing an experiment, building in another independent variable and making the experiment do double duty may not require much additional effort, particularly if building the apparatus or obtaining the subjects is tedious to begin with. Another reason for adding a variable is that you may have more than one rival hypothesis, as in the fuzzy, colorful, noisy toy example.

A third and more important reason to study two or more variables in a single experiment is that the effect of one variable may depend on the value of another. For example, increasing a subject's motivation may improve performance on an easy task such as crossing out every *e* on a sheet of paper, but it may have the opposite effect on more difficult tasks like solving math problems. In such a situation we say that there is an *interaction* between the two independent variables in their effect on behavior. We discussed many examples of interaction in Chapter 3. When an interaction occurs between two independent variables, you must vary both in the same experiment in order to understand the effects of even one. You do this by using a factorial design.

Factorial design research design that involves all combinations of at least two values of two or more independent variables; can be tested within or between subjects or in a mixed design using both within- and between-subjects variables

A **factorial design** is one in which two or more variables, or factors, are employed in such a way that all of the possible combinations of selected values of each variable are used. In the simplest case we have two variables, each of which has two values, or levels. This is known as a two-by-two (2 × 2) factorial design because of the two levels of each variable. The 2 × 2 design gives rise to four combinations, as shown in the front surface of Figure 7–2. (Table 7–9 also represents a 2 × 2 factorial design.) If there were two levels of one variable and three of another, we would have a 2 × 3 factorial experiment.

In our discussion of the fuzzy, colorful, noisy toy we used three conditions, which was the minimum number necessary to find out which attribute was responsible for the child's attraction to the toy. Because there were two levels of three variables, we could have performed a 2 × 2 × 2 factorial experiment using all eight possible combinations instead

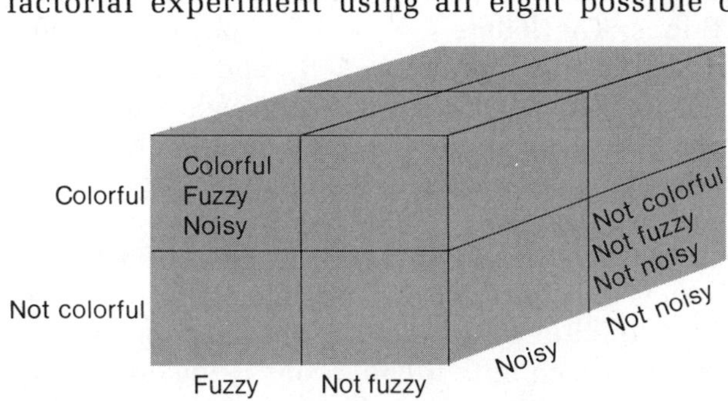

FIGURE 7–2. A 2 × 2 × 2 factorial design using all possible combinations in the fuzzy, noisy toy example.

TABLE 7–9 A factorial design.

		Factor *A*	
		A_1	A_2
Factor *B*	B_1	A_1B_1	A_2B_1
	B_2	A_1B_2	A_2B_2

of only three. Such an experiment would have permitted us to determine if some combination of variables was responsible for the child's attraction to the toy, instead of one acting alone. For example, the child might have liked the toy because it was colorful and fuzzy but would have been indifferent to a toy that was only colorful or fuzzy.

Of course, you can have as many factors and levels as you desire, but the increasing complexity begins to require much more time to conduct the experiment. In addition, the large number of interactions to be considered taxes the mind, defeating the purpose of doing the experiment in the first place. Most experiments use two or three factors, with two to six levels on the various factors.

Factorial experiments may be conducted either within subjects or between subjects, although between-subjects factorial designs may be more common. In fact, sex of subject, a between-subjects variable, is one of the most common variables in factorial designs. We will give examples of both within-subjects and between-subjects experiments as well as a *mixed design*. A mixed factorial is one that has at least one within-subjects variable and at least one between-subjects variable.

We will illustrate the three types of factorial designs in the following several tables. Table 7–9 illustrates a factorial experiment, in which factors *A* and *B* are the two independent variables. Each independent variable has two values, or levels (for example, A_1 and A_2). The two levels of the two variables give us four possible combinations of the independent variables (A_1B_1, A_1B_2, A_2B_1, A_2B_2). Thus we have a 2 × 2 factorial design. If Table 7–9 is taken to represent a within-subjects experiment, then each subject experiences each condition. Table 7–10 shows the same information, indicating that the same group of subjects, eight in this case, experiences all conditions. The letters J, K, L, M stand for the four conditions, with J standing for the combination A_1B_1, and so forth.

Table 7–11 shows one way that eight subjects could experience the four conditions in counterbalanced order. Subjects S_1 through S_4 together constitute a balanced Latin square because each condition occurs once in each ordinal position and follows every other condition once (see Chapter 5). Subjects S_5 through S_8 constitute another balanced Latin square. This example is only one way of showing how eight subjects could experience the four conditions. In this case the experimenter winds up with eight responses to each of four conditions using eight subjects.

TABLE 7–10 A factorial within-subjects design.

	A_1		A_2	
B_1	S_1, S_2, . . . , S_8	(J)	S_1, S_2, . . . , S_8	(K)
B_2	S_1, S_2, . . . , S_8	(L)	S_1, S_2, . . . , S_8	(M)

A between-subjects factorial design is illustrated in Table 7–12. This example is also a 2 × 2 design. Separate groups of eight experience each condition, thus requiring 32 subjects in order to get eight responses to each of four conditions. Table 7–13 shows another way of representing the information from Table 7–12.

A mixed factorial design is illustrated in Table 7–14. Variable *A* is the within-subjects variable and Variable *B* is the between-subjects variable. Subjects experience either B_1 first, together with A_1 and then with A_2; or they experience B_2 first, together with A_1 and then with A_2. Suppose that the *A* variable is two types of music and the *B* variable is sex. The dependent variable is degree of liking. Individual subjects would indicate their

TABLE 7–11 Possible sequence of conditions experienced by eight subjects in the factorial experiment illustrated in Table 7–10.

Subjects	1	2	3	4
S_1	J	K	L	M
S_2	K	M	J	L
S_3	L	J	M	K
S_4	M	L	K	J
S_5	K	J	L	M
S_6	M	L	J	K
S_7	J	M	K	L
S_8	L	K	M	J

TABLE 7–12 A factorial between-subjects design.

	A_1	A_2
B_1	S_1 S_2 . . . S_8	S_{17} S_{18} . . . S_{24}
B_2	S_9 S_{10} . . . S_{16}	S_{25} S_{26} . . . S_{32}

TABLE 7–13 Another representation of the between-subjects factorial design in Table 7–12.

Subjects	Group
S_{1-8}	A_1B_1
S_{9-16}	A_1B_2
S_{17-24}	A_2B_1
S_{25-32}	A_2B_2

TABLE 7–14 A mixed factorial design.

	A_1	A_2
	(within-subjects variable)	
B_1	S_1 S_2 . . . S_8	S_1 S_2 . . . S_8
(between-subjects variable) B_2	S_9 S_{10} . . . S_{16}	S_9 S_{10} . . . S_{16}

degree of liking for the two types of music, A_1 and A_2. Individual subjects, however, could only experience two conditions: Males (B_1) could rate their preference for music A_1 (Condition A_1B_1), and they could rate their liking for music A_2 (Condition A_2B_1). Females would respond likewise. An individual subject could not provide data in all four conditions.

The way the 16 subjects would experience the conditions is illustrated in Table 7–15. This particular example is actually a quasi experiment because sex is one of the factors. It was chosen, however, to show a situation in which you would have to use a mixed design because doing otherwise would be physically impossible. Mixed designs are also used when using the same subjects in all conditions is possible but not desirable. Suppose the *A* factor is two different sets of experimental instructions. The *B* factor might be the answer to two questions asked during the experimental session. The *A* factor would be studied better between subjects, but the *B* factor easily could be studied within subjects.

Comparing Tables 7–10, 7–12, and 7–14 shows one of the relative advantages of the within, between, and mixed designs. The within-subjects design requires only eight subjects in order to obtain eight responses in each of the four conditions. The mixed design requires 16 subjects to obtain the same number of responses. The between-subjects design is the least efficient, requiring 32 subjects. When presenting each condition to every subject is possible, the within-subjects design should be considered, as long as order and sequence effects are not expected. This choice is especially applicable if recruiting enough subjects is a problem.

Factorial, within Subjects. An experiment by Joseph Stevens and Lee Rubin (1970) provides an elegant example of a within-subjects factorial design. Stevens and Rubin studied the size-weight illusion, a well-known effect in which large objects feel lighter than small objects when both have the same weight. You may have noticed that a large empty suitcase feels lighter than a full handbag even though both weigh the same. Table 7–16 provides a schematic of the essential features of the experiment. Subjects were asked to lift containers that varied in both volume and weight. Some

TABLE 7–15 Another representation of the mixed design in Table 7–14.

Group	*Subjects*	*Order*
B_1	S_{1-4}	A_1B_1, then A_2B_1
	S_{5-8}	A_2B_1, then A_1B_1
B_2	S_{9-12}	A_1B_2, then A_2B_2
	S_{13-16}	A_2B_2, then A_1B_2

TABLE 7–16 Simplified design of the Stevens and Rubin experiment.

Heavy	0	X	X
Medium	X	X	X
Light	X	X	0
	Small	Medium	Large

combinations of volume and weight were not tested inasmuch as it was not possible to make very small containers heavy enough or very large ones light enough to complete the factorial.

Figure 7–3 shows idealized data from the experiment. Apparent heaviness is plotted against volume, with physical weight as a parameter. You can see that containers having the same weight seem lighter the larger they are, thus showing the illusion. Because the curves are not parallel, you conclude that there is an interaction between volume and heaviness in the size-weight illusion. The nature of the interaction is clearer when apparent heaviness is replotted, this time as a function of weight, with volume as a parameter (Figure 7–4). The size-weight illusion is greater with large lighter containers and is less with small heavy ones. In fact, the effect disappears

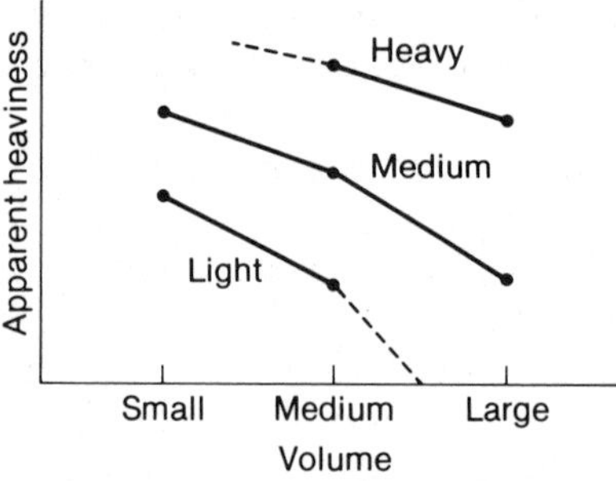

FIGURE 7–3. Idealized data from the Stevens and Rubin experiment illustrating the size-weight illusion.

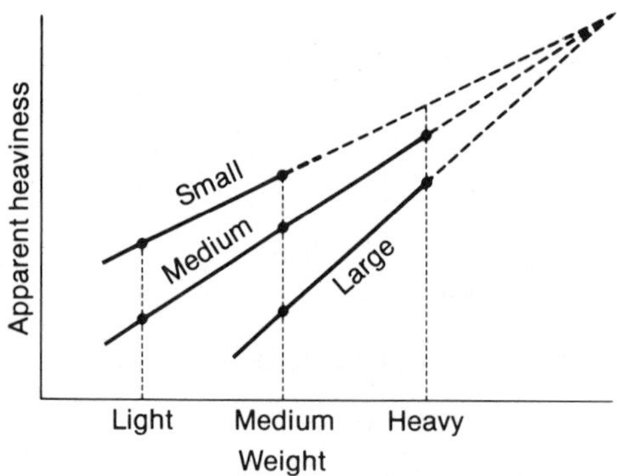

FIGURE 7–4. Data shown in Figure 7–3 replotted.

at the point where the lines come together, which happens to be about the heaviest weight that can be lifted. In other words, the heaviest weight that you can lift feels the same apparent weight no matter how large or small a container it is in.

Factorial, between Subjects. An interesting example of a between-subjects factorial experiment is given by Richard Barnes, William Ickes, and Robert Kidd (1979). They studied the conditions under which students would give help in the form of lending class notes to a fellow student. They varied the *intentionality* of the need to borrow notes by having subjects say that they either lacked ability (unintentional) or had not put out the effort (intentional) to take good notes. They varied the *stability* of the need by having subjects say that they always (stable) took poor notes or sometimes (unstable) took poor notes. Thus they had a 2 × 2 design, with intentionality and stability of need varied between subjects. (In addition, sex of the subject and sex of the person making the request were included in the design for the purpose of counterbalancing these extraneous variables. These two variables did not produce any effects, so we will not consider them further.)

The design of the experiment is summarized in Table 7–17. As you might expect, more help was offered when the person making the request said that the reason for poor notes was lack of ability rather than effort. In addition the subjects were more likely to comply when the need was seen as stable rather than unstable. No interaction occurred between the two independent variables. This experiment is reproduced in Chapter 11 as an example of how to write an experimental report. You may turn there for further details.

TABLE 7–17 Design of the Barnes, Ickes, and Kidd study.

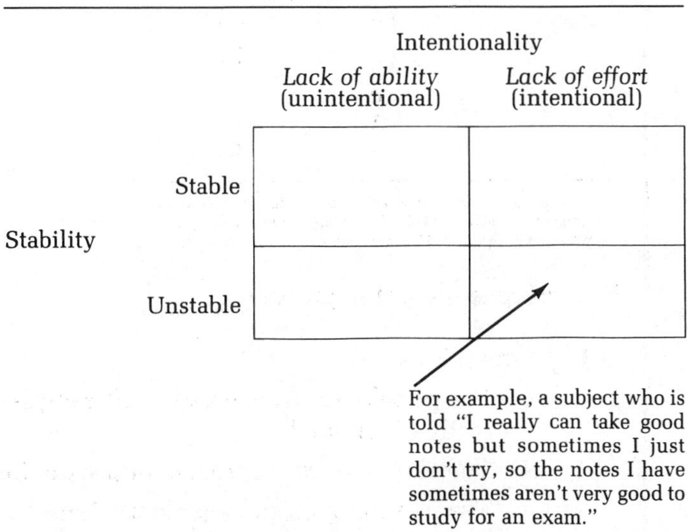

BOX 7-3 Example of a 2 × 2 Factorial Analysis of Variance, between Subjects

This example analyzes fake data that might have been obtained by Barnes, Ickes, and Kidd (1979) in their study of helping behavior by students in the form of lending class notes. The following table shows the fake data.

Hypothetical data from the Barnes, Ickes, and Kidd study.

	Intentionality	
Stability	Unintentional	Intentional
Stable	4.4	3.6
	4.0	3.2
	4.5	3.7
	3.9	3.0
	4.6	3.8
	3.8	2.9
	4.7	3.9
	3.7	2.8
	4.8	4.0
	3.6	3.1
Unstable	3.7	2.9
	3.3	2.5
	3.8	3.0
	3.2	2.4
	3.9	3.1
	3.1	2.3
	4.0	3.2
	3.0	2.2
	4.1	3.3
	2.9	2.1

Note. Hypothetical data for ANOVA, 2 × 2 factorial, between subjects. ($I = 2$ levels of stability; $J = 2$ levels of intentionality; $K = 10$ subjects per cell; $N = 40$ observations.)

Following is the 8-step procedure:

1. Assumptions
   a. The population from which each sample is drawn is normally distributed.
   b. The variances of the treatment populations are equal.
   c. The four samples and ten observations in each sample are randomly and independently drawn.

2. H_0: Our null hypothesis is that helping behavior is not affected by either the intentionality or the stability of the need.
3. $\alpha = .01$.
4. Refer to the following table.

ANOVA: Sums of squares calculation formulas.

Source	df	SS	MS	F
Between I	$I - 1$	$\frac{\sum_j X_{i..}^2}{JK} - \frac{X_{...}^2}{IJK}$ *	$\frac{SS_I}{df_I}$	$\frac{MS_I}{MS_{err}}$
Between J	$J - 1$	$\frac{\sum_j X_{.j.}^2}{IK} - \frac{X_{...}^2}{IJK}$	$\frac{SS_J}{df_J}$	$\frac{MS_J}{MS_{err}}$
$I \times J$ interaction	$(I-1)(J-1)$	$\frac{\sum_{ij} X_{ij.}^2}{K} - \frac{\sum_i X_{i..}^2}{JK} - \frac{\sum_j X_{.j.}^2}{IK} + \frac{X_{...}^2}{IJK}$	$\frac{SS_{I\times J}}{df_{I\times J}}$	$\frac{MS_{I\times J}}{MS_{err}}$
Error	$IJ(K-1)$	$\sum_{ijk} X_{ijk}^2 - \frac{\sum_{ij} X_{ij.}^2}{K}$	$\frac{SS_{err}}{df_{err}}$	
Totals	$IJK - 1 = N - 1$	$\sum_{ijk} (X_{ijk} - \bar{X})^2$		

*See note on dot notation page 152.

5. Sampling distribution, $F(1, 36)$. (F distribution with $V_1 = 1$ and $V_2 = 36$ degrees of freedom.)
6. Look in an F table under $\alpha = .01$.

   $F_{.01}(1, 36) = 7.40$. If the F calculated in step 7 is > 7.40, reject H_0.
7. Refer to the following table.

ANOVA: Data Summary Table.

Source	df	SS	MS	F
Between stability	$I - 1 = 1$	$\frac{9620}{20} - \frac{(138)^2}{40} = 481 - 476.1 = 4.9$	$\frac{4.9}{1} = 4.9$	$\frac{4.9}{.20} = 24.5$*
Between intentionality	$J - 1 = 1$	$\frac{9650}{20} - \frac{(138)^2}{40} = 482.5 - 476.1 = 6.4$	$\frac{6.4}{1} = 6.4$	$\frac{6.4}{.20} = 32.0$*
Stability × intention	$(I-1)(J-1) = 1$	$\frac{4874}{10} - 481 - 482.5 + 476.1 = 0.0$	0	n.s.
Error	$IJ(K-1) = 36$	$494.6 - 487.4 = 7.2$	$\frac{7.2}{36} = .20$	
Totals	$N - 1 = 39$	18.5		

*$p < .01$

8. Since 24.5 > 7.40 and 32.0 > 7.40, we may conclude that helping behavior is significantly affected by both intentionality and stability of need. We also may conclude that no interaction is present between the two need variables.

A Mixed Factorial Design. The next example of a factorial design has one between-subjects variable and one within-subjects variable and thus is a mixed factorial design. Gordon Bower, Stephen Gilligan, and Kenneth Monteiro (1981; Bower, 1981) studied the effect of mood on learning. They hypothesized that subjects would notice events in stories that matched their moods and would remember such events better than events that did not match their moods. By posthypnotic suggestion they made their subjects either happy or sad and then had them read a story about two men, Andre and Jack. Everything connected with Andre in the story is happy, but everything to do with Jack is sad. After the subjects finished reading the story, the experimenters asked them which character they identified with. Subjects identified with the character whose mood matched their own. The

BOX 7–4 Example of a 2 × 2 Mixed Factorial Analysis of Variance (ANOVA)

This example analyzes fake data that might have been obtained by Bower, Gilligan, and Monteiro (1981) on the effect of mood on the recall of happy and sad facts. The following table shows the fake data.

Hypothetical data from the Bower, Gilligan, and Monteiro study.

Mood	Fact recalled: Happy	Fact recalled: Sad
	54	52
	56	51
Happy	58	50
	60	49
	62	48
	18	74
	19	77
Sad	20	80
	21	83
	22	86

Note. Hypothetical data for 2 × 2 factorial, mixed. (I = 2 mood levels; J = 2 fact types; K = 5 subjects per cell; N = 20 observations.)

Following is the 8-step procedure:*

1. Assumption

   The two samples of five subjects are randomly assigned to an induced-mood group (happy or sad).

2. Hypotheses

   a. H_0: Our null hypothesis is that mood has no effect on type of fact recalled.

   b. H_1: The alternative is that mood does affect type of fact recalled.

3. $\alpha = .01$.

4. Refer to the following table.

*For a more complete discussion of this analysis, see Kirk (1968, p. 266).

ANOVA: Sums of squares computation formulas.

Source	df	SS	MS	F
1. Between subjects				
2. Between moods at fact 1 (happy)	$I - 1$	$\frac{\sum_i X_{i1.}^2}{K} - \frac{X_{.1.}^2}{IK}$ *	$\frac{SS_2}{I-1}$	$\frac{MS_2}{MS_4}$
3. Between moods at fact 2 (sad)	$I - 1$	$\frac{\sum_i X_{i2.}^2}{K} - \frac{X_{.2.}^2}{IK}$	$\frac{SS_3}{I-1}$	$\frac{MS_3}{MS_4}$
4. Within cell	$IJ\,(K - 1)$	$\sum_{ijk} X_{ijk}^2 - \frac{\sum_{ij} X_{ij.}^2}{K}$	$\frac{SS_4}{IJ\,(K-1)}$	
5. Within subject				
6. Between facts at mood 1 (happy)	$J - 1$	$\frac{\sum_j X_{1j.}^2}{K} - \frac{X_{1..}^2}{JK}$	$\frac{SS_6}{J-1}$	$\frac{MS_6}{MS_9}$
7. Between facts at mood 2 (sad)	$J - 1$	$\frac{\sum_j X_{2j.}^2}{K} - \frac{X_{2..}^2}{JK}$	$\frac{SS_7}{J-1}$	$\frac{MS_7}{MS_9}$
8. Facts × mood	$(I - 1)\,(J - 1)$	$\frac{\sum_{ij} X_{ij.}^2}{K} - \frac{\sum_i X_{i..}^2}{JK} - \frac{\sum_j X_{.j.}^2}{IK} + \frac{X_{...}^2}{IJK}$	$\frac{SS_8}{(I-1)(K-1)}$	$\frac{MS_8}{MS_9}$
9. Fact × subject within mood	$I(J-1)(K-1)$	$\sum_{ijk} X_{ijk}^2 - \frac{\sum_{ij} X_{ij.}^2}{K} - \frac{\sum_{ik} X_{i.k}^2}{J} + \frac{\sum_i X_{i..}^2}{JK}$	$\frac{SS_9}{I(J-1)(K-1)}$	

*See note on dot notation, page 152.

5. Sampling distribution: $F\,(1, 16)$ for between subjects and $F\,(1, 8)$ for within subjects.

6. Look at an F table under $\alpha = .01$.

   $F_{.01} = 11.26$. If the F calculated in step 7 (under within subject) is > 11.26, reject H_0.

7. Refer to the following table.

ANOVA: Data Summary Table

Source	*df*	*SS*	*MS*	*F*
1. Between subjects				
2. Between moods at fact 1	1	$\frac{94100}{5} - \frac{(390)^2}{10} = 18820 - 15210 = 3610$	3610	385.1*
3. Between moods at fact 2	1	$\frac{222500}{5} - \frac{(650)^2}{10} = 44500 - 42250 = 2250$	2250	240*
4. Within cell	16	$63470 - 63320 = 150$	9.375	
5. Within subjects				
6. Between facts at mood 1	1	$\frac{146600}{5} - \frac{(540)^2}{10} = 29320 - 29160 = 160$	160	19.69*
7. Between facts at mood 2	1	$\frac{170000}{5} - \frac{(500)^2}{10} = 34000 - 25000 = 9000$	9000	1107.69*
8. Fact × mood	1	$63320 - 54160 - 57460 + 54080 = 5780$	5780	711.38*
9. Fact × subject within mood	8	$63470 - 63320 - 54245 + 54160 = 65$	8.125	

*$p < .01$

8. Type of fact recalled *is* significantly affected by mood.

next day when they were in a neutral mood, the subjects were asked to remember as much of the story as they could. The experimenters found that subjects remembered more facts connected with the character whose mood matched their own at the time they read the story. Refer to Figure 7–5. The subjects' mood when reading the story was the between-subjects variable. Whether the facts were happy or sad was the within-subjects variable.

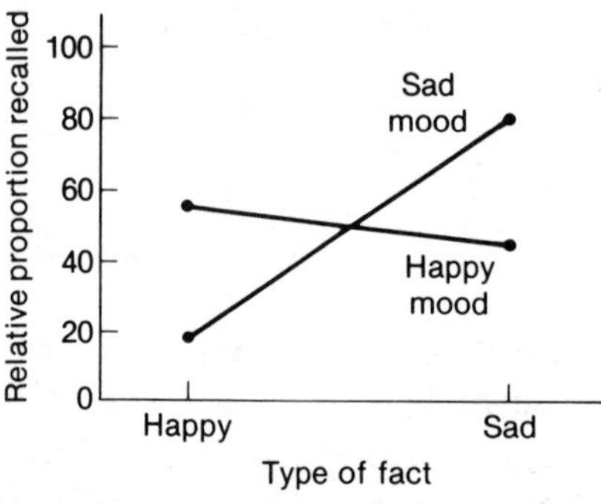

FIGURE 7–5. Relative percentages of recall of facts about the happy character versus the sad character.

Note. From "Mood and memory" by G. Bower, *American Psychologist,* 1981, *36,* 129–148. Copyright 1981 by the American Psychological Association. Reprinted by permission of the publisher and author.

SUMMARY

1. In a true experiment the experimenter has complete control over the experiment. A quasi experiment is one in which the experimenter lacks some degree of control. The most important difference is that in a true experiment the subjects are assigned to conditions, whereas in a quasi experiment the subjects are selected for conditions from previously existing groups.
2. The two basic elements of good experimental design are: the existence of a control group or a control condition and the random allocation of subjects to various conditions (for between-subjects experiments).
3. Some designs to avoid are the one-group posttest only design, the posttest only design with nonequivalent control groups, and the one-group pretest-posttest design.
4. The simplest possible true experiment has two conditions tested within subjects. All subjects experience both conditions in counterbalanced order.
5. Another simple design is the two-conditions experiment tested between subjects. This design is used when a significant interaction between conditions would occur if tested within subjects.
6. Multiple-conditions experiments are conducted when the hypothesis is not a simple yes-or-no question, when determining the shape of a function is desirable, or when multiple rival hypotheses must be ruled out.
7. Multiple-conditions, within-subjects experiments are common in perception research, as when one scales the brightness of different intensities of a light.
8. Multiple-conditions, between-subjects experiments are common in social psychology, as in the experiment on the effects of long and short hallways on social interaction in a dormitory.
9. Factorial designs are employed when one wishes to study the joint effect of two or more independent variables.
10. A factorial design may save time by studying more than one condition per experiment, or it may be used when ruling out more than one rival hypothesis, or when one is interested in possible interaction between the independent variables.
11. Factorial designs may be conducted either as within-subjects or between-subjects experiments, or they may be used in mixed experiments that have one within-subjects and one between-subjects variable.
12. The within-subjects factorial design requires the fewest subjects to achieve a particular degree of power, the mixed design the next fewest, and the between-subjects design the most.
13. The example given of a within-subjects factorial design was a study of the size-weight illusion in which size and weight of lifted containers were the independent variables.
14. The example given of a between-subjects factorial design was a study of

helping behavior by students in which the independent variables were the intentionality and the stability of the need to borrow notes for a class.

15. The example given of a mixed factorial design was a study of mood and memory in which the between-subjects variable was the mood of subjects when they read a story and the within-subjects variable was the happiness or sadness of facts in the story.

SUGGESTIONS FOR FURTHER READING

For advice on true experiments the best place to go is journals or books on particular research areas. Analyze the methods of actual experiments to see how problems of validity were controlled for in experimental situations.

READING BETWEEN THE LINES

The following problems are presented for you to solve. See Reading Between the Lines in Chapter 1 for an introduction to them. The answers are given in Appendix A.

15. SUBLIMINAL SEDUCTION

In his popular book *Subliminal Seduction* (1973) Wilson Bryan Key describes many ways in which the advertising industry attempts, by subliminal advertising, to motivate people to purchase products. One example concerns an ad in *Playboy* for subscriptions to that magazine. The two-page spread shows a naked woman kneeling and holding a large Christmas wreath. Key says that of the approximately 100 men who had read the entire magazine, over 95 percent remembered seeing the ad. He states further that "over 70 percent specifically remembered the wreath, but could provide only vague ideas about the blonde's description. Over 40 percent of those who recalled the ad were not even certain that she was a blonde" (p. 40). Key's explanation for why the men remembered the wreath better than they remembered the woman is that the wreath was made of nuts, which on close inspection of an enlargement are seen to be drawn so as to resemble male and female genital parts. What alternative explanations can you think of for the reason that the men would remember the wreath better than they remembered the woman?

16. THIRST IN BRAIN-DAMAGED RATS

Normal rats will respond to an intraperitoneal (into the body cavity) injection of salt solution with a marked increase in water drinking in order to restore their normal salt balance. Blass and Epstein (1971), however, reported that rats with lesions of a part of the brain known as the lateral preoptic area did not drink in response to this stimulus. The result was not surprising in light of considerable other evidence that this brain area is involved in regulation of drinking in response to salt levels.

Christopher Coburn and Edward Stricker (1978), on the other hand, suspected that another interpretation of the data might be possible. They knew that these brain-damaged rats also respond abnormally to other ways of making rats drink that should not have anything to do with the supposed function of the lateral preoptic area. First, they repeated the experiment of Blass and Epstein and found the same results. Then they showed that the brain-damaged rats responded normally to several other ways of changing salt balance. What might be some plausible explanations for the difference between the brain-damaged rats and the normal rats in their response to the intraperitoneal injections and the other ways of inducing thirst?

17. MEMORY FOR WORDS

The study of how words are remembered and later recalled is an active research area. One way this question is studied is by using the sentence verification procedure, in which subjects are asked whether statements such as "All robins are birds" are true or false. Variations in the speed of their responses between different pairs of concepts are taken to indicate how the words are related in memory. One theory says that the speed of response depends on how similar the concepts are to each other. Similarity is defined by how many characteristics the two concepts have in common. For example, a robin is a typical bird and so would share many characteristics with the concept *bird:* has feathers, sings, perches in trees, and eats berries. On the other hand, a penguin has fewer of these characteristics, even though it is a bird. Michael McCloskey and Sam Glucksberg (1979) tested this theory, using the sentence verification procedure. Their sentences were of the type "All As are Bs." In some of the sentences the words shared many characteristics: "All robins are birds" or "All oaks are trees." In other sentences the concepts shared fewer characteristics: "All penguins are birds" or "All mahoganies are trees." They found that subjects responded more quickly to the sentences containing the highly related concepts, supporting their theory. Can you think of anything else about the words that could explain the differences in reaction times?

8

QUASI EXPERIMENTS

As you recall from Chapter 7, a true experiment is one in which the experimenter has complete control over the who, what, when, where, and how of the experiment. A quasi experiment, on the other hand, does not permit the experimenter to control the assignment of subjects to conditions. The example we gave of a quasi-experimental variable in Chapter 7 was sex of subject, over which the experimenter has no control. Thus when an experimenter uses sex as a variable in an experiment, the possibility exists that sex may be confounded with many other variables, such as differential learning experiences, parental expectations, and other cultural influences. This chapter deals with strategies that are useful in achieving control over the threats to validity found in quasi experiments.

In addition to not being able to control the who of an experiment, the experimenter in some instances cannot completely control the what, when, where, and how. Often data must be collected at a particular time or not at all. For example, an experimenter who wishes to study the effects of changing work schedules on productivity must do so when the management of the plant decides to make the changes. The problem with such an experiment is that productivity already may have been changing because of some outside variable. Similarly, the experimenter may wish to do parts of the experiment in certain ways but cannot because of practical limitations. Any of these considerations may lead us to regard a piece of research as a quasi experiment. The boundaries between true and quasi experiments are not always distinct. If the experimenter has good control over all aspects of the experiment, we can call it a true experiment. If enough compromise of experimental control takes place, the research is considered a quasi experiment.* When the experimenter has no control over the presentation of the independent variables but can only record what happens in a certain situation, we call the research nonexperimental.

The presence of uncontrolled or confounded variables reduces the validity of a quasi experiment but does not necessarily render it invalid. The experimenter must evaluate the likelihood that the confounding variables are responsible for the outcome. This appraisal involves the use of the experimenter's judgment, as does the evaluation of all research. The true experiment is generally preferable to the quasi experiment, but many situations exist in which randomly assigning subjects to conditions is not possible. Then a quasi experiment is performed simply because doing it is better than doing no experiment at all. For example, does the advantage of using two preexisting classes to study the effects of different teaching methods outweigh the difficulty of randomly constituting two new classes? The experimenter must weigh the costs and benefits of each choice made in designing a piece of research.

NONEQUIVALENT CONTROL GROUP DESIGNS

Nonequivalent control group design research design having both an experimental and a control group wherein subjects are not randomly assigned to groups

If both an experimental and a control group are part of an experiment but subjects have not been allocated randomly to the two groups, we have a **nonequivalent control group design**. Of the quasi experiments this is the most typical. The problem with this design is how to compare results between the experimental and control groups when they were not equivalent to begin with.

Recall the discussion in the previous chapter of designs to be avoided. In the example of the company that wished to evaluate the effect of a new work schedule, we said that the study would be improved by having a second plant as a control group. Any change in productivity in the experimental plant that followed the switch in work schedule could be more confidently attributed to the new work schedule if a second plant showed no change over the same time interval. This example of a *nonequivalent control group design with pretest and posttest* is a typical quasi-experimental design. It is diagrammed in Table 8–1. Because the subjects were

TABLE 8–1 Nonequivalent control group design with pretest and posttest.

	Allocation of subjects and groups	Pretest	Treatment	Posttest
Group 1	Any method that is not random	yes	yes	yes
Group 2		yes	no	yes

*We have adopted a broader definition of quasi experiment than Cook and Campbell (1976), who defined it as an experiment that does not permit random allocation of subjects to groups. Our definition includes lack of control over other aspects of the experiment, as does their discussion of particular quasi-experimental designs.

not randomly allocated to the two groups, we do not have good reason to believe that they were equivalent before the experimental manipulation was performed. Therefore we must consider the likelihood that alternative hypotheses may account for the results. For example the workers in the experimental plant may have been less experienced on the average than those in the control plant. Their increase in productivity may have been caused by the experience they gained between pretest and posttest. The control subjects, on the other hand, may already have been working at their maximum.

Quasi experiments that employ nonequivalent control groups with pretest and posttest may be interpretable or may not. Whether they can be interpreted depends on whether the pattern of results obtained can be accounted for by possible differences in the groups or by something else in the experiment. The pattern of results we would like to see from this design is shown in Figure 8–1. Here the two groups showed the same performance on the pretest. The experimental group improved on the posttest, but the control group did not change. Although the experimental and control groups were not equivalent in all respects because they were not randomly constituted, their performances can be compared and the results interpreted because their behavior was the same at the beginning.

Figure 8–2 shows one kind of uninterpretable pattern of results. These results could be those of the factory study we just discussed. In this example the experimental group improved but the control group did not. Notice that the control group was superior to the experimental group on both occasions. This difference could result from the operation of a ceiling effect. If it was not possible for the control group to perform any better, then we cannot attribute the improvement in the experimental group to the experimental manipulation.

Another pattern of results that may be uninterpretable is given in Figure 8–3. These results could represent a learning experiment in which the experimental group performed better than the control group on the pretest. Both groups showed improvement on the posttest, but the experimental group showed twice as much improvement. Can we attribute

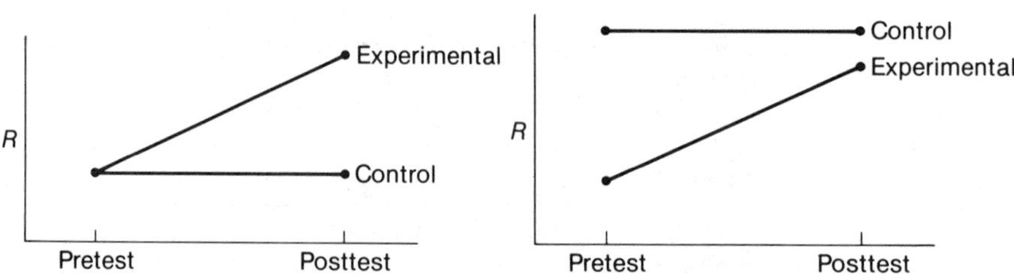

FIGURE 8–1. Desired pattern of results for a nonequivalent control group design with pretest and posttest.

FIGURE 8–2. One kind of uninterpretable pattern of results in a nonequivalent control group design with pretest and posttest.

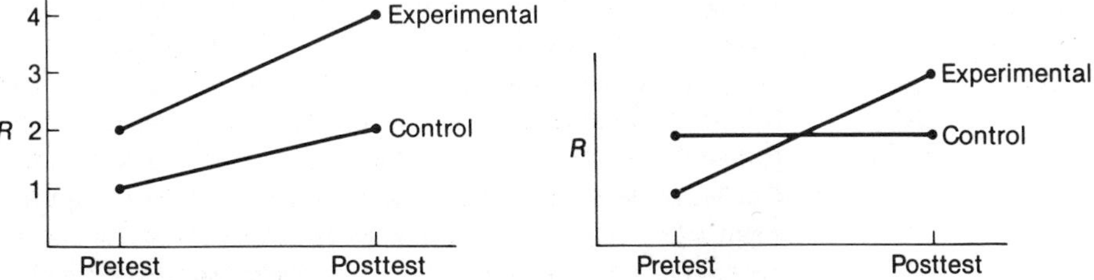

FIGURE 8–3. Another kind of uninterpretable pattern of results in a nonequivalent control group design with pretest and posttest.

FIGURE 8–4. A generally interpretable pattern of results in a nonequivalent control group design with pretest and posttest.

the difference in rate of improvement to the experimental manipulation? No, we cannot, because although the experimental group improved more, both groups showed the same *proportional* improvement. On the posttest both doubled their previous performance. Their improvement likely was caused by maturation or some other variable that had nothing to do with the experimental manipulation.

A pattern of results that usually is interpretable is given in Figure 8–4. Here the experimental group was lower than the control group on the pretest but was higher on the posttest. Determining a rival hypothesis for this pattern of results is difficult. You might suppose that the experimental subjects were as good as the control subjects to begin with and did worse on the pretest simply by chance. In that case you would expect them to do the same as the control group on the posttest if the experimental manipulation were not effective. You would have no reason, however, to expect them to do *better* than the control group on the posttest by chance alone. Therefore it is usually safe to conclude that a pattern of results such as those in Figure 8–4 shows the effectiveness of the experimental manipulation.

Two Examples of the Nonequivalent Control Group Design

The two examples of the nonequivalent control group design that we will consider next are very different. The first is rather unconventional; the second is more typical.

Delayed control group design nonequivalent control group design in which the testing of one group is deferred

The Delayed Control Group Design. A creative quasi experiment by David Marks and Richard Kammann (1980) illustrates the **delayed control group design**. These researchers were interested in studying the alleged psychic powers of Uri Geller, the Israeli magician. Among his many feats are spoon bending, mind reading, starting broken watches, and determining the contents of sealed envelopes. Because Geller, like most psychics, performs only when he is confident that he can convince anyone present, studying his methods is difficult. Marks and Kammann interviewed Geller under loose conditions and observed his routine but were unable to get him into their laboratory. They appeared to be stymied in their attempt to do a controlled study until Marks was on a radio talk show with Geller. Among the feats Geller achieved was to perceive two pictures through a sealed envelope (although he failed on a third picture).

After the show Marks retrieved the papers from the wastebasket. Marks and Kammann hypothesized that Geller had been able to perceive the pictures through the envelope by ordinary means. Later they showed the same pictures inside the envelopes to 48 students, who were asked to examine the envelopes and draw the picture without looking inside the envelope. On one of the pictures the students did a little worse than Geller and on another they did a little better, as rated by independent judges. Most revealing, perhaps, was the picture on which Geller failed. Not only did the students also fail, but their attempts looked strikingly like Geller's attempts.

From this experiment Marks and Kammann concluded that Geller uses ordinary sensory means to perceive pictures inside envelopes. Other conclusions are possible, of course. The students could also have extrasensory perception, but this conclusion is highly strained. At the least the results show that ordinary people can do essentially as well with the same materials and the same conditions as a person who claims to be a psychic. For the purposes of experimental design, the students constitute a nonequivalent control group for Geller. The fact that they did about equally well, when Geller would be expected to do much better according to the psychic hypothesis, makes it unlikely that he has any powers that the students do not also have.

Null hypothesis statement saying that there is no real difference between the groups tested; treatment had no effect

Interestingly, the conclusion that he did not differ from the students constitutes an example of accepting the **null hypothesis**, or accepting the conclusion that the two groups are no different. Ordinarily scientists avoid drawing a conclusion on the basis of accepting the null hypothesis, because proving the *non*existence of some effect is theoretically impossible. Any given experiment may not be sensitive enough to detect a real difference. Marks and Kammann were trying to prove that Geller was *not* psychic, which is equivalent to proving that there is no Santa Claus. However, one could conclude on the basis of their experiment that Uri Geller's abilities could not be distinguished from those of a naive student, or from a fraud.

Because Marks and Kammann were interested only in testing whether Geller had psychic powers, they did no experimental manipulation and therefore no before-after comparison. Thus the experiment could be considered a simple after-only design.

A Mixed Factorial Design. The next example of a nonequivalent control group design is from an experiment on anxiety. Norman Endler (1977) wanted to test an interaction theory of anxiety. He believed that the state of anxiety was the result of a trait for anxiety that interacted with anxiety-provoking situations. Persons who were high on the anxiety trait would not be in the anxious state all the time but would respond more to certain situations than would other people. He tested this theory by administering a test of the anxiety trait to students. Those who scored high and those who

TABLE 8–2 Design of the Endler study.

		State-anxiety Low	State-anxiety High
Trait anxiety	High anxiety	S_1	S_1
		S_2	S_2
		.	.
		.	.
		.	.
		S_{19}	S_{19}
	Low anxiety	S_{20}	S_{20}
		S_{21}	S_{21}
		.	.
		.	.
		.	.
		S_{37}	S_{37}

scored low were placed in two groups. Then they were tested for their measured anxiety, or state, in a threatening situation: a major psychology exam. The measure of anxiety state was pulse rate. Two weeks later Endler tested the same subjects in a nonthreatening situation.

The design of this experiment is a mixed factorial because it has one between-subjects variable and one within-subjects variable. The between-subjects variable is trait anxiety, because subjects were either high or low on trait anxiety. The within-subjects variable is situational anxiety, because subjects could experience both conditions at different times. The design is illustrated in Table 8–2. Endler found that students who were high or low on the anxiety trait as measured by the questionnaire did not differ in measured anxiety state in the nonthreatening situation. They did differ considerably, however, just before the test. The data are shown in Figure 8–5.

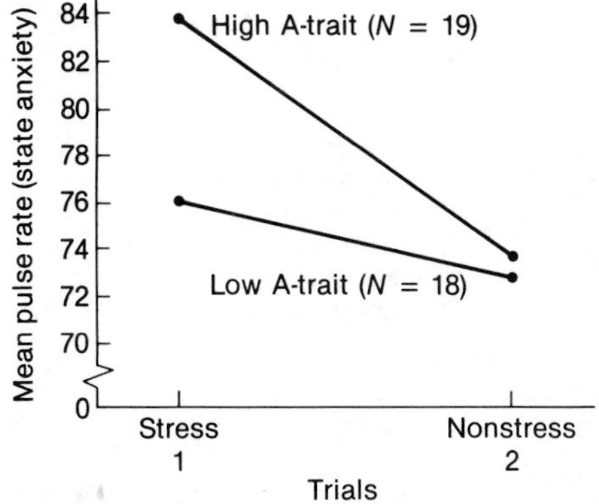

FIGURE 8–5. State anxiety (pulse rate) for subjects high or low in trait anxiety in the high- or low-stress situation.

Note. From "The role of person-by-situation interactions in personality theory" by N. S. Endler. In *The structuring of experience,* ed. I. C. Uzgiris & F. Weizmann (New York: Plenum, 1977). Copyright 1977 by Plenum. Reprinted by permission of the publisher and authors.

REGRESSION DISCONTINUITY DESIGNS

Regression discontinuity design quasi-experimental design that uses a score on a pretest as a criterion for administering a manipulation whose effect is shown in the discontinuity in the regression line relating the pretest and posttest

Researchers may want to evaluate the effect of an experimental manipulation on two groups that are known to differ to begin with. Some experimenters have attempted to evaluate such situations by taking into consideration that there is a correlation between the scores on the two variables over all subjects. Suppose that a manipulation is introduced following a pretest on one variable. Suppose also that some value on the variable is used as a criterion for the presentation of the manipulation. Then the posttest is administered. We can plot the correlation between the pretest and the posttest for all subjects as in Figure 8–6. Note, however, that some value on the pretest was used as a criterion by which to place subjects into the experimental and control groups. So we know in advance that the experimental and the control groups are not equivalent. However, we have plotted a single regression line relating the pretest scores to the posttest scores. If the experimental manipulation had no effect, then a single line would satisfactorily describe the data. If the manipulation did have some effect over and above the correlation between the pretest and the posttest, the effect would be seen as a discontinuity in the data at the value of the pretest that was used as the criterion. Then we would need two separate regression lines to adequately describe the data. Such an experiment is an example of a **regression discontinuity design.** See Figure 8–6.

For example, suppose the dean of a college wants to know if recognizing students who have achieved high grades in one term will cause them to

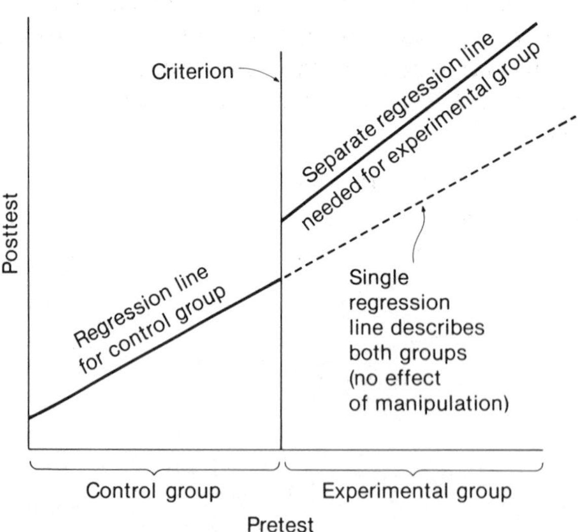

FIGURE 8–6. Regression discontinuity design when there is a difference between the experimental and control groups (solid line to the right of the vertical line) and when there is no difference (dashed line).

do better the next term.* How would the dean evaluate the effect of seeing one's name on the dean's list when the two groups of students are by definition not equivalent to begin with? Let us begin by considering that a correlation in the grades between one term and the next is present for all students, not just the dean's-list students. We might look at the scatterplot of grades for all students on two successive terms to see if there is a break in the trend of scores at the dean's-list cutoff. Such a scatterplot is shown in Figure 8–7. The vertical line is the cutoff for the dean's list. The longer line below the cutoff is the best-fitting line for students who did *not* achieve the dean's list in term one. The shorter line to the right is the best-fitting line for students who *did* appear on the dean's list in term one. The two lines are discontinuous; that is, the line for the dean's-list students falls above the other line at the cutoff and has a steeper slope. This occurrence is called a regression discontinuity because the two best-fitting lines, also known as regression lines, are discontinuous.

Although you may agree with the dean's conclusion that publishing the list of outstanding students had a beneficial effect on those students' next-term grades, such a conclusion has problems. Take a closer look at the actual data points in the figure. Notice that they seem to be curving upwards throughout the whole range of scores. Perhaps, instead of breaking at the vertical line, the last three points simply reflect a trend that occurs throughout the range. A safer conclusion may be that these data do not show a regression discontinuity but that they fit a single curved line that goes through the entire range of scores. Regression discontinuity designs can thus be tricky to interpret. Unless the data points cluster tightly so as to

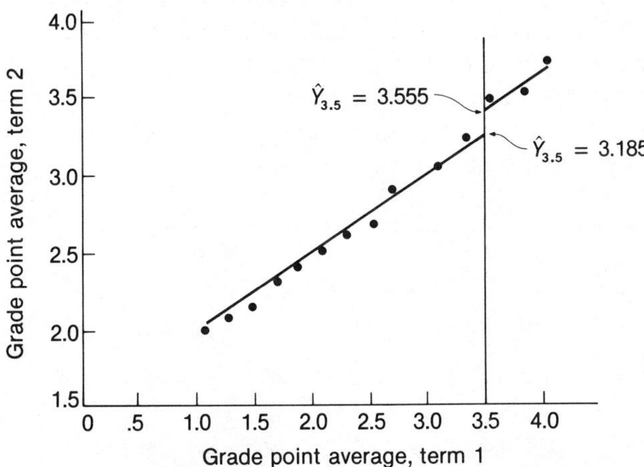

FIGURE 8–7. Relationship of grade point average in term two to grade point average in term one for students who did or did not achieve the dean's list in term one.

Note. From *Quasi-experiments: nonequivalent control group designs* by T. D. Cook & D. T. Campbell (Boston: Houghton Mifflin, 1979). Copyright 1979 by Houghton Mifflin. Reprinted by permission of the publisher and authors.

*This discussion is based on an example in Cook and Campbell (1979).

form an obvious line, deciding exactly where the line should be drawn or what shape it should have may be difficult.

DESIGNS WITHOUT CONTROL GROUPS

Sometimes no control group can be obtained that can be considered comparable enough to be useful. Then a design that allows the same group to be compared over time can be used. We will discuss two such designs: the interrupted time-series design and the repeated treatments design.

Interrupted Time-Series Designs

In Chapter 7, when we discussed designs to be avoided, we said that measurement of a single group before and after the manipulation is not good design. One way to improve on the one-group before-after design is to consider the *trend* of the data before and after the manipulation, rather than the average data as a whole. For example the manager of the plant that is changing its work schedule might keep a weekly record of output for the years preceding and following the change. Management could then look not only for average differences between the two periods but for trends that might appear. Seasonal changes or other cyclical changes in output may be important, as well as any overall trend toward higher or lower productivity that occurred around the time of the change.

The ideal situation would be a flat and stable baseline before the change, followed by either an abrupt change to a new level or a gradual change to a new level. See Figure 8–8 for typical patterns. Evaluation of such time series is a difficult procedure that requires different statistical tools than those generally used for analyzing group data. Interrupted time-series experiments are similar in design and interpretation to many single-subject designs and to the nonexperimental methods, topics we will discuss in Chapters 9 and 10.

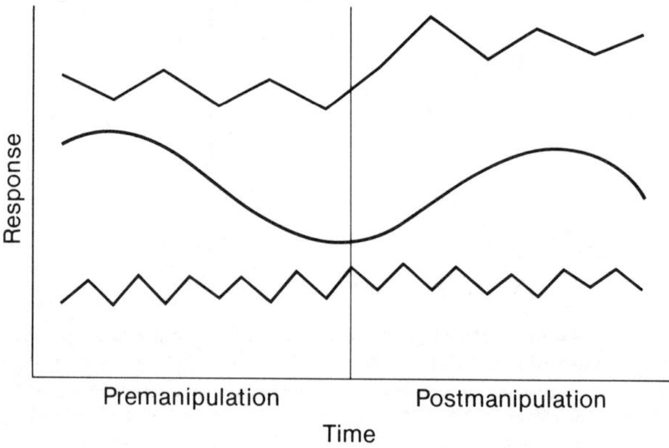

FIGURE 8–8. Typical patterns of results from time-series designs.

Interrupted time-series design research design that allows the same group to be compared over time by considering the trend of the data before and after experimental manipulation

We will talk about two examples of **interrupted time-series designs** in this chapter. Because the authors of both studies examined existing records to obtain their data rather than manipulating some independent variable, the studies technically are examples of nonexperimental research rather than quasi-experimental study. Nevertheless they present good examples of the advantages and disadvantages of interrupted time-series research. In addition similar nonexperimental studies are commonly described under the heading of quasi experiments in books on design (for example, Cook and Campbell, 1979).

The debate over the effects of pornography on sex crimes gives an example of some of the difficulties in interrupted time-series research. In the mid-1960s a relaxation of legal restrictions in Denmark resulted in the increase in availability of pornography. Researchers reported that this increased availability of pornography was followed by a decrease in sex crimes in Copenhagen (Kutchinsky, 1973). Several questions complicated the issue, however. First, the rate of sex crimes had been decreasing since 1956, although the trend accelerated around 1965. Thus the decrease may simply have been the result of a preexisting trend that had nothing directly to do with the increase in pornography. Second, attitudes toward sex crimes may have changed during the period, with fewer people bothering to report such crimes.

Kutchinsky considered this latter hypothesis and concluded tentatively that although some of the decrease could have been caused by changes in attitudes, some was real. By analyzing the rate of sex crime in various categories, he showed that child molesting had decreased even though public attitudes toward the severity of this crime had not changed significantly. More recently another report (Court, 1976) maintains that rape substantially increased in the mid-sixties after a long period of stability. Even if that trend is real, other questions should be asked. For example, did the population of Copenhagen change in some way that might explain an increase in rapes? Because most violent crimes are perpetrated by younger people, rape might have increased along with other violent crimes purely as a result of demographic trends. Further, is rape a good indicator of sex crime? Many investigators feel that rape reflects aggressive motivation more than sexual. Perhaps child molesting would be a more appropriate crime to analyze. The continuing controversy (Cochrane, 1978) over the effects of pornography on sex crimes illustrates some of the difficulties inherent in interrupted time-series research.

Another example of an interrupted time-series design is given by Alexander Wagenaar's (1981a, 1981b) study of the effect of raising the drinking age in Michigan on alcohol-related traffic accidents. Michigan, along with many other states, lowered the drinking age from 21 to 18 in the early 1970s after the voting age had been lowered to 18 in all 50 states. The change was followed by a 35 percent increase in the number of alcohol-related crashes among Michigan drivers aged 18 to 20. Therefore in January 1979 the state returned the drinking age to 21. Wagenaar wanted to know whether alcohol-related accidents had decreased following the change back to age 21 and whether this decrease could be attributed to the change.

Ordinarily one would want to make a series of observations both before and after the intervention to check for trends in the data, as we mentioned above. However, in this situation assessing the effects of raising the drinking age needed to be done as soon as possible for reasons of public policy. Therefore Wagenaar did his study only one year after the change back to age 21. He found that in 1979 drivers aged 18 to 20 were involved in 26 percent fewer accidents that were reported by the police as "had been drinking" compared with 1978. This figure was the lowest in five years.

Several alternative hypotheses would have to be ruled out, though, before the change in drinking age could be concluded to have caused the decrease in accidents. For example, police officers might have changed their criterion for reporting that the driver in an accident had been drinking. Or the occurrence of an economic recession in Michigan and higher gasoline prices both might have reduced the amount of driving. Or the fact that the winter of 1979 had relatively mild weather might have made driving safer. In order to rule out rival hypotheses, Wagenaar compared data on accidents reported as "had been drinking" with other similar data.

The first alternative hypothesis concerned a change in police officers' criterion for reporting drivers who "had been drinking." To test this hypothesis, Wagenaar compared the original data (drivers aged 18 to 20 who were in accidents in which the driver was reported as "had been drinking") with late-night, single-vehicle accidents involving drivers in the same age group. Of such accidents 60 percent are known to be alcohol related, which means that statistics on these accidents would not be affected by police officers' judgments of drinking. Wagenaar found that these late-night, single-vehicle accidents had also decreased. The alternative hypotheses about the recession, the price of gasoline, and the winter weather were tested by comparing the accident data for drivers aged 18 to 20 with drivers in age groups who were not affected by the change in the law (see Figure 8–9). The other age groups actually showed an increase in alcohol-related crashes.

A second test of the hypothesis that police officers might have changed their criterion for reporting "had been drinking" was possible by comparing single-vehicle, nighttime crashes to similar daytime crashes for the 18-to-20-year-olds. It is known that fewer daytime crashes are alcohol related than nighttime crashes. Wagenaar found that both categories of crashes decreased after the change in the drinking age, but the nighttime crashes decreased twice as much as did the daytime crashes. A similar result was found by comparing crashes in which the police did not report that the driver had been drinking with those in which the police did so report.

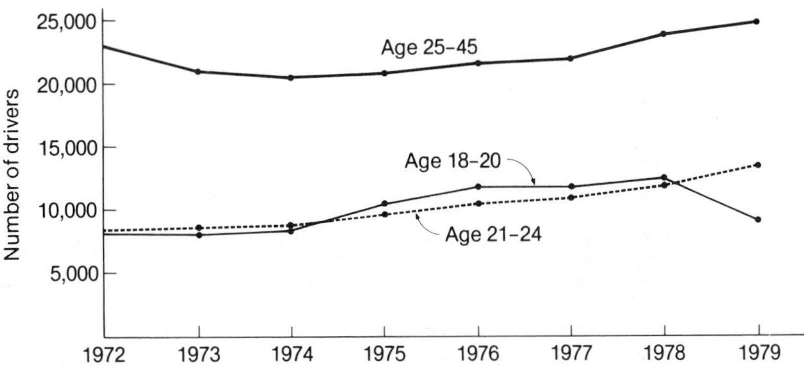

FIGURE 8–9. Crash-involved drivers in Michigan reported as having been drinking alcoholic beverages.

Still it was possible that the results were caused by some factor other than a change in drinking age. Wagenaar therefore compared the Michigan results with another state that also raised the drinking age, Maine, and two that did not, New York and Pennsylvania. The results in Maine paralleled the Michigan results, whereas no change occurred in the accident rate in New York or Pennsylvania at the time that Michigan changed its law.

In addition to making the comparisons we have just discussed, Wagenaar used sophisticated statistical methods to test all conclusions. Together, the various comparisons make it reasonably certain that the change in the Michigan law did produce the decrease in number of traffic accidents. Because Wagenaar compared his group of 18-to-20-year-olds with several different groups that were not randomly assigned to conditions, his study is a multiple nonequivalent-control-group design. A complete description of the design would be a multiple nonequivalent-control-group time-series design.

Repeated-Treatment Designs

Repeated-treatment design research design that allows the same group to be compared over time by measuring the subjects' responses before and after repeated treatments

As the name implies, **repeated-treatment designs** attempt to improve the validity of the experiment by presenting the treatment more than once. The subject's response is measured before and after the introduction of a treatment, then the treatment is withdrawn and the whole process begun again. Table 8–3 shows the general design. This design has an obvious limitation: The treatment must be one that can be withdrawn without causing complications in the analysis of data.

TABLE 8–3 Example of a repeated treatments design.

Pretest_1	Treatment	Posttest_1	Withdraw treatment	Pretest_2	Treatment	Posttest_2

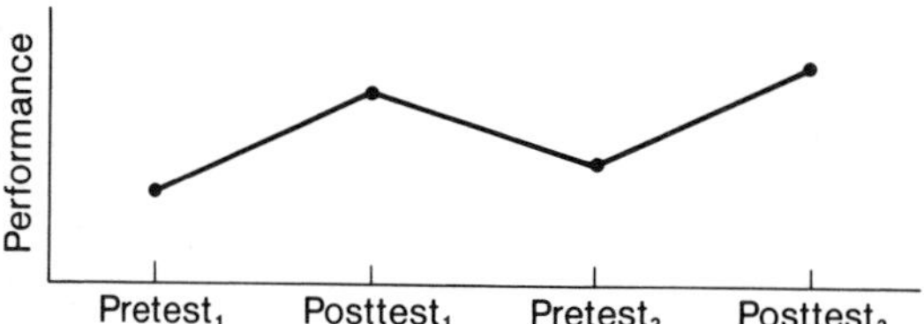

FIGURE 8–10. Desired pattern of results for a repeated-treatments design.
Note. From "Effects of the raised legal drinking age on motor vehicle accidents in Michigan" by A. C. Wagenaar, *HSRI Research Review,* 1981, *11*(4), 1–8. Copyright 1981 by *HSRI Research Review.* Reprinted by permission of the publisher and author.

Suppose an instructor is going to give four hour-long tests in a course. She wants to find out if giving extra credit for turning in homework will improve grades on the tests. If she instituted the extra credit between the first and second test, she would then have a pretest and a posttest to permit her to examine the effect of the treatment. In order to repeat the treatment, she would have to stop giving the extra credit after the second test (Posttest *1*). The third test then could be considered to be Pretest *2*, after which she would reinstitute the extra credit and look for improvement between Pretest *2* and Posttest *2*. This design might be good, except that the students would likely rebel at having the extra credit taken away. If the instructor went ahead with the plan anyway, the students might be demoralized enough that their performance would suffer on the later tests.

Figure 8–10 shows the pattern of results that is desired with a repeated-treatment design. Whatever change is found between Pretest *1* and Posttest *1* should be in the same direction as that between Pretest *2* and Posttest *2*. It is desirable that there be a reversal in any previous trend of response between Posttest *1*, when the treatment is withdrawn, and Pretest *2* to rule out the possibility that there would have been a continuous change in performance over the four tests regardless of treatment. Like the interrupted time-series design, the repeated-treatment design is one that is used in single-subject experiments, as we will discuss in Chapter 9.

SUMMARY

1. The boundaries between true experiments, quasi experiments, and nonexperiments are not particularly sharp, but the distinctions depend on the relative amount of control that the researcher is able to maintain.
2. Quasi experiments may be performed when a true experiment would be impossible or when the advantages of a quasi experiment outweigh its disadvantages.
3. The most common quasi-experimental situation is to have nonequivalent control groups. Such experiments are sometimes uninterpretable, depending on the pattern of results.
4. One example of the nonequivalent control group design was the delayed control group design employed to test the so-called psychic Uri Geller.

5. An example of a mixed factorial design was the study of anxiety. Trait anxiety was the quasi-experimental variable and state anxiety was the true experimental variable.

6. The regression discontinuity design is used to study nonequivalent groups by considering the correlation between subjects' scores on the pretest and posttest. If the experimental treatment is given to those who meet some criterion on the pretest and if the treatment is effective, the regression line between the two variables will be discontinuous.

7. Interrupted time-series designs consider the trend of the data before and after some manipulation in a study with no control group. The ideal situation is to have a stable baseline before the manipulation, followed by an abrupt or gradual change to a new stable level.

8. Repeated-treatment designs improve on the validity of an experiment by presenting the treatment more than once. The ideal result is for each presentation of the treatment to produce a change in the same direction, with a reversal of the effect when the treatment is removed.

SUGGESTIONS FOR FURTHER READING

Campbell, D. T., & Stanley, J. C. *Experimental and quasi-experimental designs for research*. Chicago: Rand McNally, 1963. This book is the classic reference on quasi experimentation.

Cook, T. D., & Campbell, D. T. *Quasi-experimentation: Design and analysis for field settings*. Chicago: Rand McNally, 1979. This book updates the material given in Campbell and Stanley, above.

READING BETWEEN THE LINES

The following problems are presented for you to solve. See Reading Between the Lines in Chapter 1 for an introduction to them. The answers are given in Appendix A.

18. AGGRESSION AND XYY MALES

Some males have a genetic abnormality that results in an extra Y chromosome. One study found that these XYY males, as they are known, were overrepresented in a prison population and concluded that the XYY condition caused persons to be overly aggressive. This finding gave rise to speculation and research into the possible causes of the apparent connection between the XYY condition and aggression.

One such study was conducted at the Boston Hospital for Women, which is connected with Harvard University. Between 1965 and 1975 over 16,000 male infants born at the hospital were screened for chromosome abnormalities as part of a large study funded by the Center for the Study of Crime and Delinquency, a federal agency. Before giving birth the mothers were presented with a booklet that contained the following paragraph: "In this hospital all male infants are undergoing chromosome analysis. This new and simplified test allows the doctors to do an accurate screening examination of your baby's chromosomes and if any serious abnormalities are found, you will be so informed. It is hoped that in time this test . . . will become a universal test on all infants" (Chorover, 1979, p. 176). Another paragraph of the booklet refers to the chromosome test as a "service" and points out that there is no charge for it.

The study identified six male infants with the XYY condition out of the more than 16,000 babies tested. A pediatric psychiatrist visited the homes of all of the XYY children and informed the parents that "their children have extra chromosome material" and the baby's pediatrician was "fully informed about the child's variation" (p. 186). What ethical and design problems can you find with this study?

19. OBESITY AND CONTROL OF EATING

Schachter's theory of obesity (Schachter and Rodin, 1974) states that obese persons are controlled more by external factors such as the amount of food in front of them or the time indicated on a clock than they are by internal factors such as the amount of food in the stomach or blood sugar level, compared with normal-weight subjects. His theory has been supported by a number of studies, such as those in which persons are given a high caloric drink to consume before they eat a meal. The theory predicts that normal-weight people would reduce their intake of the meal because their stomachs would provide information that they had eaten. Obese persons, however, would pay less attention to such information compared with normal-weight subjects.

The obese subjects were found to eat more after such a preload than did normal-weight subjects. Hibscher and Herman (1977) hypothesized that the obesity per se may not be responsible for the failure to reduce intake following a preload. Rather, the cause may be the fact that obese persons are more likely to be habitual dieters, having tried, and failed, to control their weight more than have normal people. Can you think of a plausible reason why this might be the case?

SINGLE-SUBJECT EXPERIMENTS

Up to this point in the book we have talked as if using groups of subjects were the only way to do research. It is true that most psychological research involves groups of subjects, but this approach is not the only way to do research. This chapter deals with strategies for achieving control in experiments using single subjects.

Research using single subjects not only is common, it has a long tradition as well. In fact scientists have used single subjects in research for longer than they have used groups. Gustav Fechner, who some historians say is the founder of experimental psychology, worked extensively on individual subjects—himself and his brother-in-law. Beginning in 1860, Fechner invented the basic psychophysical methods that are still used today to measure sensory thresholds and discovered principles of psychophysics that are still taken seriously. Twenty-five years later, inspired by Fechner's work, Hermann Ebbinghaus did his experimental work on memory. Following Fechner's example, he used himself as his own subject. Wilhelm Wundt, who is credited with founding the first psychological laboratory in 1879, conducted experiments measuring various psychological and behavioral responses in individual subjects. Wundt's famous student, E. B. Titchener, espoused the use of introspection, which is the careful reporting of one's own experience. Because this procedure required a great deal of training, much of his work was done using one or a few individuals. Finally, I. P. Pavlov did his pioneering work on conditioning using individual dogs. The list of psychologists who relied on individual subjects is long and includes most of those working before about 1930, when modern statistical methods were developed.

These early researchers used single subjects in the time-honored scientific tradition. In any case, modern statistical methods did not then exist. Their solution to the problems of reliability and validity was to make extensive observations and frequent replication of results. A traditional assumption of researchers doing single-subject experiments has been that individual subjects are essentially equivalent and that one should study additional subjects only to make sure that the original subject was not grossly abnormal.

In contrast the modern statistical methods that have become an integral part of present-day research grew out of a different tradition. A Belgian astronomer, Adolphe Quetelet, discovered that human traits followed the normal curve. From this he concluded that nature strove to produce the "average man" (Hersen & Barlow, 1976). The variability around the mean that is always found was considered to be a result of nature's failure to achieve the ideal average person in every case. The individual differences tradition of Galton and Pearson grew out of this thinking. According to the individual differences tradition, variability between subjects is inevitable. The task then becomes how to separate the effect of the experimental manipulation from this inherent variability. During the 1930s, statistician R. A. Fisher, a mathematician working on problems of genetics, invented many statistical methods such as the analysis of variance that have become standard in psychological research. These techniques dominated psychological research to such an extent that the single-subject tradition almost disappeared for several decades.

Nevertheless, certain psychologists continued to work in the single-subject tradition during that period, notably B. F. Skinner. Skinner disdained the use of statistics, claiming that he would rather study one animal for 1,000 hours than study 1,000 animals for an hour each. Skinner's philosophy of research is described in the classic book by Murray Sidman (1960). Sidman makes clear the difference in attitude between the single-subject approach and the groups approach to research. The single-subject tradition assumes that most variability in the subject's behavior is *imposed* by the situation and therefore can be *removed* by careful attention to experimental control. The individual-differences group-research tradition assumes that much of the variability is *intrinsic* and should be *statistically controlled and analyzed.*

We cannot settle the debate between these two positions. Psychologists began using statistical methods to evaluate the results of experiments in which removing all sources of variability was not feasible. Careful scientists use statistics also to avoid being fooled into thinking that data are more reliable than they really are. In addition, we should note that employing single-subject methods is not completely incompatible with statistical analysis inasmuch as statistical methods are being developed to handle data from individual subjects (for example, Kratochwill, 1978).

ADVANTAGES OF THE SINGLE-SUBJECT APPROACH

Although we acknowledge that the group comparison approach has a rightful place in psychology, we will point out several advantages of the single-subject approach. We should keep these advantages in mind whenever we are designing research.

Focusing on Individual Performance

Whenever data are averaged over many subjects, the possibility occurs that the average picture is a distortion of the behavior of the individual subjects. Consider Figure 9–1. Suppose this represents a learning curve of a group of subjects on some task. Because the curve is a smooth ogive (S-shaped curve), we might conclude from the group data that learning was a gradual, continuous process. However, look now at Figure 9–2. This graph shows the individual data of the five subjects who make up the group data in the previous graph. Here we get a different picture. Each subject learns suddenly, going from no to yes on a single trial. Subjects learn on different trials, however. Subject 1 goes from no on Trial 6 to complete mastery on Trial 7; Subject 2 goes from no on Trial 9 to complete mastery on Trial 10; and so forth. When the data of the whole group are averaged, though, the learning appears gradual. Although this example is extreme, it occurs fairly often in laboratory situations.

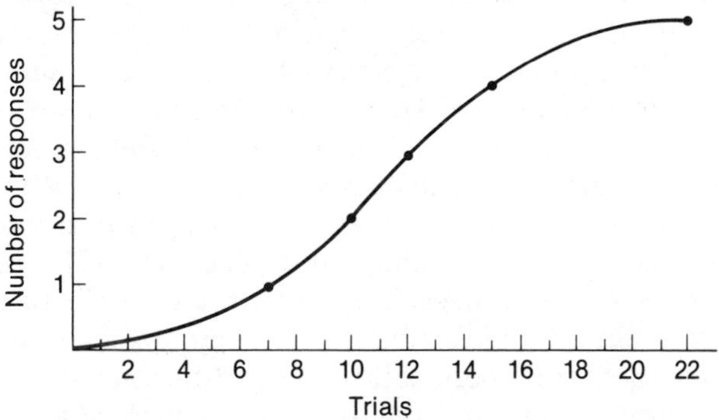

FIGURE 9–1. Hypothetical learning data for a group of subjects.

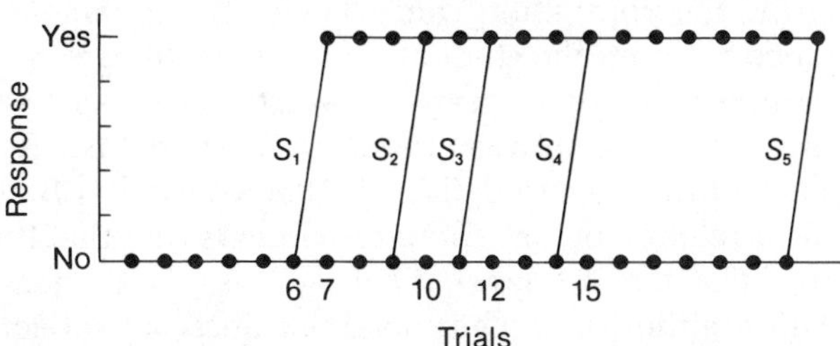

FIGURE 9–2. Hypothetical learning data for the individual subjects whose group data were shown in Figure 9–1.

Focusing on Big Effects

An experiment that employs large groups of subjects will be likely to discover that an independent variable has an effect even if the effect is a minor one. For example, given enough subjects, it might be possible to show that a clinical treatment produced improvement in 55 percent of the subjects, whereas 50 percent of the control subjects improved spontaneously. A therapist is not likely to adopt a treatment that shows such a marginal difference in success rate. The experiment would have little **clinical significance** even if it had plenty of statistical significance (Hersen & Barlow, 1976). Some researchers in nonclinical situations feel this same reluctance. They would rather not spend time investigating the effects of variables that produce small effects but would rather find the powerful variables that produce large effects. Because the effect of a minor variable is less likely to be discovered in a single-subject experiment, the experimenter will not be distracted by it. In addition, the researcher can spend time reducing variability, so that the effect of a given variable will be maximized, instead of spending time testing more subjects.

Clinical significance the practical importance of a result

Statisticians use the term **power** to refer to the probability that a statistical test will find a significant difference when there actually is a difference in the population from which the data are drawn. The power of a test depends on the size of the difference that exists in the population and the size of the sample drawn from the population. Therefore a researcher has two ways of increasing the probability of finding a significant result in an experiment: increasing the size of the effect or increasing the size of the sample (the number of subjects or the number of observations per subject). In Chapter 6 we discussed how increasing the number of subjects decreases the variability of the data. The other tactic, and the one favored by single-subject researchers, is to increase the size of the effect. For example, suppose that you are interested in whether the students at Alma Mater College are smarter than those at Rival College. The larger the number of students sampled from each college, the greater the likelihood of finding a difference in intelligence between the groups. Eventually, if you include every student from both colleges, any difference you find is "statistically significant" because it is not based on a sample at all. You have measured the whole population and you are performing not an inferential statistic but measuring the population value itself. This statement is true even if the difference between the students at the two colleges is barely measurable.

Power the probability that a statistical test will find a significant difference when a difference exists in the sample population

Suppose that two researchers work on the same problem; each measures the correlation between the same two variables. Researcher A uses 10 subjects and finds a correlation of .765. Researcher B uses 50 subjects and finds a correlation of .361. Both researchers find that their correlations are significant at the .01 level. That is, there is 1 chance in 100 that the correlation either researcher obtained does not reflect a true correlation between the two variables in the populations studied. The question now is:

In which researcher's findings should you have greater trust? Should you put more confidence in Researcher B's results because more subjects were used? The answer is that you should feel more confident with Researcher A's results because the same level of significance was obtained with fewer subjects. Remember that each had the same probability that the results were spurious: 1 in 100. In order to get the same level of significance with fewer subjects, Researcher A had to obtain a larger effect. This fact is shown by A's correlation being larger than B's. The square of the correlation coefficient gives us the percent of the variance in the data that is accounted for by the independent variable. Researcher A's correlation of .765 accounts for 58.5 percent of the variance, whereas Researcher B's correlation of .361 accounts for only 13 percent of the variance. Researcher A obtained a larger correlation and the independent variable accounts for a greater percent of the variance even though fewer subjects were used. Researcher A must have had better control over the sources of variability in the experiment.

Avoiding Ethical and Practical Problems

Whenever research involves testing the efficacy of a treatment that is expected to benefit the participant, an ethical question arises over placing some participants into a control group that will not receive treatment or that will receive inferior treatment. In clinical psychology this area is particularly touchy when the client's situation can be life-threatening, as with suicide-prone persons. One solution is to treat all of the participants but to evaluate them from a single-subject standpoint.

Another situation that calls for a single-subject experiment is when the researcher cannot locate enough subjects to constitute a group to study. Perhaps the researcher is testing the efficacy of a clinical treatment. If there are not enough people suffering from the same condition, subjects will have to be studied on a single-subject basis.

Flexibility in Design

An experiment on a group of subjects must be designed so that all subjects receive the same experience in order for them to be comparable. This necessity can result in a design that is not the best one for all subjects. In the course of an experiment on behavior modification, an experimenter may discover that a subject does not respond to a reinforcer that has worked on previous subjects. If the design is a single-subject one, the experiment can be modified on the spot by switching reinforcers or by altering the instructions.

Another problem that can be solved by a design modification is when a large change occurs in the subject's behavior that the experimenter suspects is caused by an outside event rather than by the experimental manipulation. The experimenter can immediately switch the conditions and see if the behavior changes correspondingly. A groups-design experiment, on the other hand, would call for continuing all subjects in the same procedure and hoping that the outside events would cancel each other out.

BASIC CONTROL STRATEGIES IN SINGLE-SUBJECT RESEARCH

Just as there are standard ways of controlling for rival hypotheses in group experiments, there are standard strategies in single-subject experiments. We will discuss the most important of them. Others are discussed in Hersen & Barlow (1976).

Obtaining a Stable Baseline

When you are using a group design, you compare one group of subjects against another, or a group of subjects in one condition against the same subjects in another condition. The assumption that the groups were equal before the treatment is the basis of your attributing the effect to the manipulation rather than to something else. This assumption can be tested by statistically analyzing the differences between the groups. When you have only one subject, however, you must use a different strategy to compare differences between conditions. That strategy is to compare the behavior that occurs before and after the introduction of the experimental manipulation. The behavior before the manipulation must be measured over a long enough time span to obtain a stable **baseline** against which the later behavior may be compared.

Baseline
the measure of behavior before treatment that establishes a reference point for evaluating the effectiveness of treatment

Suppose that you want to measure the effectiveness of a treatment for anorexia nervosa, a disorder characterized by voluntary self-starvation. You would need to measure the patient's weight and food intake for a period of time before initiating the treatment in order to show that the weight was stable and that the patient had not begun gaining weight spontaneously. How long this baseline measure should be continued is difficult to say. The judgment of stability is a subjective one. However, the experiment would be useless unless it were evident that the patient had not begun gaining weight before the treatment. If the baseline behavior is not stable before treatment, a declining baseline may be acceptable if the treatment is expected to cause an increase in the behavior and vice versa. For a patient with anorexia nervosa, a decrease in weight in the absence of treatment is not unusual and would constitute an acceptable baseline for comparison with a treatment. This example illustrates another consideration in obtaining baseline measures. Sometimes the existing condition is harmful to the subject, or even life-threatening, so that the goal of a stable baseline may be overridden by other factors.

Using the Withdrawal of Treatment (ABA Designs)

If you simply measure the baseline behavior and introduce a treatment, you would not know whether other variables may have produced the change in behavior. In fact, you would have the single-subject equivalent of the quasi-experimental design that we called the one-group, before-after design. The inference that the treatment is the cause of the change is considerably strengthened if the treatment is withdrawn after a period of time and the behavior shows a return toward the baseline. This use of treatment withdrawal is often referred to as an **ABA design**.

ABA design research design involving a baseline period and a treatment period, followed by withdrawal of treatment

Two principal problems are associated with an ABA design. First, the effect of the manipulation may not be fully reversible. If the treatment were a lesion of the brain that causes obesity, clearly it would be impossible to reverse the lesion. Or if a learning procedure causes a more or less permanent change in a subject's behavior, that too would not be reversible. In fact, many procedures are tested because a permanent improvement in a person's behavior is desired after the treatment is ended.

The second problem with the ABA design is that you may wish to leave the subjects in the new condition rather than return them to their original state. Treatments involving weight control, phobias, compulsive behaviors, and the like are typical examples. In such cases the experimenter may withdraw the treatment temporarily before the behavior change has reached the desired level. After the behavior shows some reversal of the trend toward improvement, treatment is reinstated. In any case experimenters in behavior modification seldom end an experiment with the baseline, or withdrawal, condition. Rather, they reintroduce the treatment in order to produce maximum benefit for the client.

Repeating Treatments (ABAB Designs)

In the examples we've just discussed, the treatment was repeated after the withdrawal phase in order to leave the subject with the full benefit of the training. This repetition of treatment also has the advantage of providing another opportunity to evaluate the effect of the treatment. This kind of experiment in which treatment is repeated is called an **ABAB design**. Repeated presentation and withdrawal of a variable can produce strong evidence for the validity of the independent variable's effect. Anyone who watches a pigeon that has been trained in a Skinner box to respond to the presence of a light and not to respond in its absence is impressed by the control that the light exerts over the animal's behavior. The light appears to turn the behavior on and off as though by a switch.

ABAB design an ABA design with treatment repeated after the withdrawal phase

An interesting example of an ABAB design is given by the work of Edward Carr and Jack McDowell (1980). They wished to treat Jim, a 10-year-old boy who scratched himself so much that he caused sores on his body. Jim's behavior had begun when he got into poison oak, causing a dermatitis that lasted a few weeks. Three years later, however, Jim was still scratching himself. The first step in the experiment was to observe Jim's behavior in various settings. The observer noticed that Jim scratched himself mostly when other people were around. Carr and McDowell surmised that the scratching was an operant response reinforced by attention from his parents. This hypothesis was confirmed in a session in which an experimenter observed the family. In the first part of the session the parents were instructed to ignore Jim's scratching. Then for a period of time they were to tell him to stop whenever he scratched himself. Finally, the session ended with another period in which they were to ignore his scratching. The experimenters found that Jim's scratching *increased* dramatically when he received social attention for it and that the scratching declined during the phase in which it was ignored (Figure 9–3).

Because Jim's parents were unable to ignore his scratching for long periods of time, the experimenters decided to use a time-out technique. Whenever Jim scratched himself, he was sent to the utility room for 20 minutes. The condition is called time out from positive reinforcement because no reinforcement of social attention could occur while Jim was in the utility room. In addition, Jim was to receive a reinforcer of his choice (a trip to the science museum) at the end of any week during which the number of sores was reduced by two from the previous lowest number.

Figure 9–4 shows the number of sores on Jim's body over the 18-month span of the experiment. First was a baseline period that was kept brief because of the undesirable nature of Jim's condition. Then treatment

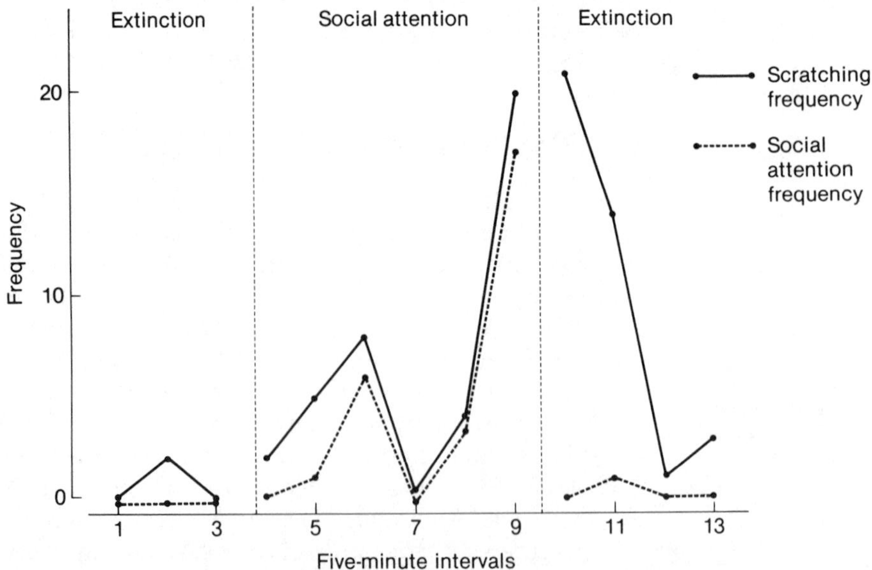

FIGURE 9–3. Frequency of scratching during consecutive 5-minute intervals.
Note. From "Social control of self-injurious behavior of organic etiology" by E. G. Carr & J. J. McDowell, *Behavior Therapy*, 1980, *11*, 402–409. Copyright 1980 by the Association for Advancement of Behavior Therapy. Reprinted by permission of the publisher and authors.

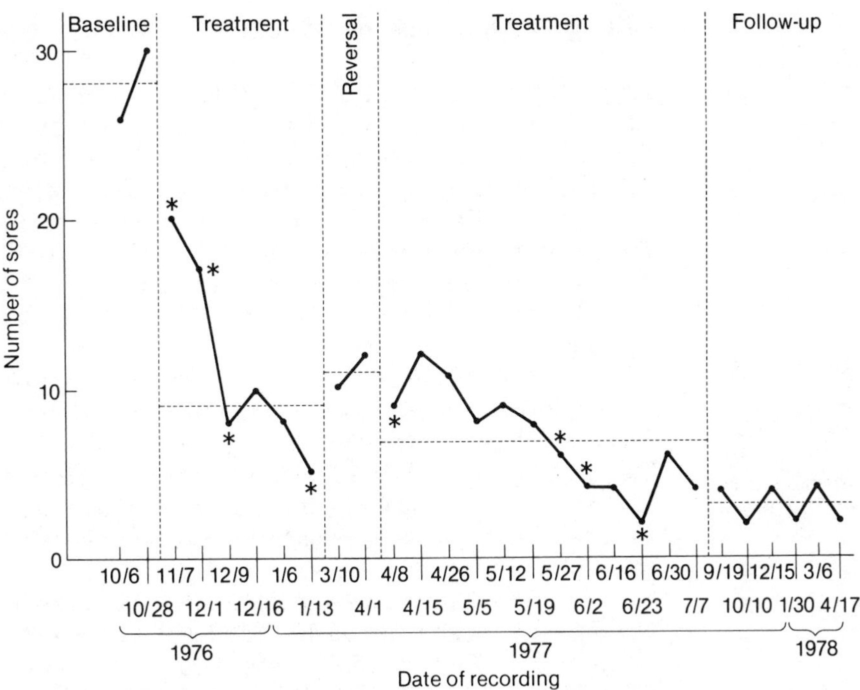

FIGURE 9–4. Number of body sores recorded over the 18-month period.

Note. From "Social control of self-injurious behavior of organic etiology" by E. G. Carr & J. J. McDowell, *Behavior Therapy,* 1980, *11,* 402–409. Copyright 1980 by the Association for Advancement of Behavior Therapy. Reprinted by permission of the publisher and authors.

proceeded for two months, during which the number of sores decreased dramatically. A natural reversal occurred when Jim's parents both lost their jobs and could not afford time or money for treatment. Following this 2½-month reversal, treatment was continued for a 4½-month period, after which no treatment was given for a 9-month follow-up period. You can see that the number of sores on Jim's body decreased steadily during treatment, increased during the reversal, decreased again during the second treatment to a low level that continued after treatment was discontinued.

Interesting features of the design are that time-outs were given contingent on the behavior of scratching, but reinforcers were given contingent on reducing the number of sores. In addition, progress of the treatment was monitored by recording the number of sores, which is only an indirect measure of the scratching behavior. Also, practical concerns dictated recording the number of sores on an irregular basis (the time axis of the graph is not measured in equal units), as well as the treatment reversal that occurred when Jim's parents lost their jobs. Neither of these features was likely to improve Jim's progress, yet the treatment was successful. In any case the reversal strengthens the conclusion that the time out for scratching and/or the reinforcements for reducing the number of sores had an effect on the scratching behavior.

Changing Only One Variable at a Time

An important rule of single-subject research is to vary only one thing at a time. If two variables are changed simultaneously, it is impossible to decide whether the change in behavior was caused by one or the other, or by the two together. If there are two variables, called *B* and *C*, and the baseline condition is labeled *A*, then an acceptable sequence of presenting the conditions would be A-B-A-B-BC-B-BC. Notice that the conditions were presented in such a sequence that every condition was both preceded and followed by the same condition at least once and that only one variable changed at a time.

Interaction design single-subject research design that manipulates variables one at a time to determine their effect

The A-B-A-B-BC-B-BC design is often called an **interaction design**. Notice, though, that all possible combinations of *B* and *C* are not presented, because C is never presented alone (*A* represents the absence of *B* and *C*). Thus, it is not possible to assess the presence of an interaction as defined in Chapter 3. (Analyzing for an interaction requires at least a complete 2 × 2 factorial design.) What is tested by this procedure is whether C has an effect *in addition to* that of *B* alone.

Suppose that you want to know whether praise for making a correct response (C) has an effect on a child's learning in addition to the effect of a token reward (*B*). If you find that praise plus token reward has a greater effect than a token reward alone, you will have information useful for designing a learning situation for the child. However, you will not know the effect of praise when presented alone. Praise alone may have worked as well as the token reward plus praise. On the other hand, praise alone may have been ineffective. (Nothing except practical considerations prevents the use of C alone. The sequence would be: A-B-A-B-BC-B-BC-C-BC, somewhat long for many situations.)

A study by Ansley Bacon-Prue, Ronald Blount, Connie Hosey, and Ronald Drabman (1980) provides a good example of an experiment that examines the effect of more than one variable. Bacon-Prue et al. wanted mentally retarded persons in an institution to make their own beds. First, they took baseline measures of the percent of residents who spontaneously made their beds. Then they instituted a procedure to remind the residents each evening, when they were all together, to make their beds in the morning.

As you can see in Figure 9–5, the instructions caused a slight, temporary increase in bedmaking. In the next phase the experimenters placed photographs of the residents who made their beds on a given day on a conspicuously placed poster that was titled "The Bedmakers" and that showed a picture of two made beds. The instructions continued to be given as well. Figure 9–5 shows that the percentage of made beds jumped suddenly and continued to increase thereafter. Next there was a second instruction-only phase, during which the percentage of made beds decreased steadily. A second instruction-plus-photograph phase reversed the decline.

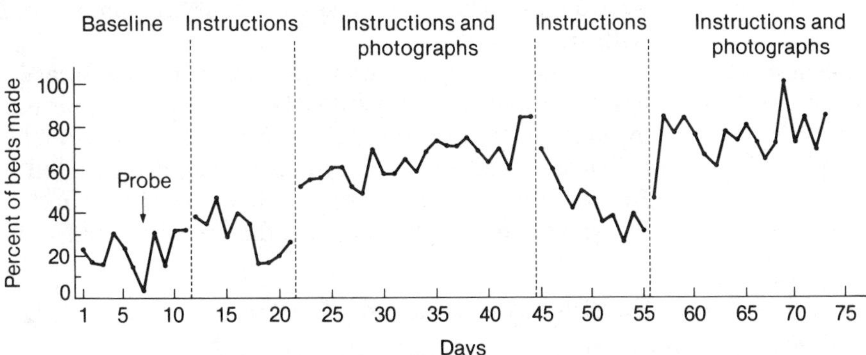

FIGURE 9–5. Percent of beds made during the various experimental phases.
Note. From "The public posting of photographs as a reinforcer for bedmaking in an institutional setting" by A. Bacon-Prue, R. Blount, C. Hosey, & R. S. Drabman, *Behavior Therapy*, 1980, *11*, 417–420. Copyright 1980 by the Association for Advancement of Behavior Therapy. Reprinted by permission of the publisher and authors.

Although this experiment involved changing only one variable at a time, Bacon-Prue et al. did not arrange that every condition was both preceded and followed by the same condition. In other words, the design was A-B-BC-B-BC, rather than A-B-A-B-BC-B-BC. Besides saving time that would have been required by two additional conditions, the design is justified by the fact that the B condition (instructions only) did not have any permanent effect over that of the baseline condition. Therefore there was no reason to return to baseline before introducing the additional manipulation (photographs). On the other hand, the results suggest that a photographs-only condition might have been worth trying. If it were successful in maintaining the bedmaking behavior, it probably would have saved staff time and effort in the future. Then the design would have been A-B-BC-B-BC-C. An interesting aspect of this experiment is that it is a single-subject design applied to a large group of subjects.

Using Multiple Baselines

Another effective way to demonstrate that the manipulation caused the behavior change is to introduce the manipulation at different times for each of several different behaviors to see if the onset of behavior change coincides with the manipulation. For example, suppose a researcher is trying to determine if rewarding a retarded child for doing certain personal tasks is effective. If the researcher begins rewarding toothbrushing, face washing, hand washing, and hair combing all at the same time, it is possible that the presence of the experimenter, the attention received, or a spontaneous decision to turn over a new leaf was responsible for the change. The researcher, however, could begin rewarding only toothbrushing the first week, toothbrushing and face washing the second week, and so forth until, after four weeks, all behaviors are being rewarded. This sequence would make it possible to see whether the increase in behavior coincides with the reward.

Multiple-baseline design research design that introduces the experimental manipulation at different times for different behaviors to see if behavior change coincides with manipulation

This design is known as a **multiple-baseline design**. The separate baselines may be different behaviors in the same individual, as in this example, or the same behaviors in different individuals. A third possibility is to test the same behavior in the same individual but in different settings. An example of this latter approach will be given shortly. Multiple-baseline designs are especially useful if the behavior change is irreversible.

Employing a Changing Criterion

Another way of showing that the manipulation caused the behavior change is to change the criterion for reward over time. After a baseline measurement a reward can be given for meeting a lax criterion of the behavior. After the behavior stabilizes at that level, the criterion can be raised until the behavior stabilizes again, and so forth. If the behavior begins to change after each change in the criterion, then the conclusion that the reward is the cause of the improvement is rather convincing.

Changing-criterion design research design that introduces successively more stringent criteria for reinforcement to see if behavior change coincides with the changing reinforcement

Suppose that a child is unable to sit still in class. The teacher may reward the child for sitting still for 5 minutes at a time until the performance becomes stable. Then the criterion may be set at 10 minutes, later at 15, and so forth. The behavior at each criterion becomes the baseline against which to evaluate the effect of the manipulation at the next criterion. Like the multiple-baseline design, a **changing-criterion design** is useful when the behavior change is irreversible.

AN EXAMPLE OF A MULTIPLE-BASELINE DESIGN WITH WITHDRAWAL OF TREATMENT

As an example of a single-subject design, we will discuss an experiment conducted by Nirbay Singh, Maryan Dawson, and Paul Gregory (1980). They desired to stop a profoundly retarded 18-year-old female from hyperventilating. This problem, in which a person breathes too deeply, can have serious medical consequences. Several treatments had been attempted on the subject without success, including reprimand and medication.

Singh, Dawson, and Gregory decided to punish episodes of hyperventilation by briefly presenting ammonia (smelling salts) to the subject every time she hyperventilated. The design was a multiple-baseline design, with withdrawal of treatment as a test probe. Baseline recordings were made for 5 days in each of 4 different settings (classroom, dining room, bathroom, and dayroom). Experimental sessions lasted 2 hours per day (30 minutes in each of 4 settings). During this time all instances of hyperventilation were recorded but not punished. Then the baseline recordings were continued in three of the settings, and punishment was administered to any episodes

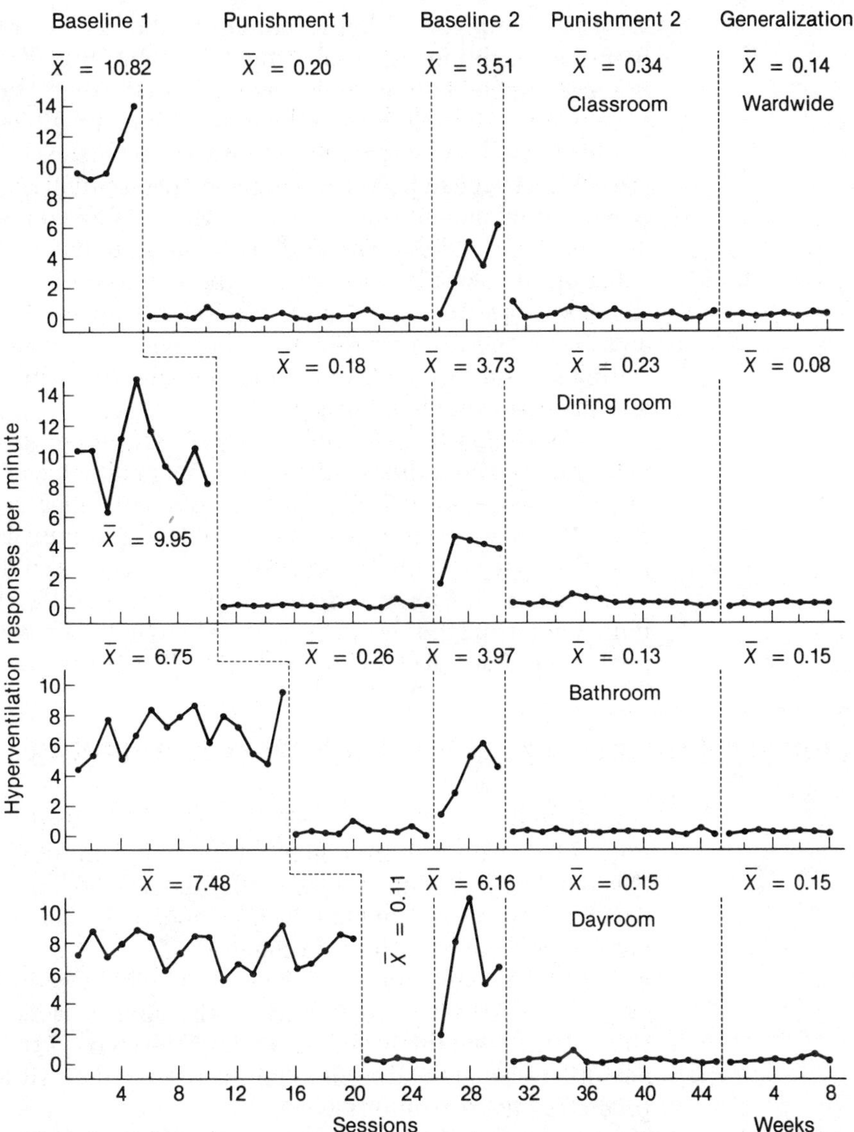

FIGURE 9–6. Number of hyperventilation responses per minute across experimental phases and settings.

Note. From "Suppression of chronic hyperventilation using response-contingent aromatic ammonia" by N. N. Singh, M. J. Dawson & P. R. Gregory, *Behavior Therapy*, 1980, *11*, 561–566. Copyright 1980 by the Association for Advancement of Behavior Therapy. Reprinted by permission of the publisher and authors.

of hyperventilation that occurred in the classroom. After 5 more days, punishment was instituted for episodes occurring in the dining room as well as in the classroom, and baseline recording continued in the bathroom and dayroom. After 5 more days, punishment was extended to the bathroom and then to the dayroom after another 5 days.

The data from this experiment are indicated in Figure 9–6. You can see that frequency of hyperventilation did not decrease in any of the baseline conditions. In each situation when punishment was initiated, however, hyperventilation decreased dramatically. After punishment had been continued for 5 days in the last setting, punishment was withdrawn but the episodes of hyperventilation were still recorded. You can see that the subject began hyperventilating again in all situations but ceased abruptly when punishment was reinstated. After 15 more days of punishment for any instance of hyperventilation in the 4 settings, the procedure was generalized. Instead of having one experimenter administer punishment in the 4 settings during a 2-hour session, all nurses in the ward were to administer punishment whenever they observed hyperventilation in any setting during an 8-hour day. This practice was instituted to consolidate and maintain the previous gains.

The study illustrates how to test the effectiveness of an experimental manipulation on a single subject in an unambiguous manner. Because the manipulation was instituted at four different times in four different settings, the researchers would have to have used four different alternative hypotheses to account for the decreases in hyperventilation that occurred. The increase in hyperventilation that occurred following the removal of punishment and the abrupt decrease when punishment was reinstated give further evidence of the effectiveness of the treatment.

A SINGLE-SUBJECT EXAMPLE FROM PSYCHOPHYSICS

Our previous example came from the Skinnerian tradition. This next example comes from another major tradition employing single subjects, psychophysics. We mentioned earlier that Gustav Fechner, the founder of psychophysics, used single subjects extensively. This practice is still common in psychophysical experiments.

Brian Wandell and E. N. Pugh, Jr. (1980) measured the threshold for detection of a flash of colored light seen against a background of a different color. They were interested in whether the color of the background made any difference in the threshold for the flash in their situation. Their theory predicted that it would not.

The threshold for detection of the flash was measured at each combination of several background colors and intensities. The flash was presented in one of two temporal intervals and the subject was to guess in which interval it occurred. The intensity of the flash was varied from trial to trial depending on whether the subject had been correct or incorrect on the previous trial, thus giving a type of staircase method. A typical staircase sequence is shown in Figure 9–7. The intensity was increased after an error and decreased after two correct responses in a row. The staircase procedure continued until 12 reversals in the staircase had been made. The threshold was taken to be the average intensity of the combined reversals. This

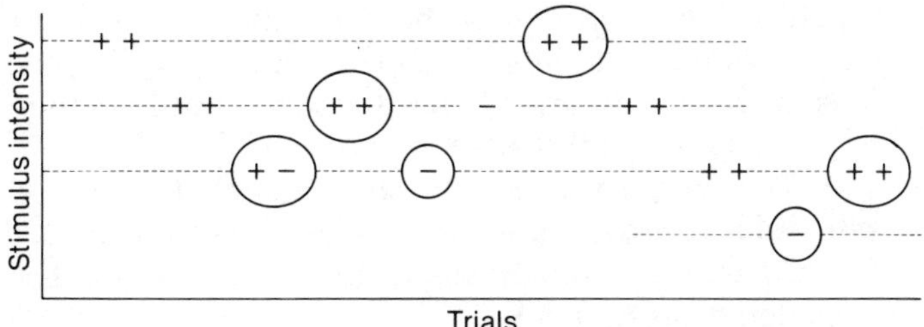

FIGURE 9–7. Typical sequence of responses obtained when measuring thresholds by the staircase method.

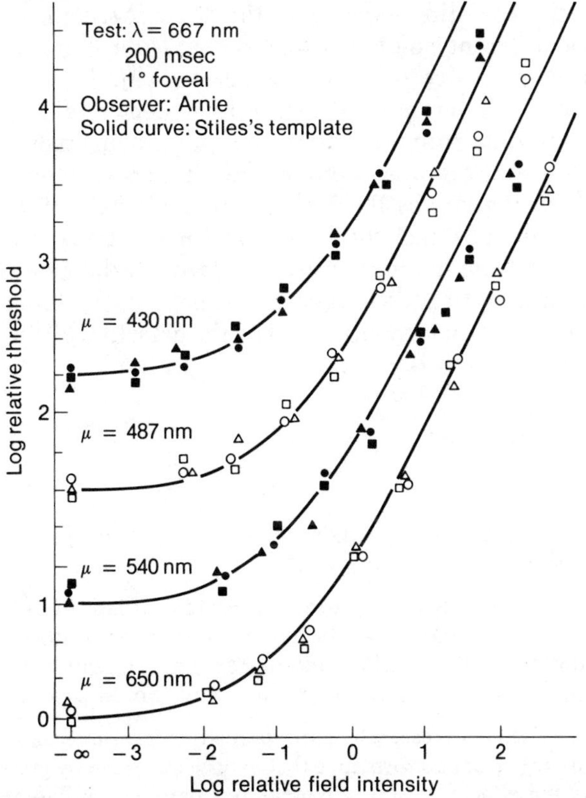

FIGURE 9–8. Graph of threshold as a function of field intensity for one subject.
Note. From "A field-additive pathway detects brief-duration long-wavelength incremental flashes" by B. A. Wandell and E. N. Pugh, Jr., *Vision Research,* 1980, *20,* 613–624. Copyright 1980 by Pergamon Press. Reprinted by permission of the publisher and authors.

procedure was repeated for each combination of background intensity and color.

No report is made of the order in which combinations were tested. This omission, common in psychophysical research, stems from the fact that the likelihood of finding significant order or sequence effects in such a study is minimal. Wandell and Pugh used two subjects in their experiment, a paid subject and one of the experimenters. This practice of using an experimenter as a subject also is common to psychophysical research inasmuch as the methods used make it unlikely that knowledge of the hypothesis will influence the outcome.

The design was a factorial experiment in that all combinations of selected background intensities and colors were used. It differs from most factorial experiments because it used only two subjects whose data were considered separately.

The results of the experiment for one subject are shown in Figure 9–8. The abscissa shows the intensity of the background against which the flash was seen. The ordinate shows the threshold for seeing the flash. Each curve is for a different color of background. Note that each curve has been displaced vertically from the next curve by .5 units on the ordinate to make it possible to differentiate the data from each condition. The lowest curve shows the data from all conditions pooled together. The curves drawn through the data points were derived from the pooled data.

From the curves the authors concluded that the color of the background did not affect the threshold for detecting the flash under their conditions. Note the impressive regularity of the data. The data points fit the line well with little variability. There is little doubt that Wandell and Pugh's conclusions are supported by the data. In addition, the data from the other subject were similar.

SUMMARY

1. Experiments using single subjects have been performed for as long as psychology has existed.
2. The single-subject tradition assumes that variability is imposed by the situation and therefore can be removed by careful attention to experimental control. The individual-differences group-research tradition assumes that much of the variability is intrinsic and should be statistically analyzed.
3. Single-subject research has several advantages over group research: focusing on individual performance that may be obscured by group research, focusing on big effects, avoiding ethical and practical problems in forming control groups, and permitting greater flexibility in design.
4. Averaging the data in group experiments may obscure individual performance because the average data may not resemble the performance of any single individual.
5. Group experiments that find small but significant effects may have little clinical or practical significance.
6. The term *power* refers to the probability that a statistical test will find a significant difference when there actually is a difference in the population

from which the sample is drawn. A researcher can increase the power of an experiment by increasing the sample size or by increasing the size of the effect. The single-subject tradition prefers to focus on increasing the size of the effect.

7. Basic control strategies in single-subject research include: obtaining a stable baseline, using withdrawal of the treatment, repeating treatments, changing only one variable at a time, using multiple baselines, and employing a changing criterion.

8. Withdrawal of the treatment is called the ABA design. Two major difficulties with the design are that the treatment may be irreversible, or that the experimenter may wish to leave the subjects in the new state rather than return them to the original condition.

9. When treatment is repeated, the experiment is called an ABAB design. The ABAB design removes one of the objections to the ABA design in that it leaves the subject in the trained state.

10. When a single-subject experiment has several variables, only one variable should be changed at a time.

11. The A-B-A-B-BC-B-BC design is often called the interaction design, although it does not permit the testing for an interaction as defined earlier in this book. Every condition is both preceded and followed by the same condition at least once, and only one variable is changed at a time.

12. The multiple-baseline design is an effective way of demonstrating that the manipulation caused the behavior change. The manipulation is introduced at different times for different behaviors to see if the onset of behavior change coincides with the manipulation for each behavior.

13. The changing-criterion design introduces successively more stringent criteria for reinforcement over time. It is useful when the behavior change is irreversible.

14. The first example given of a single-subject experiment came from a clinical application of operant techniques to eliminate hyperventilation.

15. The second example came from psychophysical research on color vision.

SUGGESTIONS FOR FURTHER READING

Hersen, M., & Barlow, D. H. *Single case experimental designs*. New York: Pergamon Press, 1976. The emphasis in this book is on clinical research.

Johnston, J. M., & Pennypacker, H. S. *Strategies and tactics of human behavioral research*. Hillsdale, N.J.: Erlbaum, 1980.

READING BETWEEN THE LINES

The following problems are presented for you to solve. See Reading Between the Lines in Chapter 1 for an introduction to them. The answers are given in Appendix A.

20. ELECTRICAL INHIBITION OF AGGRESSION IN A CHARGING BULL

Jose Delgado (1969) received a great deal of publicity for a demonstration in which he entered an arena with a bull that had an electrode implanted in a part of the brain known as the caudate nucleus. The electrode was connected to a radio receiver attached to the bull's horn. When Delgado pressed a button, an electrical stimulus would be transmitted to the bull's brain. First, Delgado induced the bull to attack him. Then, while the bull was charging him, Delgado pressed the button, which caused the bull to turn sharply to one side and stop. Delgado claimed that he had stopped the charge by inhibiting the part of the brain that was involved with aggression. What other reason could account for the bull's sudden change of heart about goring Delgado?

21. THE PHYSIOLOGY OF ATTENTION

The advances made during the 1950s in the knowledge of brain function led many investigators to look for the physiological bases of psychological functions. One such investigator was Raoul Hernandez-Peon, who sought the physiological basis of attention (Hernandez-Peon, Scherrer, & Jouvet, 1956). He put electrodes into the cochlear nuclei of the brains of cats. This part of the auditory system was a likely place to look for the mechanism of attention to auditory stimuli, based on previous research. Another part of the brain was believed to control the activity in this nucleus much like a switch turns off a light. Hernandez-Peon recorded the activity in the cochlear nucleus when sounds were presented to the cat. He found a big response to novel stimuli that decreased when the cat became bored with the tone. He also found that the response to the tone was less when the cat was distracted by a mouse. These results were taken as evidence that the cochlear nucleus is involved in the mechanism of attention to auditory stimuli. Auditory information is believed to be switched off before it reaches the rest of the brain. Can you think of any other explanation for the reduction in activity in the cochlear nucleus?

NONEXPERIMENTAL RESEARCH

A chapter on nonexperimental research might seem out of place in a book on experimental methods in psychology. Recall, though, that we defined experimental psychology somewhat broadly to encompass scientific psychology, which would allow a place for nonexperimental methods in science. We have held up the experiment as the most desirable way to investigate behavior, when feasible, because it allows the most unambiguous conclusions to be drawn about the causes of an observed effect. When a true experiment is not feasible, then a quasi experiment is next best because it retains certain features of experimental control. As we lose control over more and more aspects of the research situation, we eventually reach a point at which the research becomes nonexperimental. Exactly where to draw the line is not especially clear or important. In this chapter we will discuss four popular types of nonexperimental research: naturalistic observation, surveys, archival research, and case studies.

Nonexperimental research has two main characteristics. The first is that no attempt is made to manipulate an independent variable. Perhaps we have an effect whose cause or causes we are seeking to discover. For example, we might wish to know if hot summer weather is the cause of riots. The second characteristic is that the data collection procedure often must compromise some degree of control in return for obtaining the data. For example, in purely observational research we may have to permit all kinds of extraneous variables to go uncontrolled during the observation period. Or, we decide to examine public records that may be almost, but not exactly, in the form we desire. Or, we must keep a questionnaire short in order to gain the cooperation of subjects.

Correlational research nonexperimental research that measures two or more variables to determine the degree of relationship between them

Observational research study method in which the researcher observes and records ongoing behavior but does not attempt to change it

Survey assessing public opinion by the use of questionnaire and sampling methods

Archival research study method that examines public records to obtain data and test hypotheses

Case study exploratory study of an existing problem as a means of creating and testing hypotheses

Nonexperimental research often is called **correlational research** because it seeks causes of behavior by looking for correlations among variables. The term is somewhat misleading, however, because all research is correlational to the extent that it seeks functional relationships between variables (compare Cook & Campbell, 1979). Calculating correlations among variables does not make the research "correlational" in the strict sense. We often calculate correlations among variables in the truest of experiments. What makes research "correlational" in the loose sense is the inability to independently manipulate some variable. In "correlational" research relationships are studied among variables, none of which may be the actual cause. On the other hand, alternative causes are easier to rule out in an experiment because of the ability to manipulate variables.

Just as it is not fruitful to distinguish sharply between quasi-experimental and nonexperimental research, there is no point in trying to be precise about types of nonexperimental research. It is convenient, though, to distinguish several varieties of nonexperimental research. The first may be called **observational research,** in which the researcher simply observes ongoing behavior. Examples are field observation of ducks from a blind or television monitoring of people in a store. The second category of nonexperimental research is the **survey,** in which the subject is requested to cooperate by responding to questions. Nearly everyone has experienced a survey.

The third category is **archival research,** in which public records are examined in order to test hypotheses about the causes of behavior. The fourth category we will call the **case study.** This category is different from the others in that the research investigates a particular existing problem that comes to the attention of the researcher. The problem may be a practical one that must be solved as soon as possible, or it may be an event that intrigues a researcher. Case studies are typified by the opportunistic, ad hoc nature of the methods used to study the problems. We will consider examples of each of these four types of nonexperimental methods.

OBSERVATIONAL RESEARCH

Naturalistic observation observational research of subjects in their natural environment carried out so as not to disturb the subjects

Observational research involves the recording of ongoing behavior without attempting to influence it. This method takes two general forms: naturalistic observation and participant-observer research.

Naturalistic Observation

Naturalistic observation is research conducted in such a way that the subject's behavior is not disturbed by the observation process. Observational research has played a prominent role in the related science of biology but is not employed much by psychologists. Perhaps the fact that psychologists and their favorite object of study are the same species accounts for the difference. We tend to assume, often incorrectly, that we have a great deal of insight into the important categories of human behavior and their causes. Careful observation of naturally occurring behavior might suggest many fruitful hypotheses for research and might help prevent half-baked experiments.

An excellent example of the use of naturalistic observation is found in the work of Erving Goffman (for example, 1971). He has described such naturally occurring behavior as how people avoid bumping into each other on public sidewalks. He finds that people engage in rituals of looking at each other and giving signals to indicate their intention to pass on one side or the other. Many people would not be aware that they engage in these behaviors. Because Goffman's studies do not include the kind of objective records that would allow one to evaluate the generality of his findings, we should probably classify them as casual observation, rather than strictly objective naturalistic observation. However, his insights have led other investigators to conduct more objective tests of his ideas. In a similar but looser way investigators have turned to the writings of a Shakespeare or a Dostoevski for hypotheses which they then verify in a more rigorous fashion.

A particularly good example of how Goffman's suggestions have led to more rigorous work is given by a naturalistic observation study by Peter Collett and Peter Marsh (1974). They placed a videotape recorder on the seventh floor of a building overlooking a busy pedestrian intersection. They recorded and later analyzed instances when two people met in such a way that both had to move in order to avoid collision. They noticed a striking difference in the way men and women maneuvered in passing. Men tended to turn so as to face the other person, whereas women tended to turn away. The differences were large. Of the men 75 percent passed in the facing orientation, compared with only 17 percent of the women. Collett and Marsh hypothesized that the women turned away in order to avoid brushing the other person with their breasts. This hypothesis was confirmed by examining the frequency with which men and women held an arm across their bodies as they passed. Women used the arm cross more often than men, particularly in those instances when they were turned toward the other person as they passed. This occurrence was not related to whether they were carrying anything in their hands.

Another example of naturalistic observation is given by Don Zimmerman and Candace West (1975). They were interested in whether patterns of conversational speech would reflect power and dominance between individuals. In particular, they were interested in looking for sex differences in interruptions and other turn-taking behavior in conversations. They tape-recorded conversations between sets of two persons in public places around a university, such as a coffee shop. They chose conversations that could be overheard easily in the normal course of being in a public place.

They studied 10 female-female pairs, 10 male-male pairs, and 11 cross-sex pairs. Whenever possible, they obtained the permission of the conversationalists to use their recordings. Sometimes, however, people left before the researchers could approach them. All personal identifications were edited out of the transcripts of the recordings. Zimmerman and West found that 96 percent of interruptions in the cross-sex pairs were made by the males. These investigators decided to learn whether this finding was limited to the type of setting or to people who might be already acquainted. They conducted a laboratory experiment in which pairs of people were asked to chat and get acquainted "before the experiment begins" (1978, unpublished). In five conversations between males and females, all of the males did more interrupting, with the men doing 73 percent of the interrupting on the average. The amount of interrupting was unrelated to which person talked first.

The Zimmerman and West research illustrates a typical and admirable progression in observational research from idea to naturalistic observation to laboratory. This move to the laboratory allows researchers to rule out sources of confounding that would occur in the original naturalistic situation.

As we mentioned earlier, naturalistic observation has been a popular method with biologists. Perhaps the most famous examples of naturalistic observation come from scientists who work in ethology, the branch of biology that deals with the study of behavior. Although ethology is synonymous in many people's minds with naturalistic observation of animal behavior, ethology concerns itself with behavior as a product of natural selection and as a tool in studying the evolution of species. Much important ethological work is observational, yet an increasing amount of ethological work is conducted in the laboratory.

An example of naturalistic observation by ethologists is given by the work of Konrad Lorenz (for example, 1958) on the courtship behavior of ducks. Most people who watch ducks in a pond or zoo simply see a mass of random activity. After observing the behavior of ducks for countless hours and taking motion pictures, Lorenz was able to identify about 20 different specific behaviors. One of these is the grunt-whistle, described here for the mallard and pintail: "The male flick[s] its bill backward and upward through the water, throw[s] a shower of droplets toward the 'courted' bird, then rear[s] up and back in the water, and finally shak[es] the tail after settling back to the normal position. . . . A whistle is uttered during the display, followed by a low grunt" (Sharpe & Johnsgard, 1966, p. 263).

By studying these behaviors in many species of ducks, Lorenz was able to clarify the evolutionary relationships among them. The assumption is that species of ducks that share more specific behaviors are more closely related. The validity of the behavioral method is confirmed if the animals that share similar behaviors can be crossbred and the behavior of the resulting offspring studied. Behaviors that both parent species share should appear in the offspring, but behaviors that only one parent displays should be absent or present in a weakened or distorted form.

Roger Sharpe and Paul Johnsgard successfully crossbred mallard and pintail ducks. The offspring varied among themselves in the degree to which they resembled the two parent species. Some were much like mallards and some were mostly pintail, but the majority fell somewhere in between. Observation of the offspring showed that their behavior was closely related to their appearance; those that were mostly mallard showed mostly mallard behavior, and so forth. According to the prediction, behaviors shown in only one of the parent species were weakened or absent. Thus the importance of heredity on behavior was demonstrated and the predictions of ethological theory were confirmed.

The Sharpe and Johnsgard study is an interesting blend of observation and experiment. The researchers manipulated the genetics of the animals but did not present stimuli to them. They simply observed the natural behavior of their subjects after having created them to specification!

Naturalistic observing has few hard and fast rules. Two that should be mentioned are: careful record keeping and care for privacy of the subjects. Careful record keeping is what separates naturalistic observation from casual impression formation. The observer should keep a record of all behaviors of interest and the times at which they occur. This recording of information is facilitated by using movie cameras, videotape or audiotape recorders, or other devices. Many times using slow-motion or speeded-motion recording is helpful to make behavior patterns easier to see; stop-action recording can freeze critical moments. In the study of pedestrian passing, motion was frozen at the instant of passing. In the study of conversations, all tape-recorded utterances were transcribed to paper for analysis.

Participant-Observer Research

Participant-observer research observational research in which the observer joins and participates in a group in order to record behavior

One kind of observational research that has provided important results is **participant-observer research,** where investigators join naturally occurring groups and record their observations. One of the most famous of these studies was that of Leon Festinger, H. W. Riecken, and Stanley Schachter (1956), who joined a group that believed the world would come to an end at a certain time. Group members believed that they would be rescued by a flying saucer. The psychologists carefully observed interactions between group members and the effect the disconfirmation of their prediction had on their behavior. Surprisingly, when the world did not end, the group members began to be more open and less analytical about their beliefs. This research was instrumental in the development of Festinger's theory of cognitive dissonance, which predicts how people deal with conflicting beliefs. We should note that careful records and diaries are crucial in evaluating participant-observer studies because of the increased possibility of subjectivity in these situations.

Problems in Observational Research

Two important problems are present in participant-observer research. First, by entering the group, the observer by definition changes it to some extent. Therefore the act of observing the behavior changes the behavior to be observed. A large group may not be influenced much by an observer's presence, whereas a small group may be influenced considerably. In general, participant-observer research is done in unusual groups that can absorb an observer whose presence would have little effect.

The second problem is the ethical question of invasion of privacy. Participant observers cannot always obtain informed consent from their subjects. Some researchers hold that participant-observer research is therefore always unethical. Others point out that professionals such as journalists are permitted to engage in this type of practice. They argue that if psychologists do not perform participant-observer research, they are withholding the application of psychological techniques and insights to important social problems.

The care for the privacy of subjects was discussed in Chapter 6 under the category of research ethics. Here we will only note that naturalistic observation may involve recording behaviors that, even though conducted in public, may still be of a private nature. In one study a researcher feigned homosexuality in order to study the behavior of homosexuals. He gained their confidence by serving as a lookout in a public washroom while they engaged in sex. Later, having noted the license numbers of their cars, he obtained identities from the department of motor vehicles by subterfuge. Then, in disguise, he joined a research team and interviewed his subjects as a public health worker (Holden, 1979). Although the investigator did not reveal the identities of the subjects and his conclusions are supposed to be sympathetic to homosexuals, he did obtain the data under false pretenses and subjected the persons he studied to risk. This study later was discussed at a conference on research ethics as a prime example of research that should not be conducted (Holden, 1979).

SURVEY RESEARCH

Conducting research via surveys is sometimes useful. Often the purpose of a survey is simply to determine how people feel about a particular issue such as gun control or the performance of the president of the United States. Other surveys may attempt to find out the effect of some event on people's behavior. For example, surveys conducted after the Three Mile Island nuclear accident attempted to determine who evacuated the area and for what reasons. In addition, surveys provide an opportunity to examine correlations among the subjects' responses and to look for possible patterns of cause and effect.

A major function of surveys is to dispel myths. One such myth is that women whose children have grown up and left home suffer a kind of depression called the empty nest syndrome. Lillian Rubin (1979) surveyed 160 women in this situation in life and found that, rather than being depressed, virtually all of them experienced a sense of relief. Other surveys surprise us by indicating how widespread child abuse and wife beating are.

Because survey research is technical and complex, we will give only a brief overview here. Nevertheless, it is important to have an idea of the techniques because survey research is so often used.

Types of Samples

Surveys differ greatly in value according to how the respondents are sampled. We will discuss three types of samples: uncontrolled samples, haphazard samples, and probability samples.

Uncontrolled Samples. Magazines and radio stations often publish questions for their audiences to respond to. Obviously these broadcast surveys lack reliability. One station says, "Our poll is not a scientific survey but a rough estimate of the views of our listeners." The results from an **uncontrolled sample** are worse than a rough estimate, however. All of the data come from people who are motivated to respond. Most listeners feel moderately in favor of some issue such as gun control, but a few are strongly, perhaps violently, opposed. An uncontrolled survey will be biased in the direction of the more vocal persons.

Uncontrolled sample population subgroup that the researcher has no control in selecting

The British magazine *New Scientist* polled its readers on their attitudes toward ESP (Evans, 1973). The results showed that 67 percent of those responding considered ESP to be either "an established fact" or a "likely possibility." This sounds like impressive evidence in favor of the scientific credibility of ESP until one discovers that the return rate on this questionnaire was only about 2 percent. People who believe in ESP likely would be more motivated to respond than nonbelievers, thus giving biased results.

Although a survey with an uncontrolled sample can be considered a special type of sample, rate of return is an important consideration in all survey research. Refusal to cooperate, failure to return a questionnaire, or unavailability of target persons should be recorded. Possible biases thereby introduced should be kept in mind when the research is evaluated.

Haphazard Samples. Sometimes the surveyor has control over whom to sample but uses haphazard methods of obtaining people. A teacher may survey a class as a representative sample of college students; a television station may send a crew out to interview 10 people on the street with instructions to include 5 women, 2 blacks, 3 teenagers, and 1 adorable little girl. These **haphazard samples** are almost as worthless as uncontrolled samples. Perhaps the most famous haphazard survey was conducted by the now defunct *Literary Digest,* which obtained respondents from telephone books and automobile registration lists. This survey predicted that Landon would win the 1936 presidential election over Roosevelt by a landslide. It overlooked the fact, however, that during the Great Depression people who could afford telephones and automobiles were more likely to vote Republican.

Haphazard sample population subgroup that the researcher may have control over selecting but uses hit-or-miss methods for selection

Probability Samples. The most satisfactory surveys obtain their respondents on a probability basis. The researcher makes an effort to assure that each person in the population has an equal chance of being represented. The most straightforward technique is **simple random sampling.** According to this method, a list is made of all members of the population and a random sample is drawn from the list. Suppose that you wish to know student attitudes toward coeducational dorms at a particular college. You would obtain the student directory of the college and compare its list of names with a list of numbers in a random-number table. If you wanted to sample 10 percent of the students, you could take every name that matched up with a particular digit, such as 0. If you wanted 1 percent of the students, you could compare the names with pairs of digits, taking names that matched up with one pair, such as 00.

Simple random sample group chosen from an entire population wherein the selection is unbiased among individuals

If you are surveying a population that has identifiable subgroups that are likely to differ markedly in their responses, you can improve accuracy by obtaining a **stratified random sample.** Suppose you are interested in attitudes toward women's right on a certain college campus. Men and women are likely to differ widely in their responses. If the college has 55 percent men and 45 percent women students and you want a sample of 100, you would randomly select 55 men and 45 women. Thus by stratified random sampling you have ensured that the proportion of men and women matches the college population.

Stratified random sample group chosen to proportionately represent certain segments in a larger population

Random samples are extremely accurate. A sample as small as 1,000 individuals will allow a survey researcher to estimate within plus or minus 3.2 percent the attitude of a population as large as that of the United States (Weisberg & Bowen, 1977).

Random samples are not always feasible, however. For instance, making a list of every person in the United States would be impossible. Even random sampling of a college may be difficult. Suppose there is no student directory. You may decide to obtain the students from classes. Rather than taking every tenth student in each class, sampling every student in one-tenth of the classes would be more efficient. This method is an example of **cluster sampling.** You would obtain a list of all classes at the college. Next you would stratify the classes into sciences, humanities, and

Cluster sample group selected by using clusters or groupings from a larger population

so forth, as well as into lower and upper division courses. Then you would randomly select one-tenth of the classes in each category. Even though the students that you sample by clustering probably would be more alike than in a purely random sample (because students within classes are likely to be similar in background), the larger sample you obtain would offset the disadvantages of not having a purely random sample. Commercial polls, such as the Gallup Poll, use a sophisticated version of cluster sampling. They are able to determine attitudes with a margin of error of plus or minus 4 percent with a sample size of 1,000, compared with 3.2 percent for a simple random sample of the same size (Weisberg & Bowen, 1977).

How a Questionnaire Is Designed

We will briefly indicate some basic principles of questionnaire construction so that you will be aware of the major pitfalls. The principal concern is that the questionnaire items be unambiguous. Each item should address a single question and do so in a clear manner. The following item is ambiguous: "College students should receive grades in their courses because this prepares them for the competitive world outside of college." This item contains both an opinion about grading and a reason for grading. A person might agree with giving grades but disagree with the reason stated for grading students. It would be better to phrase the item, "College students should receive grades in their course work." Another item could be addressed to the desirability of preparing students for a competitive society.

The next consideration is to write the question in a way that will not bias the results. Two congresspersons each may survey their constituents on attitudes toward abortion. The first one's newsletter asks, "Do you believe in killing unborn babies?" The second one's newsletter asks, "Should women be forced to bear unwanted children?" Even if the people in the two congressional districts had identical attitudes toward abortion, the congresspersons could quote their respective survey results as indicating dramatically opposite attitudes toward abortion.

Bias often enters when respondents perceive one alternative as more socially acceptable than the other, a phenomenon called *social desirability*. Researchers avoid this occurrence by wording questions so that each alternative appears equally socially desirable. The question on abortion might better be structured as follows: "Women should be permitted to decide for themselves whether to continue a pregnancy." In order to balance out people's natural tendency to agree with any question, an experimenter could include a question that presents the matter the other way: "Abortions should be permitted only for certain specified reasons."

Attitudes elicited by questionnaire items frequently are measured on a seven-point scale. Seven categories of agreement are the maximum that can be distinguished on most dimensions. The item might be laid out as follows, with instructions for the respondent to place a check in the space that most closely corresponds with his or her attitude:

Women should be permitted to decide for themselves whether to continue a pregnancy.

Agree ___ ___ ___ ___ ___ ___ ___ Disagree

The numbers need not be indicated but can be assigned later when the responses are scored.

ARCHIVAL RESEARCH

Archival data factual information that exists in public records

The term *archival research* refers to research conducted using data that the researcher had no part in collecting. **Archival data** are those that exist in public records, or archives. The researcher simply examines or selects the data for analysis. Archival research is appropriate in many instances. Data that bear on the hypothesis may already exist, and collecting new data would be wasteful. Or, ethics or logistics may make it infeasible to conduct an experiment relating the variables of interest. In a moment we will consider archival research on suicides and sex crimes, both topics inappropriate for experimental research.

On the other hand, archival research has limitations. First, most archival data are collected for nonscientific reasons. Governments and private agencies collect the data for their own purposes, and such data often do not suit the purposes of the scientist. In order for archival data to be scientifically useful, the agency collecting the data must ask questions similar to the scientist's or must inadvertently collect data that is of value to the scientist. Second, because archival research is by nature carried out after the fact, ruling out alternative hypotheses for particular observed correlations may be difficult. A researcher who relies on archival data is at the mercy of any biases that occur in collecting the data. Police records are notoriously subject to bias. Many categories of crime are seldom reported to the police. Only one in four rapes, for instance, is reported (Court, 1976). A 400 percent increase in rapes would suddenly seem to have occurred if every rape were reported. Police, in turn, use latitude in determining whether to record a particular incident as a criminal act or to look the other way. Accordingly, crime statistics can vary because of a crackdown motivated by an upcoming election or by individual officers' being concerned over their own efficiency ratings.

A successful use of archival research is given by David Phillips's analysis of motor vehicle fatalities (1977). Authorities have long suspected that many automobile fatalities are suicides rather than accidents. Phillips hypothesized that if suicides are triggered by reports of other suicides, then motor vehicle fatalities should increase just after publicized suicides. He studied all motor vehicle fatalities occurring in California during the week that followed the reporting of suicides on the front page of the state's two largest newspapers. Then he compared the fatalities with those in a control period in another year. He found a 9 percent increase in the number of fatalities in the week following the suicides, with a maximum increase of 30 percent on the third day after the stories appeared. By correlating the increase in fatalities following each story with the total circulation of all newspapers that covered the story, he showed that the publicity was responsible for the increase. Further analyses bolstered his conclusion that the increase was the result of a correlation with the publicized suicides. Details were similar between the suicide stories and the type of accidents that increased following the stories. For example, if a murder/suicide was reported, there was an increase in multiple-fatality accidents, and so forth (Phillips, 1979).

CASE STUDIES

All of the types of research we have discussed so far involve planning on the part of the researcher. In fact, a good research program is usually well thought out in advance. Many case studies, however, result from problems that present themselves to researchers as opportunities that must be grasped quickly or lost. Little time may be available for planning, and the study often must be conducted under difficult conditions. Case studies defy characterization because of their ad hoc nature.

An example of case-study research is the study of "assembly-line hysteria" or "mass psychogenic illness" by Michael Smith, Michael Colligan, and Joseph Hurrell, Jr. (1978). In this phenomenon, which occasionally occurs in factories or schools, many people suddenly suffer such physical symptoms as headache, nausea, and blurred vision. Typically, the outbreak is triggered by a strange odor, but investigation reveals no toxic substance that can account for the sickness. Colligan and his team at the National Institute for Occupational Safety and Health (NIOSH) investigated a number of such incidents, along with physicians and industrial hygienists.

After interviewing many people who experienced the symptoms and after administering a wide variety of psychological tests and comparing the results to a control group of workers who were not affected by the outbreak, the NIOSH team concluded that the main cause of mass psychogenic illness is physical or psychological stress in the workplace. This stress provides the setting for a potential outbreak. The trigger is a strange odor or other stimulus to which someone reacts with physical symptoms that increase the distress. For example, the person may begin hyperventilating, which causes dizziness. Someone then attributes the cause of the distress to the strange odor, and the symptoms quickly spread to other workers (Colligan and Stockton, 1978). Investigation showed that the affected workers had been experiencing more boredom, social isolation, and physical stress than had the unaffected workers.

This study of mass psychogenic illness is typical of case studies. The efforts of the NIOSH team were directed toward practical problem. Cases appeared unpredictably and required prompt attention. A multidisciplinary team approach was used. Members of each discipline used several techniques to rule out various explanations and narrow down the possible causes. A special questionnaire was developed for use in succeeding cases. Other case studies are as varied as this one. In fact, one of the few generalizations possible about case studies is that it is difficult to generalize about them.

SUMMARY

1. Nonexperimental research has two main characteristics: no attempt is made to manipulate an independent variable, and the data collection procedure often must compromise some degree of control.
2. Although nonexperimental research is called correlational research, all research is correlational in that it seeks to find relationships between variables.
3. Nonexperimental research methods include: observational, survey, archival, and case study.
4. Observational research involves recording a subject's behavior without attempting to influence it.
5. Naturalistic observation involves recording a subject's behavior in such a way that the behavior is not disturbed by the process of making the observation.
6. Participant-observer research requires the observers to join naturally occurring groups and to record their observations. Invasion of privacy poses an ethical problem in participant-observer research. A practical problem is the likelihood that the researcher may influence the group as well as observe it.
7. Surveys are useful ways to determine the attitudes of people on particular questions, to determine the effect of some natural event, or to look for patterns of cause and effect among many variables.
8. Surveys may use uncontrolled samples, haphazard samples, or probability samples.
9. Probability samples include: simple random samples, stratified random samples, and cluster samples. Simple random samples are feasible only with relatively small populations. Stratified random samples permit the researcher to assure that various segments of the population are represented proportionately in the sample. Cluster samples are commonly used with large surveys.

10. Questionnaires must be written so that the items are unambiguous and unbiased. One prominent bias is that some answers have greater social desirability than others.
11. Archival research involves the examination of public records. Advantages are that the data do not need to be collected by the researcher and that the research afforded may be on problems not amenable to experimentation. Disadvantages are that the researcher is limited to the types of questions asked by the agency that collected the data and by any biases present in the collection procedure.
12. Case studies are ad hoc studies of existing problems. They take many forms and cannot be neatly classified.

SUGGESTIONS FOR FURTHER READING

KIDDER, L. *Research methods in social relations* (4th ed.). New York: Holt, Rinehart, & Winston, 1981. This book has several chapters devoted to nonexperimental techniques: observational methods, questionnaires and interviews, archival research, and sampling of individuals from a population.

WEBB, E. J., CAMPBELL, D. T., SCHWARTZ, R. D., & SECHRIST, L. *Unobtrusive measures.* Chicago: Rand McNally, 1966. This book contains thought-provoking discussions of observational and archival research, with emphasis on methods that do not cause the subjects to be aware that they are being studied.

READING BETWEEN THE LINES

The following problems are presented for you to solve. See Reading Between the Lines in Chapter 1 for an introduction to them. The answers are given in Appendix A.

22. CLEVER HANS

In the early 1900s in Germany a sensation was caused by a horse that had amazing intellectual abilities. Although horses are not usually known for their intelligence, Mr. von Osten's horse Hans was able to add, subtract, multiply, and divide. Hans could tell all of the factors of a number and could even add fractions. He could tell the day of the week on which a certain date would fall. In addition, he had perfect pitch and could identify chords played on a musical instrument. If the notes played did not constitute a pleasing chord, he would indicate which notes should be removed.

He could read German but not Latin or French. In short, Hans was able to do many things that a college graduate might well have trouble doing.

Hans answered questions by tapping with his hoof to indicate numbers and by moving his head for yes, no, and various directions. He demonstrated his ability to read either by choosing one card that contained the desired word out of several or by tapping to indicate the rows and columns of a specially prepared table of the alphabet. When asked a question, Hans would first nod if he understood or shake his head if he did not. No wonder he was called Clever Hans and was the subject of numerous newspaper and magazine articles. Hans was studied by many people, including zoologists, a circus manager, an animal behaviorist, a sensory physiologist, and a psychologist, all prominent in their fields. They concluded that no trick was involved and that Hans was genuine. What could these well-educated people have overlooked that would explain Hans's amazing abilities?

23. ORCHESTRA CONDUCTORS LIVE LONGER

A study found that orchestra conductors lived longer than average and concluded that the life that conductors lead somehow enables them to live longer. The important factor could be the effect of staying active throughout life, because maestros tend to retire late or not at all. Or, perhaps it could be the effect of making music. Can you think of any other explanation for the longevity of orchestra conductors?

REPORTING THE RESULTS

Of all the steps in the research process, the most crucial may be the communication of the findings to others. The most perfect experiment in the world makes no contribution to science if the results are not reported to the scientific community. As we discussed in an earlier chapter, science is a social enterprise. It grows by the public discussion and assimilation of knowledge contributed by individual scientists.

Scientific communication takes place in different ways. We think of the article published in a scholarly journal as the standard form of scientific communication. This form is known as archival publication because these journals are publicly available in places such as libraries. Archival publication is the permanent record of science. As such it clearly serves a vital function, but it is not the only way scientific findings are published.

Invisible college informal communication network of persons having common scientific interests

Another important type of communication goes on informally over the telephone, by mail, by visits to laboratories, and at professional meetings. The people who communicate in this way about their research are said to form **invisible colleges**, informal networks of people with common scientific interests. Through this informal communication new ideas and results are usually first discussed. Published papers typically appear one or two years after the information is available to the invisible college. Informal communication not only allows scientists to keep up with what is happening in other laboratories, it also permits researchers to present their ideas in a tentative form before committing themselves in archival publications. For these reasons, it is important for scientists to be aware of the role of the invisible college and to become part of the one that operates in their area of research. Many a young scientist has been frustrated by the difficulties of "breaking into the club" by relying on archival communication. Therefore we will discuss how to present findings at scientific meetings as well as via the standard article in an archival journal.

THE WRITTEN REPORT

In this section we will discuss the writing of a formal report as it is submitted to a scientific journal. We will follow the American Psychological Association format because it is used by most psychological journals as well as by other publications. Once you are familiar with APA format, it is convenient to work with. A full discussion appears in the *Publication Manual of the American Psychological Association* (1974), which you can refer to for details. Another way to learn how to prepare a paper for publication is to look through a recent issue of the journal that you wish to submit your paper to and study its format.

General

Writing a scientific report is not easy. From reading a few research articles, many students get the feeling that it should be easy—just use a lot of big words and long sentences, stick with the passive voice, and above all sound dull and pompous. Sometimes these attributes, unfortunately, are typical of scientific writing. The purpose of scientific writing, though, is the same as that of all good writing: to convey a message clearly, concisely, and interestingly. It is true that scientific writing must conform to a certain format in the interest of economy. Yet every writer should try, within that format, to write as well as possible, and this takes effort. Many scientists with reputations as good writers testify that they must work hard to make their writing seem effortless.

Scientific writing, like other expository writing, aims to persuade as well as to inform (Sternberg, 1977). If you simply throw your results and theory down on paper and "let them speak for themselves," you will be disappointed with the outcome. Young scientists sometimes underestimate the importance of good writing in gaining acceptance for their ideas. Repeatedly in the history of science the person who wrote more clearly and persuasively was remembered and the one who wrote poorly was forgotten. We can capture the essence of good report writing in three words: clarity, brevity, and felicity. The first two terms are familiar; the word *felicity* means pleasingness of style.

Clarity. The most important element of writing a scientific paper is to say exactly what you mean as directly as possible. You must look at each sentence and ask whether someone could mistake its meaning. Sometimes this approach means avoiding common usages, such as the word *hopefully* when you mean to say "it is hoped." Consider the following sentence:

"Hopefully, the subjects followed the instructions." Does it mean that the author hopes the subjects followed the instructions or that the subjects followed the instructions eagerly or full of hope? Eliminating such problems requires work and practice. Ask someone else to read a draft of your paper to suggest places where the meaning is unclear.

Brevity. Next, work at brevity. Does every word, phrase, and sentence contribute to the paper? Years ago, research papers were long and discursive. Today, because of space shortage in journals, papers must be as brief as possible. Although the need for brevity can sometimes lead to an unfortunate terseness of style, brevity can also be an aid to good communication. Pascal once apologized to a correspondent, "I have made this letter longer than usual because I lack the time to make it shorter." Writers sometimes attempt to clarify by repeating instead of by revising material so that it is clear in the first place. Remember that your intended reader is a busy person whose time you are competing for. If you had an appointment with your reader in person, you would be careful not to waste his or her time.

Felicity. Felicity, or pleasingness of style, may seem out of place in scientific writing, but scientific reporting, too, needs liveliness and grace. Although many forms of humor are best avoided because they can distract from the message or even backfire, there is a place for wit. A well-known paper in vision research was entitled, "What the frog's eye tells the frog's brain" (Lettvin, Maturana, McCulloch, & Pitts, 1959). The title conveys the topic of the paper in such a way that people want to read it. This paper has become a classic in its field, helped in part by its catchy title.

Documenting Your Paper

An essential feature of scientific writing is that certain types of statements must be documented.

What to document. First, you must give credit to ideas that are other people's. Second, you need to show where your ideas fit into a larger framework. Third, your reader may want to know where to go for further information about the theory, methods, or data you discuss. It is not necessary to document statements that are common knowledge among your audience. For example, you do not need to document a reference to Pavlovian conditioning or Freudian theory. Beyond this generalization, however, one cannot give a clear rule on what to document. Perhaps one way of answering the question is to recall what it is like to read about scientific topics in popular literature. When scientific claims are made but not documented, readers who wish to learn more will be unable to do so. Who found this phenomenon? What methods were used? Under what conditions does it occur? What theories does it relate to? What do other scientists think of these ideas? All of these questions are unanswerable without documentation.

APA style of documentation. In APA style the authors of the work you are citing are named in the text, followed by the date of the publication:

Jones and Smith (1982) found that

Or you may say:

Recent work (Jones & Smith, 1982) shows that

Note that when the names appear outside of the parenthesis you use the word "and," but when they are inside the parenthesis you use the ampersand (&). If there are two authors, always list both names whenever you cite their work in the text. If there are three or more authors, list all names the first time you refer to the work:

Jones, Smith, and Brown (1981) found

Thereafter, list only the first author, followed by *et al.* and the year of publication:

Jones et al. (1981) found

The reference list will contain an entry for each work cited in the paper. There must be no entries in the reference list that are not cited in the paper and vice versa. A reference has three major parts: author(s), title, and facts of publication. Each part is separated by a period. Other information is separated by commas. For example:

Miller, G. A. The magical number seven, plus or minus two: Some limits on our capacity for processing information. *Psychological Review*, 1956, *63*, 81–97.

This particular example is of a journal article. The author data appear in the same form for all kinds of references (that have individual authors). The point to remember about titles is that the title of a book is underlined but the title of an article is not. The publication data may differ from one type of publication to the next, as the following examples show.

A reference to a journal article contains the following information: author(s), title, journal (underlined), year, volume (underlined), pages. Refer to the previous example for the appearance of a reference to a journal article. Most journals number all pages of a volume consecutively even though each volume may have several issues. Some journals, however, such as *Scientific American,* begin each issue with page one. For such publications it is necessary to give the issue number, as follows:

Parker, D. E. The vestibular apparatus. *Scientific American,* 1980, *243*(5), 118–135.

The following information is given for a book: author(s), title (underlined), city in which it was published, publisher, year. Here is an example of a reference to a book:

McBurney, D. H., & Collings, V. B. *Introduction to sensation/perception.* Englewood Cliffs, N.J.: Prentice-Hall, 1977.

Note that when the book is not published in a major city, you must give the state or country also.

When the work cited is a chapter in a book that contains chapters by different authors, the book is considered an edited volume. The following information is given for a reference to a chapter in an edited volume: author(s), title of chapter, editor(s), title of book (underlined), city in which it was published, publisher, year. Here is an example of a reference to a chapter in an edited volume:

Coppen, A. Biogenic amines and affective disorders. In B. T. Ho & W. M. McIsaac (Eds.), *Brain chemistry and mental disease.* New York: Plenum, 1971.

Note that the editors' names and initials are listed in forward rather than reverse order.

These three forms are the most common references, but they are by no means all of them. Refer to the *Publication Manual of the American Psychological Association* for other examples.

The Parts of a Paper

The parts of a paper are: (1) title, (2) authors and their affiliations, (3) abstract, (4) introduction, (5) method, (6) results, (7) discussion, (8) reference notes, (9) references, (10) footnotes, (11) tables, (12) figure captions, (13) figures. We have listed them in the order that they appear in a typescript submitted for publication in a journal. In the published form the footnotes, tables, figure captions, and figures are placed appropriately throughout the paper.

Each part of the paper serves a specific function, which we will consider in order. As you begin to write a paper, consult a recent issue of the journal you are writing for to see its style for a typical article.

On pages 224 to 239 we have reproduced an actual journal article (Barnes, Ickes, & Kidd, 1979) in the appropriate form for submission to a journal.* You should study this manuscript carefully for style. The numbers indicated refer to paragraphs in the *Publication Manual of the American Psychological Association.*

Following are some guidelines for typing the manuscript. Do not use erasable paper because it smudges easily and becomes messy. (If your typing is poor and you will make many mistakes, your instructor may accept a photocopy of a paper typed on erasable paper. A journal should receive an original on standard bond paper.) Leave wide margins, at least an inch all around. Double space *everything*. Start every section on a new page except for the method, results, and discussion sections. Together with the introduction, these sections form the body of the paper, which is typed straight through.

Title. The title is your chance to gain the attention of the desired audience. It should convey the main idea of the paper in a few words. Include key words that will catch the eye of a person scanning the table of contents of the journal or that will come up on computerized searches of the literature. Avoid words that do not contribute directly to the idea of the paper, such as "An experimental study of. . . ."

Authors and their affiliations. Authors usually are listed in order of the importance of their contributions to the paper, although some authors prefer an alphabetic or random listing. You will want to list your name in a form that you will be comfortable with for the rest of your career, so as to avoid having your work listed under several different names in bibliographic sources.

Abstract. The abstract is a brief (100 to 175 words) synopsis of the paper. It should summarize the problem, method, results, and conclusion. The abstract must be self-contained because it will be reproduced verbatim in *Psychological Abstracts* and other publications. Because of its condensed form, the abstract is the most difficult part of the paper to write and often is written last.

Introduction. The introduction sets the stage for the rest of the paper. First, state the general problem the paper deals with. Then briefly discuss the relevant literature in such a way that shows the present theoretical status of the problem and places your experiment in context. Although you

*From "Effects of the perceived intentionality and stability of another's dependency on helping behavior" by R. D. Barnes, W. Ickes, & R. G. Kidd, *Personality and Social Psychology Bulletin*, 1979, 5(3), 367–373. Copyright 1979 by the Society for Personality and Social Psychology, Inc. Reprinted by permission of Sage Publications, Inc.

must acknowledge the sources of the ideas you discuss, you do not need to give a thorough history of the problem. Finally, state how your study will contribute to understanding the problem. Indicate your hypothesis and expected results.

Method. The method section is the heart of the paper, and many authors write this section first. Because the method section describes what you did in the experiment, everything in this section should be stated in the past tense. The method section has two purposes. First, having read your method section, someone else should be able to repeat the experiment exactly in all essential details. Second, another person should be able to judge the validity of your conclusions by comparing them to the method section. For example, in what exact ways did you induce a certain theoretical state, such as hunger, in the subjects? How did you measure their responses? The following subsections can be convenient for organizing the method section. In order they are: subjects, apparatus, design, procedure.

Subjects. Tell how many subjects you used and how they were obtained. Describe any characteristics of your subjects that are important to the study, such as their age, sex, or student status. In the case of animal subjects such as rats, you should name the strain and supplier as well as species.

Apparatus. Indicate the materials used in the study, including the type of apparatus, and tell the values of stimuli.

Design. State the logic of the experiment, including the variables (for example: The design was a 2×2 factorial in which sex and instructions each varied between subjects). State which variables were randomized, which were counterbalanced, and so forth. Tell what the dependent variables were.

Procedure. Although procedure does not need to be a distinct subsection from design, it is helpful to remember that the design is a logical construction in your head, whereas the procedure is a sequence of steps you followed in putting the design into effect. How were the subjects assigned to conditions? What instructions were they given? You may find it helpful to think of the design subsection as what you did and the procedure subsection as how you did it. Both aspects are fundamental to understanding the method.

Results. The main function of the results section is easy to state: What did you find? Results usually are described in the past tense (for example: The rats bar-pressed more when they were hungry). First, indicate any data transformations that you made before analyzing the data. Then state what you found. Usually you will refer the reader to a table or graph of the data. Indicate which results were statistically significant and what tests of significance you used.

A common problem in the results section is to get bogged down in describing the statistics and lose sight of the results that you are trying to present. On the other hand, you should not spend time presenting results that were not statistically significant. Remember that the focus of the results section is on what you found; the statistics assure the reader that results are not likely to have been a fluke.

Usually you will summarize the results in either a table or graph. Tables have the advantage of being economical of space, precise, and easy to coordinate with the statistical analysis. Figures, on the other hand, allow the reader to get a better idea of the size of the effects and any interactions among variables. My own preference is for figures because they seem to make it easier for the reader to grasp and retain the main features of the results.

Discussion. The discussion section builds on the results by interpreting them and relating them to the literature. The focus of this section is on the theoretical contribution of the study. Describe similarities and differences between your results and those of others. Do not introduce further data from your study unless they are incidental to a comparison with other published data. The following questions are appropriate to address: What weaknesses are there in your data? What qualifications must be made to your conclusions? What has your experiment contributed to the understanding of the problem stated in the introduction? Whereas the methods and results are written in the past tense, conclusions are stated in the present tense (for example: Hunger increases bar-pressing rate).

Reference notes. If you need to cite any source that is not generally available, such as an unpublished manuscript or personal communication, refer to it in the usual way in the text—(Smith, 1981)—and include a section headed "Reference Note(s)" before the references themselves. The form of the reference notes is as similar to that in the reference section as possible (for example: Smith, D. H. Personal communication, June 1981).

References. This section contains the documentation of points made in your paper. It serves the essential function of tying your paper to the literature. Many readers will turn to the references immediately after reading the title and the abstract to see whom you cite. Be sure to reference all sources that you have drawn on for specific ideas. Remember, however, that the reference list is not a bibliography of background material not specifically cited in the text.

Footnotes. A footnote is the appropriate way to indicate mailing address for reprints, acknowledgment of financial support or technical assistance, and so forth. This type of footnote is not numbered and will appear in the journal at the bottom of the first page. Footnotes to the content of the paper should be avoided. When essential, content footnotes are numbered and will appear in the journal at the bottom of the page on which they are cited.

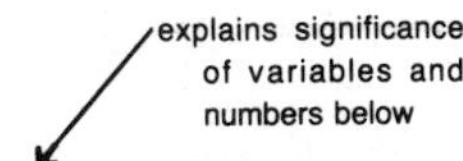

TABLE 11–1 Mean number of correct responses as a function of sex and amount of reinforcement.

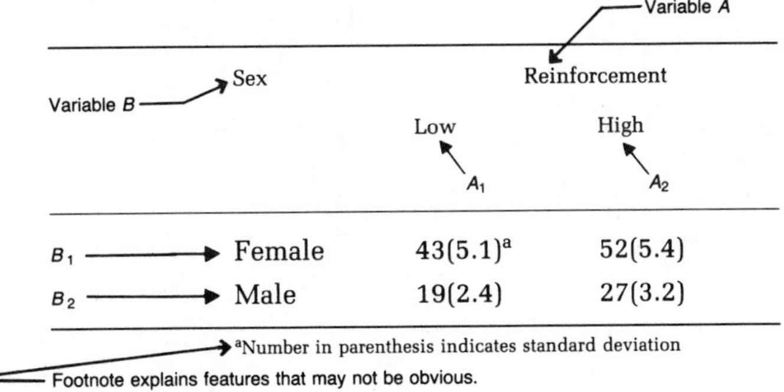

Sex	Reinforcement	
	Low	High
Female	43(5.1)[a]	52(5.4)
Male	19(2.4)	27(3.2)

[a]Number in parenthesis indicates standard deviation

Tables. Put data into a table when doing so will help to make the data clearer than being strung out in the lines of text. The best way to learn how to set up a table is to look in a journal to see how tabular material is handled. Table 11–1 shows a typical table and gives some suggestions. Tables should not duplicate material presented in the text or in figures. Indicate where a table should appear in the published paper by typing the following in the text:

Table 1 here

Figure captions. Each figure should have a caption that briefly describes the contents of the figure. The caption should be understandable by itself but should avoid repeating material from the body of the paper. Figure captions come after the tables and before the figures themselves.

Figures. Figures that are to be published in a journal should be professionally drawn. Some authors use kits to construct graphs, but most people find it difficult to get the proper combination of line width and symbol and letter sizes to make a clear and pleasing graph. For unpublished papers you will draw your own graphs in pencil on graph paper. Avoid color coding in graphs because colors do not photocopy. Different symbols should be used to indicate groups and conditions. Although the proportions of the graph will depend on the type of material, a rule of thumb is to make the ratio of height to width three to four. If you draw the graph to fill a piece of 8½-by-11-inch graph paper and orient the horizontal axis along the longer side of the page, you will usually come out well. The axes should be clearly labeled. Make the symbols and lettering large enough that the figure can be read from a distance.

Use paperclip;
no cover.

The title page is not numbered.

(4.13)

(1.2) Effects of the Perceived Intentionality and Stability

of Another's Dependency on Helping Behavior

Richard D. Barnes and William Ickes

University of Wisconsin, Madison

Robert F. Kidd

Boston University

The maximum length of title is 12-15 words.
Identify major variables.
Note capitalization.
Double-space *everything*, without exception.

Author's address at time research was conducted; not necessarily present address.

No more than 60 spaces for running head.

Running head: Dependency and Helping

(4.13)

New page

Do not indent abstract; type it in a single paragraph.

Dependency and Helping

1

(1.4)

Abstract

(4.14)

A field experiment was conducted to investigate the effects on help-giving of the perceived intentionality and stability of the cause of a dependent person's need. Subjects were asked to lend class notes to a caller whose need for help was described as due either to a lack of ability ("unintentional" dependency) or to a lack of effort ("intentional" dependency). The cause of the caller's dependency was also varied according to its perceived degree of stability (stable vs. unstable). As predicted, more help was elicited (1) when the caller's dependency was attributed to a lack of ability rather than to a lack of effort, and (2) when the dependency was seen as stable rather than unstable. The results are discussed in terms of theorizing which has attempted to relate outcome attributions to helping behavior.

Type two or three key words from title on each page. This will allow editor to reassemble pages if they get separated. Do not use author's name to identify pages.

Abstract is page one.

Set typewriter for a 6-inch line; margins should be 1-1½ inches.

Period goes outside parentheses, unless entire sentence is in parentheses.

Length of abstract is 100-175 words.

Dependency and Helping

2

(4.15)

(1.5)

Effects of the Perceived Intentionality and Stability

of Another's Dependency on Helping Behavior

Previous research on the attributional determinants of helping behavior has been guided by Heider's (1958) distinction between "internal" and "external" causes. The results of a number of studies have indicated that more help will be given when a supplicant's dependency is attributed to an external cause (i.e., bad luck) than when the same dependency is attributed to an internal cause (i.e., laziness). For example, in an experiment by Schopler and Matthews (1965), subjects gave significantly more help when a subordinate's request for help appeared to be part of the planned experimental procedure (external locus of dependency) than when it appeared to be initiated by the subordinate himself (internal locus of dependency). Similarly, Berkowitz (1969) found that subjects worked harder on behalf of a fellow subject when his poor performance on a task was attributed to an error made by the experimenter than when it was attributed to his own mismanagement. And, as "real-world" support to complement these findings, Bryan and Davenport (cited in Berkowitz, 1975) reported that readers of the *New York Times* who contributed to 100 needy people during a Christmas season gave significantly more money to people whose dependency appeared to be externally caused than to those whose outcomes could be attributed to their own moral or psychological deficiency.

Although the simple distinction between an internal versus an external locus of dependency is an important one, recent theoretical developments have indicated that there is more to attribution than the internal/external distinction, and have stressed the need for multi-dimensional causal taxonomies

Type the complete title at the beginning of the introduction. The introduction, which opens the main body of the paper, is not labeled.

Indent five spaces for every paragraph, including each footnote, figure caption, and table footnote.

Cite the source of ideas.

Abbreviations are sometimes used in parenthetical material (3.7).

Cite the source that you read.

Underlining indicates italics in printed version. Underline titles of publications. Otherwise, use italics sparingly. See 3.77 for rules.

A few neatly hand-lettered corrections are permitted (4.6).

Dependency and Helping

3

(cf. Horowitz, 1968). The first reformulation was proposed by Weiner, Frieze, Kukla, Reed, Rest, and Rosenbaum (1971). These authors noted that Heider's (1958) characterization of ability and effort as internal causes and task difficulty and luck as external causes implied a further division according to the degree to which each of these factors exhibits stability over time and situation. However, Weiner recognized that even a two-dimensional taxonomy was not sufficient to account for a number of important causal distinctions (Weiner, 1974).

To overcome some of the limitations, Rosenbaum (1972) proposed the addition of a third causal dimension--intentionality. In Rosenbaum's taxonomy, ability can be viewed as either a stable disposition or as a more variable facility. Similarly, the effort factor can take the form of a dispositional "trait" for a fluctuating, unstable "state." More importantly, Rosenbaum's scheme makes an explicit distinction between factors perceived to be under direct personal control (intentional factors) and those perceived to be under the control of other, more impersonal forces (unintentional factors). Although "controllability" might be a better term than "intentionality" in capturing the meaning of Rosenbaum's third causal dimension, we will employ Rosenbaum's terminology throughout this paper.

Following a review of the theoretical developments described above, Ickes and Kidd (1976) proposed a model to predict how the perceived stability and intentionality of a dependent person's outcome may affect his chances of being helped. It is usually assumed that a request for aid implies a failure on the part of the supplicant to independently satisfy his own needs. However, if the cause of his dependency is perceived as unstable, the potential helper may infer that the supplicant is at least sometimes able to take care of his own needs and so may question the degree to which help is really

List all authors the first time they are cited (3.51).

Abbreviation for "compare." Do not underline.

"And" is used in text citations occurring outside of parentheses. The ampersand (&) is used for citations within parentheses. See 3.51.

Use dashes sparingly.

Punctuation goes inside quotation marks at end of sentence, with few exceptions (see 4.10).

required. From the potential helper's point of view, a supplicant whose cause of dependency is unstable may be seen as in less need of help than a supplicant who has no possibility of altering his outcome without additional help.

With respect to the intentionality factor, Ickes and Kidd (1976) suggest that the separation of effort and ability ascriptions on the basis of intentionality may be an important element in the decision to help an unfortunate other. For example, suppose you are downtown standing on a corner across the street from a large electric sign showing the time. A man standing next to you turns and asks you what time it is, and you tell him to look up at the sign across the street. If his dependence on you is due to a lack of effort, he might answer, "Would you read it for me? I can see that far, but I'm not willing to try." However, if his dependence is due solely to a lack of ability, he might answer, "Would you read it for me? I'm willing to try, but I can't see that far."

In more general terms, if the supplicant's dependency is perceived as due to a lack of effort (intentional), the outcome will be seen as one the supplicant can control and the potential helper will not feel obliged to intervene. However, if the outcome is perceived as due to a lack of ability (unintentional), the outcome will be seen as one the supplicant cannot control and the potential helper will feel obliged to intervene on his behalf. Thus, helping should vary according to whether the supplicant's dependency is perceived as intentional or unintentional, with more help given in the second case than in the first. (For an elaboration of the relationships among the dimensions of internality-externality, stability-instability, and intentionality-unintentionality, see Ickes and Kidd, 1976).

Dependency and Helping

5

In summary, it is proposed that when the perceived causal locus (internal/external) of a dependent person's outcome is held constant, helping will vary according to the perceived stability and intentionality of the outcome. The expected pattern of results would be two additive main effects indicating a greater degree of helping to the extent that the supplicant's dependency is seen as (1) stable rather than unstable, and (2) unintentional rather than intentional. A field experiment was designed to test these predictions.

(4.16) (1.6) Method

Subjects were 51 male and 54 female students enrolled in introductory psychology classes. The names and telephone numbers of these students were obtained from course rosters. Prior to being called, each subject was randomly assigned to one of the various experimental conditions within the constraints imposed by counterbalancing for the sex of the subject and the sex of the confederate.

The new dimensions of outcome attribution proposed by Weiner et al. (3.7) (1971) and Rosenbaum (1972)--stability and intentionality--were independently manipulated in a between-subjects design. The perceived causal locus of the caller's dependency was held constant so that it was "internal" in all conditions. Using Rosenbaum's classification scheme, an "unintentional" dependency was defined in terms of a lack of effort or motivation. Cross-cutting this intentionality manipulation, a relatively stable need or dependency was contrasted with a relatively unstable one. Thus, including the counterbalance variables, the complete design was a 2 x 2 x 2 x 2 factorial in which perceived intentionality, perceived stability, sex of subject, and sex of confederate were varied independently. There were either six or seven subjects in each cell.

For seriation see 4.16.

Do not begin a new page when a heading occurs. Center a main heading, but do not use all capitals. Underline all headings within text. This paper uses only one level of heading. A second level of heading is typed in the same style, flush with the left margin. If a third-level heading is needed, it is typed in the same style as a second-level heading, paragraph indented, followed by a period and two spaces, with the text following on the same line (see 4.16).

Use numbers for 10 and above, except to begin sentence (see 3.20).

Do not abbreviate "subject" or "experimenter."

Note spacing.

Use words for numbers 0–9, with certain exceptions (such as the preceding sentence). See 3.20, 3.21.

In an adaptation of a procedure developed by McFall and Twentyman (1973, Exp. IV), subjects in the present study were contacted by telephone between 6:00 and 10:00 p.m. three days before their final examination in introductory psychology. Using a carefully prepared script, the caller identified him/herself as another student in the same large (300-400) lecture section and expressed a need for help in studying for the final exam. After briefly describing the reason for (cause of) his or her dependency, the confederate proceeded to make a series of five graded requests of the subject. These were structured in such a way that the cost of agreeing to help increased with each successive request. The script was as follows:

> Hi, may I speak to ________? You're taking Intro Psych, aren't you? Well, I'm (Tony Freeman/Julie Pearson). I don't think you know me, but I'm in (professor)'s section, too. I don't know anyone else in the class, so I asked in the psych office for the class roster and got your name off of it. I hate to bother you, but I really need some help before the final.
>
> I just don't seem to have the (ability/motivation) to take good notes. I really (try to/can) take good notes, but (sometimes I just can't do it/I just can't ever do it/sometimes I just don't try/I just don't ever try), so the notes I have (sometimes aren't/are never) very good to study for an exam with.
>
> (Request 1:) Do you think I could take a look at yours?
>
> (Request 2:) I think I'll need to fill in what I've missed since the last exam. I could come by your place tonight to look at them, okay?

Note periods and lowercase (3.5).

If exact instructions are crucial to the method, reproduce them as part of the procedure.

Indent long (four or more lines) quotations, but do not use quotation marks. Remember, double-space everything.

Dependency and Helping

7

(Request 3:) Actually, my notes are pretty bad, so I'll probably need to borrow yours for at least a day. Would that be all right?

(Request 4:) Great! Well, let's see ... I've got a paper for another class that's due tomorrow, so I can't pick them up tonight. Could I come by late tomorrow night [two days before the examination]?

An ellipsis is used to indicate omitted material (see 3.47, 4.12).

(Request 5:) I really don't know when I'll be through with them. Could you come by here to pick them up when I'm finished?

The script allowed for four variations in the perceived cause of caller's dependency: stable lack of ability, unstable lack of ability, stable lack of effort, and unstable lack of effort.

Although care was taken not to inform the confederates about the nature of the hypotheses under investigation, they could not be kept "blind" with respect to the experimental treatment which a given subject received. Moreover, because the confederates may have developed their own hypotheses about how the subjects might be expected to respond, it was important to minimize the likelihood of their introducing a subtle bias into the telephone interaction.

A number of alternative solutions to this problem were considered, but as most were ultimately rejected as unfeasible, we attempted to counter the problem of bias in this particular paradigm by (1) holding to a minimum the differences in the wording of the scripts used in the various conditions, (2) repeatedly stressing to the confederates the need for experimental control in the comparability of presentation of each of the versions, and (3) conducting three lengthy rehearsal sessions prior to the actual calling of subjects in which the confederates were required to "overlearn" the scripts to the point that they could be repeated in a standard, semi-automatic fashion. During these rehearsals, the confederates were carefully trained to use a similar pattern of inflection across the variable segments of the script.

After each request, the confederate noted on a response sheet whether or not the subject agreed to the request. Then, depending upon the subject's answer, the confederate either extricated himself or herself from the conversation or proceeded to the next request level. If the subject said "no" unequivocally to the first request, the confederate simply terminated the conversation by saying, "Oh ... Well, thanks anyway." If an ambiguous response was given, the confederate repeated the request and attempted to elicit a definite "yes" or "no." If the subject said "no" to any of the subsequent requests, or agreed to all of them, the confederate terminated the conversation and released the subject from any perceived obligation to help by saying, "Listen, this isn't going to work out. My schedule for the next few days is really messed up. Thanks anyway, okay?" (No notes were ever actually obtained from the subjects, and the subjects were never informed that the call was part of an experiment.)

Place question mark inside quotation marks when it is part of quoted material (see 4.10).

Period goes outside parenthesis when whole sentence is inside parentheses (see 4.10).

(1.7) Results

One problem presented by field experimentation is that of obtaining information about how participants perceived or interpreted the manipulation. Kidd (1976) has suggested that this problem may be dealt with by drawing a separate "manipulation check" sample from the same subject population, randomly assigning these subjects to the experimental treatments, inducing

Dependency and Helping

9

the manipulations, and then questioning these subjects about their perceptions of and reactions to the manipulations. In line with this recommendation, 75 additional undergraduates, representing approximately equal numbers of males and females taking introductory psychology, were called three days before their final exams and questioned about their perceptions of the dependency manipulations.

Data were obtained in the form of dichotomous repsonses, with "0" and "1" assigned to the possible responses for a given manipulation check question. As expected, subjects in the lack of effort treatment saw the caller's failure to take good notes as due to a lack of effort rather than to a lack of ability, χ^2 (1) = 59.04, p < .001. The reverse pattern of greater ability attributions than effort attributions was observed in the lack of ability conditions. Likewise, subjects felt that the caller had a chronic problem with note taking in the stable conditions, while in the unstable conditions the caller's poor note taking was seen as occurring "only sometimes," χ^2 (1) = 10.08, p < .005. There was no significant interaction between the intentionality and stability factors.

The major dependent variable in the study proper was the number of the five helping requests agreed to by the subjects over the telephone. A four-way ANOVA for this measure revealed significant main effects for both of the attribution factors (ps < .05) with no significant effects for sex of subject, sex of confederate, or any of the interaction terms. For this reason, the data were collapsed across the two counterbalanced sex variables and analyzed in a 2 x 2 factorial design.

The results of this analysis took the form of the two additive main effects predicted by Ickes and Kidd (Table 1). Significantly more requests

chi

The word "data" is generally used as a plural.

Use figures to express the actual numeral.

Describe the results, not the statistics.

Results are described in the past tense.

Chi square (χ^2) is the statistic; the degrees of freedom are indicated in parentheses; "p" refers to the significance level (see 3.14).

Identify any Greek letters by writing them in the margin and circling them.

Abbreviation for "analysis of variance." See 3.5 for use of abbreviations.

Dependency and Helping

10

were agreed to when the caller's dependency was attributed to a stable cause than when it was attributed to an unstable cause, $\underline{F}$ (1, 95) = 4.40, $\underline{p} < .05$. Helping was also greater when the dependency was perceived as due to an unintentional lack of ability than when it was perceived as due to an intentional lack of effort, $\underline{F}$ (1, 95) = 4.64, $\underline{p} < .05$.

Insert Table 1 about here

The same results were apparent when a chi square analysis was applied to the data. For this analysis, the range of possible helping responses was divided into two categories: no- or low-cost helping (0-2 requests agreed to), and high-cost helping (3-5 requests agreed to). This division is justified because (1) it exactly divides the range of possible responses in half; (2) it meaningfully contrasts low- versus high-cost helping, since the subject does not agree to relinquish physical possession and control of the notes until the third request and (3) this same request proved to be the natural breakpoint of the data in the McFall and Twentyman (1973) experiment.

The results of this analysis revealed that more subjects gave high-cost (vs. low-cost) help when the other's dependency was due to a stable cause (40 out of 51) than when it was due to an unstable cause (27 out of 48), χ^2 (1) = 5.56, $\underline{p} < .025$. Similarly, more subjects gave high-cost help when the other's dependency was due to an unintentional factor (40 out of 50) than when it was due to an intentional factor (27 out of 49), χ^2 (1) = 7.01, $\underline{p} < .01$. The interaction effect was not significant.

"F" is the statistic for analysis of variance (3.14).

Indicate where tables and figures should be placed. Use arabic numerals for tables and figures, not roman (4.20).

(1.8)

Discussion

The results of the present field experiment are consistent with Ickes and Kidd's attributional analysis of helping behavior. When the causal locus of a supplicant's dependency is held constant, the amount of help the person receives still varies according to the degree to which the cause of dependency is perceived to be stable and intentional.

In a given helping situation, of course, other factors may be expected to either combine additively or interact with stability and intentionality to affect helping behavior. The procedure used in the present study was in some ways unique in that it (1) held anticipation of future contact to a minimum, since the requests were made shortly before the final examination in the subjects' course; and (2) utilized a series of requests that escalated in cost to the subject, possibly producing a "foot-in-the-door" effect (Freedman & Fraser, 1966) that increased the level of helping in all of the experimental conditions. However, despite the possible influence of these other factors on helping, the present results clearly indicate that causal attributions made on the basis of stability and intentionality distinctions contribute significantly to observed differences in helping behavior. They also indicate that people make causal distinctions at a much more detailed level than that implied by a simple internal-external distinction.

In the discussion section compare the results to the literature.

Conclusions are given in the present tense.

Qualify conclusions, as appropriate

Use ampersand (&) when reference is within parentheses (3.51).

Show what your study has contributed and how it has helped to resolve the original problem.

Dependency and Helping

(1.9) (4.18) 12

References

Berkowitz, L. Resistance to improper dependency relationships. Journal of Experimental Social Psychology, 1969, 5, 283-294.

Freedman, J. L., & Fraser, S. C. Compliance without pressure: The foot-in-the-door technique. Journal of Personality and Social Psychology, 1966, 4, 195-202.

Heider, F. The psychology of interpersonal relations. New York: Wiley, 1958.

Horowitz, I. A. Effect of choice and locus of dependence on helping behavior. Journal of Personality and Social Psychology, 1968, 8, 373-376.

Ickes, W., & Kidd, R. An attributional analysis of helping behavior. In J. Harvey, W. Ickes, & R. Kidd (Eds.) New directions in attribution research (Vol. 1). Hillsdale, N.J.: Erlbaum, 1976.

Kidd, R. F. Manipulation checks: Advantage or disadvantage? Representative Research in Social Psychology, 1976, 7, 160-165.

McFall, R., & Twentyman, C. Four experiments on the relative contributions of rehearsal, modeling, and coaching to assertion training. Journal of Abnormal Psychology, 1973, 81, 199-218.

Rosenbaum, R. M. A dimensional analysis of the perceived causes of success and failure. Unpublished doctoral dissertation, University of California, Los Angeles, 1972.

Schopler, J., & Matthews, M. The influence of perceived causal locus of partner's dependence on the use of interpersonal power. Journal of Personality and Social Psychology, 1965, 2, 609-612.

Weiner, B., Frieze, I., Kukla, A., Reed, L., Rest, S., & Rosenbaum, R. M. Perceiving the causes of success and failure. In E. E. Jones, D. E.

References start a new page.

Capitalize main words of journal title; underline title of journal or book (3.59).

Note space between initials in a name.

Capitalize first word following a colon in a title (3.76).

Indent second and following lines of a reference three spaces (4.18).

Use ampersand in references (3.60).

For an edited book the editors' initials precede the last name.

Note that no space is used between letters.

Underline volume number of journal but not book. (Do not give the issue number unless the journal begins every issue with page 1.)

Kanouse, H. H. Kelley, R. E. Nisbett, S. V. Valins, ~~and~~ & B. Weiner (Eds.), *Attribution: Perceiving the causes of one's behavior*. Morristown, N.J.: General Learning Press, 1971.

Weiner, B. *Achievement motivation and attribution theory*. Morristown, N.J.: General Learning Press, 1974.

Do not list any source you did not cite. This is not a bibliography.

Dependency and Helping

14

(3.63)

Footnote

This research was supported in part by National Institute of Mental Health Grant MH-26646 to William Ickes. The authors would like to express their thanks to Lori Schmitz and James Wacht for serving as the confederates in this study.

Acknowledgment footnotes will appear at the bottom of the first page of the printed article; they are not numbered. See 3.63 and 3.64 for a discussion of footnotes.

Dependency and Helping

15

(3.26–3.36, 4.20)

Table 1

Mean Number of Helping Requests Agreed To

Perceived Stability of Other's Outcome	Perceived Intentionality of Other's Outcome		
	Lack of Ability (Unintentional)	Lack of Effort (Intentional)	
Stable	4.27 (26)	3.48 (25)	3.88
Unstable	3.50 (24)	2.75 (24)	3.13
	3.90	3.12	

Note: Numbers in parentheses represent the _N_ per cell.

The tables follow the footnotes, one table per page.

Use arabic numerals.

Draw lines in pencil (4.20).

If there are any figures, the figure captions begin on the next page, followed by the figures themselves, one per page. The figures are not paginated. Identification for each figure is handwritten on the back of the page.

Steps in the Publication Process

In this section we will describe the steps that a paper goes through in becoming an article in a typical journal. Our discussion will provide an overview of the publication process, rather than a detailed description. Refer to the APA *Publication Manual* for details.

Before you begin writing a manuscript for publication, you should decide which journal you are going to submit your paper to. Each journal may have slightly different requirements for style, length, and so forth that you should be aware of. Consult a recent issue of the journal for such information.

Deciding which journal to submit a paper to is not always an easy task. You want your paper to appear in a journal with wide circulation. You will also want it to appear in a journal that is read by specialists in the area that the paper concerns. Other considerations include prestige of the journal and likelihood of acceptance. As you might expect, these last two considerations generally involve a tradeoff. Two guidelines are helpful. First, choose a journal that has published other articles on the same topic. Second, choose a journal that you have cited most frequently in your reference list.

Before you submit your manuscript, consult a recent issue of the journal for the editor's address and double check the requirements for submission. Prepare a cover letter addressed to the editor, giving the title of your paper and some details about it, such as the number of tables and/or figures. Tell the editor whether it has been presented at a meeting. Give your return address and your telephone number.

When the editor receives the manuscript, he or she reads it for an initial screening and sends it out for review, usually to two other persons in the field. After the reviews are received, the editor decides either to accept the paper as is (rarely), to accept it pending certain revisions, to reject it with the suggestion that it be resubmitted with certain revisions, or to reject it outright. The editor's letter gives an overall evaluation of the paper, interprets the reviewers' comments, and suggests how you should proceed. If you are going to revise the paper, you should study the comments of each reviewer. You need not accept each suggestion, but you must give a good reason if you do not. If a reviewer is completely off base, you may say so, carefully. In extreme cases an editor will get additional reviews if you can show that the reviewer did not do a competent job.

After you have revised the paper, retype it. Resubmit it with a new cover letter that tells how you have accounted for the reviewers' comments. At this point the editor usually makes a final decision to accept or reject. Next you wait a considerable time, up to a year, while the article is scheduled into one of the journal's upcoming issues. This time period sometimes is referred to as "in press." The exact sequence of events varies from journal to journal, but the following is typical. You receive the copy-edited version of your manuscript, with editorial changes in grammar, spelling, and style, but not in substantive matters. Any corrections you wish to incorporate should be made at this point. After the copy-edited manuscript is returned to the editor and set in type, you receive galley proofs, sheets of paper containing your manuscript set into type but not arranged into pages. Read the galleys carefully for typographical errors. Next you may receive page proofs, which show how your paper will actually look in the journal. Check these to see if the galley corrections have been made and to see that nothing is out of order or lost. Shortly after you return the page proofs, your paper appears in the journal. The whole process may take about a year. The editor usually requires about three months for the initial review process. After final acceptance has been made, the publication delay may be another nine months. Many journals print a note indicating when a paper was accepted for publication. You may consult recent issues to estimate when your article will appear.

ORAL PRESENTATIONS

The oral presentation is an important means of scientific communication. Numerous regional, national, and international meetings are held each year in which the primary formal means of communication is the oral presentation of short research papers. For the student presenting a paper toward the end of a course in experimental psychology is an excellent learning experience. Many regional student psychology conferences are also held, at which papers are given.

Although the parts of an oral presentation are the same as for a research report, simply reading the manuscript of a paper prepared for publication is a mistake. The oral format requires several changes. First, the paper must be shorter, because in the 10 or 15 minutes that are usually allotted presenting all the material in a typical paper is physically impossible. Second, it is necessary to simplify the material in order for the audience to digest the ideas as they are presented. Third, written material tends to be boring to listen to. If you choose to write out your talk in order to feel prepared, focus on how it will sound when spoken. Then leave the written version at home or in your pocket and speak from an outline.

Organize your talk according to the main parts of a paper: introduction, method, results, and discussion. Make only one or two points in each section of the talk. Your introduction should set the stage in a few sentences. The method section should stick to the essential elements of design, assuming that your audience is generally familiar with how such research is done. Most of your time should be spent on the results. Be sure to emphasize the main findings. Keep the discussion section brief also, simply pointing out some of the implications of the research. Always summarize your results at the end.

Visual aids are a key element of any oral presentation. Ordinarily, visual aids are slides or overhead transparencies. In practice, it is surprising how often visual aids are the weakest part of a presentation. When you use slides, preview them to make sure they will be legible under the conditions that are typical of a convention. Also, see that they are not placed upside down in the projector. Complicated tables are not useful as slides because they are difficult to read, nor is typed material legible in slide format. If your talk is to a small group, you may choose to distribute a handout that describes the results.

Practice the talk in front of sympathetic peers. This technique helps you to know if you are on the right track, and it allows you to modify rough spots. An additional benefit is having most of the potential questions asked first by your friends instead of by strangers who may be less forgiving.

POSTER PRESENTATIONS

Posters have become a popular way of presenting research at meetings. The advantages are that people can browse among many posters, spending time on the ones that interest them, and can discuss the material in as much depth as desired with the author of the poster. Poster sessions are also ideally suited to class projects.

At meetings a vertical surface of 3-by-6 feet or 4-by-8 feet will be available for the presentation. You bring the parts of the poster and assemble it on the board with tacks. See Figure 11–1. Place a strip of paper at the

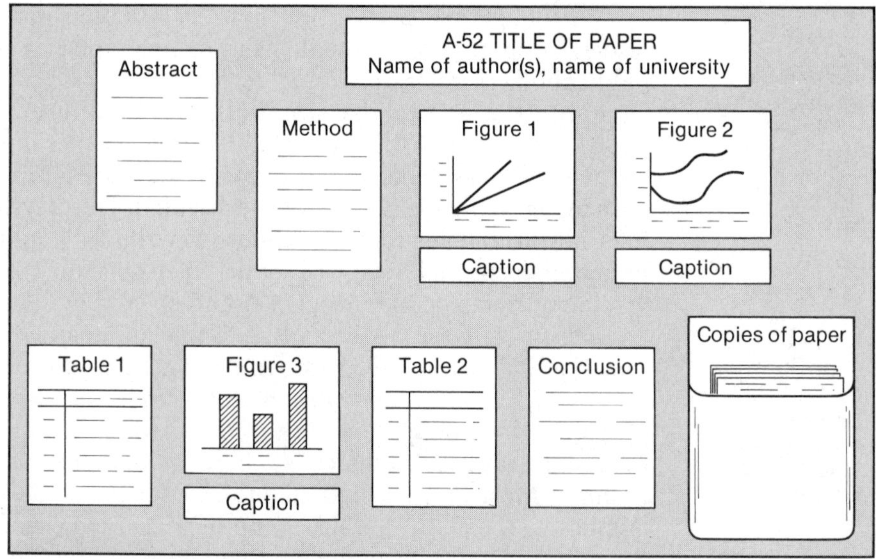

FIGURE 11–1. Typical layout of a poster.

top of the board with the title and the author's name in letters at least an inch high. Position the abstract of the paper in the upper left corner on a single sheet of paper. Type everything on a special large-type typewriter or letter the material neatly by hand. Make all tables and figures about 8-by-10 inches. Keep in mind that your poster should be readable from a distance of several feet. Place copies of the paper or of the abstract in a pocket on the board so that interested persons can take one with them.

During the poster session, stand near the poster to answer questions and discuss the material with people who stop by. Many persons who have presented posters at meetings find they prefer the personal give-and-take of the poster format to the usual oral presentation.

SUMMARY

1. Scientific communication takes place in many ways, including archival publication in scholarly journals and informal communication among groups of scientists known as invisible colleges.
2. Most psychological journals follow the *Publication Manual of the American Psychological Association*, which should be consulted for detailed matters of style.
3. A scientific report requires the same attention to good writing as does any other form of written persuasion. Key concepts are clarity, brevity, and felicity.
4. Documentation is used in a paper to give credit to the work of other authors, to show the larger framework in which your ideas belong, and to point the reader to sources of further information.
5. Authors are indicated in the text by name and the date of their publication.
6. The reference list contains an entry for each work cited in the text and no others.
7. The parts of a paper are: (1) title, (2) authors and their affiliations, (3) abstract, (4) introduction, (5) method, (6) results, (7) discussion, (8) reference notes, (9) references, (10) footnotes, (11) tables, (12) figure captions, (13) figures.
8. The title should convey the main idea of the paper in a few words.
9. The authors in your paper are listed in the order of the importance of their contributions.
10. The abstract is a brief summary of the paper and includes elements from the introduction, method, results, and discussion.
11. The introduction states the general problem the paper deals with, discusses the relevant literature, and states what the paper will contribute to the understanding of the problem.
12. The method section tells what you did in the experiment in such a way that another person can evaluate the validity of the conclusions of the study and

can repeat it in all essentials. The method section describes the subjects, apparatus, design, and procedure.

13. The results section discusses the results and their statistical analysis. Graphs and tables are described here.
14. The discussion section interprets the results and relates them to the literature. It states the contributions that the study makes to the understanding of the problem posed in the introduction, and it deals with any weakness in the data or any qualifications of the conclusions.
15. The steps in the publication process include choosing the journal, submitting the final manuscript including a cover letter, revising the paper to account for reviewers' comments, resubmitting the paper, reviewing the copy-edited manuscript, and reading the galley proofs and page proofs.
16. Oral presentations include most of the elements of the written paper in a simplified format. Practicing the talk before a sympathetic audience, preparing good visual aids, and speaking the paper rather than reading it are keys to a good presentation.
17. Poster presentations are an increasingly popular form of communication of results at scientific meetings. The various parts of the paper are placed on a vertical surface in such a way that they can be read from a distance of several feet. The author remains near the poster to discuss the results with passersby.

SUGGESTIONS FOR FURTHER READING

AMERICAN PSYCHOLOGICAL ASSOCIATION. *Publication manual of the American Psychological Association* (2nd ed.). Washington, D.C.: Author, 1974. This publication is an indispensable style guide for anyone writing in the field of psychology.

BARAFF, R. *Scientists must write: A guide to better writing for scientists, engineers, and students.* London: Chapman and Hall; New York: Wiley, 1978. This book covers all aspects of scientific writing.

STERNBERG, R. J. *Writing the psychology paper.* Woodbury, N.Y.: Barron's Educational Series, 1977. This valuable writing guide deals specifically with psychology.

STRUNK, W., JR., & WHITE, E. B. *The elements of style* (2nd ed.). New York: Macmillan, 1972. This short book, a classic in its field, concisely covers the essentials of good writing.

READING BETWEEN THE LINES

The following problems are presented for you to solve. See Reading Between the Lines in Chapter 1 for an introduction to them. The answers are given in Appendix A.

24. ANTISOCIAL BEHAVIOR UNDER HYPNOSIS

For many years people have been concerned that persons who are hypnotized might be induced to perform acts that they would not do otherwise. Loyd Rowland (1939) conducted an experiment at the University of Tulsa to test this question. He took two students whom he had hypnotized at least twice before and caused them to be deeply hypnotized. Then he showed them a rattlesnake in a box that had an invisible glass cover. The snake was prodded by a wire until it rattled and threatened to strike. Rowland told the subjects that there was a piece of coiled rubber rope in the box and that they were to reach in and pick it up. Both of the hypnotized subjects attempted to do so and were prevented only by the invisible glass. A control group of 42 persons who were of "every age and degree of sophistication" were brought into the laboratory and were asked to pick up the snake, with the instructions that it was artificial. Only one complied. When asked why she had, she replied that she was not afraid of an artificial snake. When she examined the snake, she became too frightened to go near the box. Can you think of any other hypothesis for the difference in the behavior of the two groups besides the hypnotic state?

25. LIFE EVENTS AND ILLNESS

A large amount of research exists indicating that life events can cause illness. The life events may be of the kind that are obviously stressful, such as the death of a family member, or they may be desirable events, such as marriage, birth of a baby, or a new job. Many illnesses have been studied, including depression and schizophrenia. The studies ask people who have suffered the illness to list the life events they have experienced in a period before the illness. The control group of people who have not experienced the illness are asked the same questions. The results show that persons who suffered the illness had experienced more stressful life events than had the control persons. What problems of interpretation can you think of in such retrospective research?

26. YES, BUT IS IT SIGNIFICANT?

I once testified as an expert witness in a trial in which the victim claimed she could identify the defendant on the basis of his body odor, even though she had failed to identify him visually. I was asked whether identifying a person on the basis of body odor was possible. I described an experiment I had performed in which 11 persons had worn T-shirts for two days and then had tried to identify their own shirt from among 12 shirts, the 11 dirty shirts and 1 control shirt. Three subjects correctly identified their own shirts. On a purely random basis slightly less than one correct identification would have been expected. The probability of three people identifying their own shirts by chance was .06. I testified that people have a marginal ability to identify others by odor but that this ability is unreliable. In cross-examination the district attorney asked me whether such a result was statistically significant. When I said that it was marginally significant, she asked, "Then we are able to identify people by odor, aren't we?" What would you have answered if you had been on the stand?

BIASES AND LIMITATIONS OF EXPERIMENTAL PSYCHOLOGY

We have spent much of this book talking about what experimental psychology is and how psychology can be used as a method of gaining knowledge about human behavior. Before we end the book, however, we must temper our enthusiasm somewhat by discussing a few of the problems of psychological research. Science is, after all, a human activity and therefore subject to human failings. We should have a realistic idea of what science is and is not likely to accomplish.

Let us look at the place of science in relation to the fact that science has become one of the moral arbiters of our society. With the decline of the influence of traditional religions, psychologists have entered the priestly ranks in our culture. *Psychology Today,* for example, is one of the most popular magazines in the country. In it social scientists are interviewed about moral issues from war to incest. A need for caution arises from the tendency of people to take scientific statements of how society does behave as indications of how it ought to behave. It is easy to conclude that because 85 percent of the population does something, it is right to do that particular thing. By documenting what is statistically common, we contribute to the definition of what is normal. A classic example of this phenomenon is the Kinsey report on sexual behavior, but this tendency is found in studies of everything from daydreaming to cheating on income taxes. This chapter will discuss some of the major limitations of research in experimental psychology.

BIASES

In Chapter 1 we emphasized the fact that science is a *social* enterprise. As such, science is subject to all of the types of human bias. Some of them affect the choice of problems to work on, the theories developed, and whether particular results are reported. We will consider the many sources of bias under two headings: those that cause science to be conservative and those that lead science to have a liberal influence.

Science as Conservative

As any social institution, science is conservative. Editors, reviewers, department chairpersons, and deans generally are older scientists who may be slower to change than younger ones. That new scientific ideas are adopted more readily by younger scientists is well known. Too, scientists sometimes refuse to change their positions on important theoretical issues, and thus it becomes necessary for a generation of scientists to pass before a new theory is firmly established.

Another source of conservatism is provided by the dependence of science on financial support. In the latter half of the twentieth century science entered a period known as "big science." In 1979 nearly $17 billion was spent on basic and applied research in the United States, of which 39 percent was supported by the federal government. In the same year over $4 billion was spent on research at U.S. universities and colleges, 68 percent of which was federally supported (U.S. Bureau of the Census, 1979). The impact this federal spending has on psychological research is enormous. We can get some idea of its weight by noting how many journal articles report research supported by the government. For example, 76 percent of the articles published in the *Journal of Experimental Psychology: Human Perception and Performance* for 1979 were supported by government grants. The figure for the *Journal of Personality and Social Psychology* was 41 percent. Many of these experiments required expensive equipment and facilities that would be beyond the reach of most universities, let alone individual researchers. The days when research is conducted in spare time and funded out of the researcher's pocket are largely over.

The amount of money available for various categories of research is part of the congressional budget process and therefore is subject to political pressure. Many researchers keep an eye on the types of research that are being funded and direct their grant applications accordingly. In addition, the federal government puts out periodic *Requests for Proposals* on projects it wishes to fund. Although many of the steps in the review process involve peer review by nongovernmental scientists, the final steps include political considerations. It is obvious that the type of research that gets proposed and funded is subject to political pressure, even if the pressure exists only in the mind of the scientist who decides to slant a proposal to be relevant to aging, child abuse, education, or whatever is being funded at the time. One of the least subtle forms of pressure on scientists is fear of being ridiculed on the floor of the Senate and receiving a "golden fleece award" if the research should be capable of sounding silly out of its proper context.

Given that the major support for science is from the government, it is not surprising that there is a great deal of research on how to make people more productive and little on how to make work more meaningful; much research on how to exercise power over subordinates and little on what having power does to the wielder of power; a great deal of interest in the personality patterns of prejudiced people and little on the social conditions that lead to prejudice; more study of what is wrong with students who cannot read than of schools that do not teach; and so forth. It is easy to make a case that research is funded by powerful groups and organizations in order to further their purposes.

Similarly, the results of psychological research tend to be used to control certain groups. Mental patients receive behavior modification, hyperactive children receive drugs, and prisoners receive psychosurgery. In each case a group of powerful people exists who find it necessary or desirable to control the behavior of others. Needless to say, mental patients and hyperactive children need help and society must protect itself against criminals. Yet psychologists should be aware that their work supports a social system that sometimes oppresses people.

In discussing the influence of the social context of psychology, Danziger (1979) points out that the very origin of psychology was dependent on the support of conservative forces. "In the United States [as opposed to Germany] . . . control of university appointments, research funds, and professional opportunities was vested in the hands of either businessmen and their appointees, or politicians who represented their interests. If psychology was to emerge as a viable independent discipline, it would have to be in a form acceptable to these social forces. . . . Psychologists might become acceptable if they would reasonably promise to develop the technical competence to deal with [the problems of migration, urbanization, and industrialization]" (p. 35).

Let us not assume that scientists are swept along by forces beyond their control. As society members who have a stake in the status quo, scientists are often willing servants of power. Examples of these influences are not hard to document. Danziger quotes J. B. Watson as saying that "if psychology would follow the plan I suggest, the educator, the physician, the jurist, and the businessman would utilize our data in a practical way. . . ." He says further that "the reason his [Watson's] message found such immediate and massive resonance was that most American psychologists already accepted the premise that it was the business of their discipline to produce data to be utilized 'in a practical way' by educators, businessmen, and so on" (p. 38).

One of the less savory episodes of science in the service of vested interests is that of Samuel Morton, who in the middle 1800s systematically distorted data on brain size and on race to bolster the then-fashionable notion of white supremacy (Gould, 1978). A more recent example is provided by Sir Cyril Burt, the eminent British psychologist, who systematically concocted data over a long period of time to provide evidence that intelligence is largely inherited (Hearnshaw, 1979). Burt's data went unchallenged for years even though many suspicious clues were there to be noticed. Interestingly, it took a liberal, Leon Kamin, to do the work necessary to expose the conservative bias in Burt's work. We will discuss this case in the section on fraud later in this chapter.

Science as Liberal

Although we have a clear case for science as a conservative force, we can see that science may also have a liberal influence. In fact, many people intuitively see science as a force for change directed against established institutions. This view is almost true by definition because of the objective way science operates, as we discussed in Chapter 1. Because science deals only with data that can gain the assent of every person, political and other orthodoxies are frequently challenged by science. In addition, the search for truth often leads to answers that are not palatable to society as a whole and to its powerful institutions in particular. Psychological research on the adverse effects of segregated education contributed to the Supreme Court's landmark desegregation decision in 1954. The fact that the struggle for desegregation is still going on more than 25 years later is testimony to the resistance of society to liberalizing influences, psychology among them.

Funding for research in social science was reduced in 1981 because social science was perceived to have a liberal influence. At the same time funding for the natural sciences was increased. The ideological nature of the spending cuts was made clear in the arguments in favor of the cuts. Congressman John Ashbrook, for example, said, "We have seen how scholarly works have been used to launch major new government policies or programs over recent years. It was a study on the learning abilities of schoolchildren that launched the nightmare of busing. . . . To avoid the risk of the government inadvertently aiding one side of an argument, many people, myself included, consider the best policy is for the government not to involve itself at all" (Association for the Advancement of Psychology, 1981, p. 3).

Psychology has been argued to be more radical than called for by the nature of science. Donald Campbell, whose work on validity we considered in Chapter 5, has said: "Present-day psychology and psychiatry in all their major forms are more hostile to the inhibitory messages of traditional religious moralizing than is scientifically justified. . . . The religions of all ancient urban civilizations . . . taught that many aspects of human nature need to be curbed if optimal social coordination is to be achieved; for example, selfishness, pride, greed, dishonesty, covetousness, cowardice, lust, wrath. Psychology and psychiatry, on the other hand, not only describe man as selfishly motivated, but implicitly or explicitly teach that he ought to be so. They tend to see repression and inhibition of individual impulse as undesirable" (1975, pp. 1103–1104). This bias comes through in the topics that are studied and the way they are studied. Campbell says further: "Conformity or suggestibility to majorities and prestige figures has been extensively studied from the beginnings of experimental social psychology . . . but almost always as a popular character weakness" (p. 1107).

We could give more examples of issues on which psychologists have taken a more liberal or radical stance than the prevailing public opinion, such as capital punishment, child welfare, and wife abuse. For this reason those conservatives who believe that psychologists are a liberal influence are correct, whatever the merits of the particular issues.

LIMITATIONS OF SCIENCE

When we discussed the nature of science in Chapter 1, we said that science deals with phenomena upon which every person can agree. As we noted then, this premise limits the purview of science considerably. When Yuri Gagarin, the Soviet cosmonaut and the first person to orbit the earth, returned from his historic flight, he said that there was no God because he had looked in the heavens and had not found him. To most people it is obvious that Gagarin's method was not suited to the purpose of finding God. In this section we will discuss the limitations of science in obtaining knowledge. Some of these are *essential* limitations to the nature of science and some of them are *practical*.

Essential Limitations

Yuri Gagarin's failure to find God in space is an example of the essential limitations of science. No matter how hard he looked, Gagarin would never find God from his spacecraft. He was using the wrong methods. Science must remain *agnostic* about questions that lie outside the realm of things on which every person may agree.

Science is agnostic not only concerning the existence of God but also about many questions of values. For example, a perennial political debate concerns whether tax rates should be directed more toward reducing the differences between the rich and the poor or toward providing incentives for people to work harder and thereby become richer. Psychology can discover that poverty leads to psychological distress and crime and that people will work hard for financial rewards, but it cannot tell which goal is more important. This question is one of values and its answer must come from outside science. Lively debates take place in scientific organizations over the proper balance to strike between scientific objectivity and social responsibility. The decision of the American Psychological Association that its annual convention would boycott states that had not ratified the Equal Rights Amendment is an example.

Closely related to the fact that values lie outside of science is the idea that much of science is *culturally relative*. This concept is particularly true of the social sciences. Not only is the importance of a certain question a relative matter, but the framing of questions themselves is often relative. Years ago psychologists measured masculinity and femininity on various scales and studied the relationship of these traits to psychological adjustment and the like. It was assumed that males ought to be masculine and females, feminine. Today many psychologists feel that every person should have a balance of both masculine and feminine traits and be more or less androgynous. These psychologists see the popular ideals of masculinity and femininity as exaggerations of the norm and believe that a better-adjusted society would contain a higher percentage of androgynous persons. With a similar philosophy toward cultural change, some psychologists specialize in assertiveness training for women and minorities. From another perspective these psychologists might be viewed as encouraging defiance of legitimate authority. This type of problem, arising from cultural perspective, is common in many areas of psychology.

Science is also *incomplete*. We know only a tiny fraction of what there is to know, particularly in psychology. As one of the youngest sciences and one that deals with nature's most complex phenomena, psychology is more incomplete than other sciences that have existed longer. We must be humble about making claims for the truth of psychological principles because of the slender base on which many of these claims rest. It is interesting to look at psychology books of 50, 25, or even 10 years ago. We find that social psychology hardly existed before World War II and that cognitive psychology as we know it dates from about 1960.

Because psychological knowledge is so incomplete, it is therefore *tentative*. Science textbooks are continually being revised as new information is obtained. Many times it is not simply that more becomes known about a topic but that theories are developed in areas that did not previously have theories. Also, new theories replace older ones that have been found wanting. In Chapter 2 we discussed the idea that progress in science can take place by means of revolutions that overthrow earlier theories and install new ones. One example of an earlier theory that has been discredited is phrenology, the idea that one can judge personality and intelligence from the various bumps and protrusions on the head. It is sobering to realize that some of the theories we work on today will be cited in future textbooks as examples of obvious and amusing errors of an infant science.

Practical Limitations

Certain problems remain unsolved not because of any essential limitation but for reasons outside the logic and methods of science. Perhaps the most important practical limitation of science is its *opportunistic* nature. Science progresses where the problems are easier, where techniques of study are available, and where financial support exists. Areas that are not blessed with these characteristics will remain backward. Consider the greater understanding we have of vision as opposed to olfaction. The eye is amenable to analysis by well-understood techniques such as optics, and there is money available for visual research because of the handicap that blindness causes. On the other hand, the olfactory system is difficult to study for many technical reasons, and "smell blindness," or anosmia, has not been considered to be serious. Many interesting theoretical problems in psychology wait for solutions, but they will not receive much attention as long as easier ones are present for which more financial support is available.

One major practical limitation of science is the *cost of research,* which stems from the size and complexity of many problems and the technical difficulties of research. Physics, for example, has progressed to the point where further advances require fantastically expensive apparatus, such as linear accelerators, that are so big as to be major engineering projects in themselves. Psychological apparatus has not reached that limit as yet, but the day may not be far off. Scientists who study the sense of balance and orientation would certainly like to have orbiting space laboratories to facilitate research under conditions of weightlessness. It is doubtful that such laboratories will ever be adequate to answer many questions that could be raised. Solutions to problems of abnormal personality may require the investment of more resources than our society is willing or able to provide.

Another practical limitation of science comes from the *complexity* of many problems. Traditional psychological theories are developed to account for the effect of one or two variables at a time on some behavior. When we discussed the idea of interactions, we saw how complicated describing behavior was with only two independent variables. Adding a third independent variable can make the interactions mind-boggling.

Furthermore, traditional psychological theories are not intended to deal with situations in which the dependent variable can affect the *independent* variable via a feedback mechanism. In traditional theories the stimulus produces a response, and thus we have stimulus-response psychology. In many situations, however, the response can have an effect on the stimulus as well as vice versa. One simple example is the way we respond to the sensation of cold by turning up the heat in the house. Another example of a feedback system is the way you guide a forkful of spaghetti to your mouth. Your eye guides the motion of the hand (the response) by signaling to the brain any error in direction of the spaghetti (the stimulus). A game that is popular at some parties is for a blindfolded person to try to feed another person. When the person doing the feeding gropes about for the mouth of the person being fed, that person tries to correct for the error in aim of the feeder. Most of the food inevitably winds up splattered about. The reason this mess occurs, and is supposedly funny, is the lack of feedback about the error that normally is present when one feeds oneself. This feedback permits correction of error so that the food reaches the mouth.

These and more weighty problems can be handled by a type of theory called systems theory. Systems theory has not had much impact on psychology yet for the reason that even relatively simple problems prove difficult to handle. Psychology therefore continues to deal with behavior according to theories that are known to be oversimplified and inadequate.

The results of interfering with the normal operation of a feedback system can be amusing, as in the feeding example, but they can be tragic when major social problems are dealt with in the same way. The likelihood always exists that a social change that seems desirable in itself will have unforseen effects that may be dangerous. For example, giving third-world farmers pumps for their wells encouraged them to raise more cattle, which denuded the vegetation and made the land less productive than before. Politically conservative people believe that alterations in society based on scientific research too often lead to unforseen and dangerous outcomes.

In summary science is subject to a number of limitations resulting from the essential nature of science and from the practical nature of the problems that science must deal with. Awareness of the limitations of science should make us careful in making claims for science and should help put scientific knowledge in social perspective.

FRAUD

Fraud is an unpleasant topic that no one likes to talk about. Fraud occurs in science just as in all other human activity. Psychologists have long known that honesty is not a unitary trait. People may be scrupulously honest toward their employers but may fudge on their income tax. An intriguing question is why fraud in science seems so much worse than, say, fraud in banking. One answer lies in the nature of a scientist's data. Bank records can be verified in internal and external ways, but scientific data are creations that can easily be concocted. This means that often we are utterly dependent on the scientist's honesty for the truthfulness of the data. The role of honesty in science is not stressed, but we may say categorically that the honesty of the scientist is a prerequisite for the very existence of science.

Another reason that fraud in science seems so shocking is the priestly function that scientists serve in our society. Because of this role we tend to expect scientists to have higher morals, and we are more apt to be scandalized when we find them to be human. Cases of fraud in psychology have not been many, but some have been spectacular.

In 1974 a scandal that rocked the field of ESP occurred in the parapsychology laboratory of J. B. Rhine. Walter Levy, a young physician and director of the Institute for Parapsychology in Durham, North Carolina, was caught cheating in an experiment. The experiment involved testing rats in an apparatus that was designed to allow them to use either precognition or psychokinesis (kinds of ESP) to increase the number of pleasurable brain stimulations they received. An assistant noticed that Levy seemed to be loitering needlessly about the automated apparatus. From a hiding place the assistant and two others observed Levy during a session and saw him tamper with the apparatus. Suspicions confirmed, they rigged up a second recorder that would not be affected by the tampering. Later the first recorder showed the rats receiving stimulation 54 percent of the time, but the second one showed a chance level of 50 percent. Confronted with the evidence, Levy confessed and resigned. The scandal shook Rhine, who had considered Levy the best hope for the Institute's future as well as for the field of parapsychology, because Levy's evidence had seemed the strongest yet for the existence of ESP.

The most spectacular case of fraud in psychology was perpetrated by Sir Cyril Burt, the eminent British psychologist who was knighted for his work. He published much work on the IQs of identical twins reared apart. This work purportedly showed a high degree of correlation between twins and hence suggested that heredity was the dominant contributor to intelligence. About 1974 Leon Kamin noticed that the correlations reported were identical to the third decimal place in several different reports, over which the number of twin pairs supposedly increased from 15 to 53, a mathematical impossibility. This lead was followed up by a journalist, Oliver Gillie, who discovered that at least two of Burt's coauthors either did not exist or had never worked for him. Although leading scientists such as H. J. Eysenck defended Burt against "a determined effort on the part of some very left-wing environmentalists determined to play a political game with scientific facts" (Gould, 1979, p. 104), the consensus now is that Burt was guilty of a conscious fraud over the course of many years. Burt's life and career are the subject of a biography by Leslie Hearnshaw (1979). Although Hearnshaw began his work as an admirer of Burt's, he became convinced that Burt was undoubtedly a fraud. He attributes the deviation to serious setbacks in Burt's life: a marriage gone sour, the loss of his papers in the bombing of London, and a serious illness. These blows caused an exaggeration of a tendency to paranoia and led him to cheat as a way of vindicating his ideas (Hawkes, 1979).

Parallels between the Levy and Burt cases and with other famous frauds suggest that few scientists start out as frauds. They seem to cheat when early successes are followed by failure. The need to build on past successes, whether motivated internally or by external career pressures, can provide a strong temptation to cheat.

Why are there so few frauds? The biggest factor seems to be the knowledge that successful experiments, particularly the more startling ones, frequently are replicated. This knowledge provides motivation for honesty. When word gets around that a certain person's experiment could not be replicated by several laboratories, that person loses credibility. Eventually the work is quietly forgotten and the person fades into oblivion. The problem of fraud also points to the need for good record keeping so that an author's claims can be backed up with data sheets and protocols. Even though data sheets can be faked, they can be checked for internal consistency. Nevertheless, as we discussed in Chapter 5, replication is the ultimate test for the reality of a finding and thus is the ultimate deterrent to fraud.

THE RESPONSIBILITIES OF THE SCIENTIST

Our discussion of the biases and limitations of science was intended to provide perspective on our earlier discussion of the advantages of science as a way of gaining knowledge. It should not leave you with the feeling that science is so fraught with problems that you should shy away from it. Science remains one of the most magnificent achievements of civilization. This section will round out the chapter by considering the responsibilities of the scientist as a member of society.

Scientists are given many privileges. They are permitted to work on problems that they set for themselves under conditions that they control to a large degree. They are reasonably well paid and are accorded prestige. What responsibilities accompany these privileges? First must be the goal that society will be benefited by the work. Of course, much pure research has no apparent practical significance, and one can make a strong case for satisfaction of curiosity as a valid end in itself. Nevertheless, many disciplines have struggled with the problem of balancing the uncertain long-term benefits of their work against certain near-term dangers. Atomic physics is the classic example; gene splicing is the most recent. In psychology debate has surrounded whether research on the genetic basis of intelligence should be done at all. What if particular groups were found to be genetically inferior in intelligence? Would it not be better if we did not know that? Most scientists have such strong commitment to the idea that knowledge is better than ignorance that they are willing to take the risks that new knowledge brings.

The role of free speech is crucial. Science flourishes only in an atmosphere of free exchange of ideas. When that atmosphere prevails, sufficient debate takes place that the necessary safeguards likely will be erected so that knowledge will be used wisely. Concerned scientists and lay watchdogs have so far been effective in preventing scientists from running amok. The principle of free speech also holds for scientists. They are free to study unpopular problems and propose unpopular ideas. It is up to their colleagues to refute these ideas in the open forum. Such considerations may seem hypothetical and far removed from testing rats in a Skinner box or college sophomores in a conformity study, but this philosophical arena is the larger context in which all scientists work.

Another responsibility of scientists is to educate the public about their findings. Some scientists feel that their work is done when it is published in a journal. Yet the support that society gives to science places a duty on the scientist to educate the public. It is no accident that many scientists divide their time between research and teaching. In addition, there is a long tradition of popularization of science by scientists themselves in the form of public lectures, books, and the electronic media. Scientists must present their case directly to the public and respond to the public's concerns. For example, many psychologists feel that answering questions about pseudosciences such as parapsychology is beneath their dignity. That attitude, though, simply allows the pseudosciences to flourish and justifies the ivory-tower image of the scientist.

SUMMARY

1. Because science is a human enterprise, it is subject to human bias. Some of these biases cause science to have a conservative influence and some liberal.
2. Science is conservative in the same way that any social group is conservative, as well as in its dependence on financial support from society.
3. Much research that is done in colleges and universities is supported by the federal government and is subject to political pressure.
4. Individual scientists share the biases of their society and often perform research that supports the status quo.
5. Because science rests on observation rather than authority, it challenges political and religious orthodoxies and has a liberal influence on society.
6. Science has certain essential and practical limitations in achieving knowledge.
7. Essential limitations come from three considerations: Science must remain agnostic about questions that lie outside the realm of things on which every person may agree; science is necessarily incomplete; and science is always tentative.
8. Three considerations constitute practical limitations on science: Scientists often work on problems that seem capable of solution rather than the most important ones; some research is too expensive to conduct; and some problems are too complex to study with present methods.
9. Fraud in science is a matter of serious concern because data are easily faked and scientists have so much influence in our society. Although not many documented cases of fraud have occurred in psychology, the Levy and Burt cases are instructive in their parallels.
10. The major deterrent to fraud seems to be the realization that important experiments are likely to be replicated.

11. The responsibilities of the scientist include having as the goal of research that society will be benefited by the work. One problem is justifying pure research that has uncertain future payoff against applied research that may be of immediate significance. Another problem is the risk that new knowledge presents to society.
12. Science flourishes only in an atmosphere of freedom of speech, including freedom of inquiry into unpopular ideas.
13. Scientists have the responsibility to educate the public about the nature and results of scientific research.

SUGGESTIONS FOR FURTHER READING

HOGAN, R. T., & EMLER, N. P. The biases in contemporary social psychology. *Social Research*, 1978, *45*, 478–534. This article suggests areas of social psychology in which biases have affected research.

VITZ, P. C. *Psychology as religion: The cult of self-worship*. Grand Rapids, Mich.: Eerdmans, 1977. Although this volume deals primarily with personality theorists, it shows clearly the biases that influence how researchers approach their subject areas.

READING BETWEEN THE LINES

The following problems are presented for you to solve. See Reading Between the Lines in Chapter 1 for an introduction to them. The answers are given in Appendix A.

27. THE LIBERATED FEMALE RAT

For many years researchers who studied sexual behavior in rats found that the male rat was the active partner, while the female was more passive. During these studies the rats were housed in small arenas that kept the animals close to each other. More recently, Martha McClintock and Normal Adler (1978) studied sexual behavior of rats in larger and more complex environments. They found that the female rat actually controlled the initiation and timing of sexual behavior by soliciting the male. What reasons can you think of for the failure of researchers to discover this fact for so many years?

28. THE CAUSES OF CHILD ABUSE

The causes of child abuse have been a topic of experimental interest recently. Researchers have found that child abuse more frequently is reported in poor families than in middle-class or wealthy families. Some researchers believe that poor families do not abuse their children any more than do other social classes but that they are unable to cover up the abuse as well as middle-class and upper-class families. Leroy Pelton (1978) believes there may be political bias behind the objection to the class-differences theory of the amount of child abuse. Can you think why researchers would object to a conclusion that there is a class difference in the amount of child abuse?

APPENDIX A

ANSWERS TO "READING BETWEEN THE LINES"

1. Guns Don't Kill People, People Kill People

The gun lobby assumes that people have free will and that they choose to kill. It follows from this that people who kill are different from ordinary people who would use a gun only in self-defense. The antigun lobby argues that the presence of a gun is a stimulus to use the gun. The two sides make different assumptions about the importance of determinism versus free will. One slogan might be: Guns turn people into killers. The gun control lobby's slogan, Guns don't die, people do, is less to the point but may be a better slogan because of its emotional appeal.

2. Reincarnation

The claim of reincarnation is virtually impossible to test, which seems to make it all the more appealing to some people. In the words of Lucy, of the comic strip "Peanuts": "I have the perfect theory. It can't be proved one way or the other." It is not hard to come up with alternative hypotheses, however. Hypnosis causes an increase in the ability to imagine scenes and events. Psychologists know that it is difficult to distinguish imagined events from real ones. The recall of past lives under hypnosis is just one example of the ability to imagine fictitious events. An interesting exercise is to relax and recall various scenes from your past, going back as far as you can. Then, imagine yourself 10 or 20 years from now. Most people can imagine the future about as vividly as they can recall the past. If you have little difficulty imagining what has not yet happened, what does that say about the ability to "recall" a past life? Although people may claim to be able to recall historical facts or to speak foreign languages that they could not have known in their present life, research shows that they are actually using bits of information they have learned by ordinary means in their present life which they remember by means of hypnosis.

3. Preference Tests for Beer

The Schlitz brewers were not taking much of a chance by running their test live on television. Most brands of beer taste much alike and are hard to discriminate from one another. Given this fact, the choice of beer was likely to be random. Inasmuch as the number of people preferring either beer was always close to the prediction of a random choice, what was actually proved on the live taste test was that people cannot tell the difference between their own beer and Schlitz. A preference test between two alternatives is meaningless if people cannot discriminate any difference between the alternatives. Similar tests are made in commercials for the ride or comfort of automobiles, the taste of soft drinks, and the like.

4. Imagine That ESP Does Occur

ESP challenges several basic limiting assumptions of science: that effects cannot precede causes, that we know the world only through the senses, and that mere thought cannot influence the world except via our bodies. If ESP did exist, most of human society as we know it would be impossible! There would be few secrets, and the daily lottery would be bankrupt. All banks would fail because their safes would be cracked by psychic means, and the stock market would cease to function. Most of these effects would occur even if only a few people had ESP and if it worked only part of the time. In addition, the various state lotteries that are conducted every day would not show the constant conformity to the laws of probability that they do.

5. The Authoritarian Personality

Families with high levels of status concern and repressive disciplinary procedures tend to come from the lower social classes. They are less educated and more conservative. These values are passed along to their children through principles of social learning. Thus the children learn to be prejudiced and discriminatory from their parents via such mechanisms as instrumental conditioning and modeling. This explanation is thought by many investigators to be more parsimonious than that of Adorno et al. Adorno et al. studied working-class people who generally have stricter child-rearing practices than the middle-class researchers. Racism is also a common attitude among working-class persons. Some researchers have suggested that the reason a correlation was found between authoritarianism and child-rearing practices was that the researchers had used a particular population in which these characteristics were common. According to this interpretation, authoritarianism is not a personality trait but a cultural norm.

6. Testing for Independence of Dimensions

When the light flickered at a higher rate, more light was presented per unit time than when it flickered slowly. If each individual flicker of the light could not be detected by the rat, the light would appear as a steady light whose brightness would depend on the average intensity of the light per unit time. Therefore the fast flicker would appear brighter to the rats and the dimensions of flicker rate and intensity would not be independent after all, but confounded. There is evidence that 10 flashes per second would in fact appear like a steady light to a rat.

7. Is Prayer Effective?

Galton assumed that these groups would have the same longevity, except for the effect of prayer. It is likely that being royalty is more stressful than being a scientist or a member of the gentry. Other factors could be hereditary weaknesses caused by inbreeding or simply the fact that royalty tend to be related to one another and therefore are not a random sample of the population.

8. "You Can Prove Anything with Statistics"

The *Y* axis is not labeled! The origin of the graph is actually $2,150 and the top of the graph is $2,400. Draw a rough sketch of what the graph would look like with an origin of $0 to see how much of a difference there was between the two proposals.

9. Do Younger Infants Prefer Simpler Patterns?

Because all of the cards were the same size, the less complex cards had the largest squares. In other words, size of square was perfectly confounded with complexity. Miranda and Fantz (1971, in Fantz, Fagan, & Miranda, 1975) repeated the study except that they varied the number of squares independently of the size of the squares. They presented infants with cards that had 2, 8, or 32 black squares. The size of the squares was varied such that three of the cards had the same total amount of black area. These three cards constituted the replication of the earlier study. In addition, other cards were made in which size and number varied independently. The patterns used are shown in Figure A–1.

Considering only the three cards that were similar to the previous study, Miranda and Fantz found the same results as Brennan and Moore: There was a tendency for infants to prefer the simpler patterns when the size of the square was confounded with number. However, there was also a strong trend for the infants to prefer both larger squares, when number was held constant, and more numerous squares, when size was held constant. Therefore, if number is taken as a measure of complexity, even newborn infants prefer greater complexity to less. The previous experiments had pitted two strong tendencies against one another: preference for greater size and preference for greater complexity. In that situation the preference for size had won out. In another study Fantz et al. found that older babies tended to be less controlled by pattern size and more by complexity alone, which would explain the apparent developmental trend toward greater complexity found by the previous investigators.

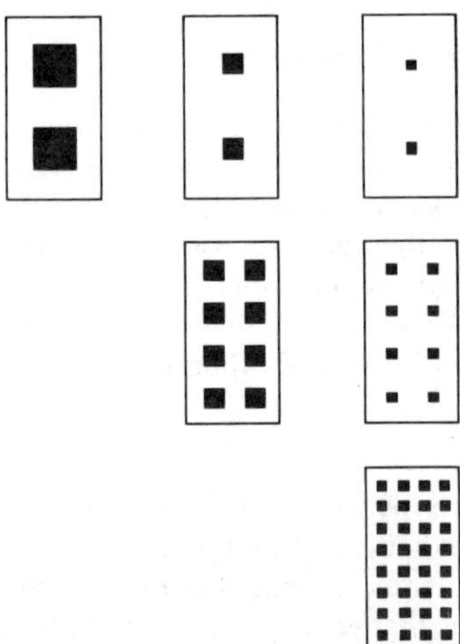

FIGURE A–1. Stimulus patterns. Number of squares varies across rows, and size of squares varies across columns. The three cards along the diagonal have the same total black area.

Note. From "Early visual selectivity" by R. L. Fantz, J. F. Fagan, & S. B. Miranda. In *Infant perception: from sensation to cognition* (Vol. 1), ed. L. B. Cohen & P. Salapatek, *Basic visual processes* (New York: Academic Press, 1975). Copyright 1975 by Academic Press. Reprinted by permission of the publisher and authors.

10. Do Women Fear Success More Than Do Men?

The subjects of the stories were in a situation that is highly sex stereotyped in our society: Most medical students are males. Women who show "fear of success" in this study may actually be showing fear of succeeding in a man's world. Imagine what might happen if the story were about a male nursing student who found himself the most popular member of his class (Tresemer, 1977).

When Horner's study was replicated using another profession, the results were reversed. Wood and Greenfield (cited in Tresemer, 1977) had male and female executives respond to the following verbal cue: "When Janet (Jeff) graduated from college, she (he) went on to get a graduate degree in business. Early in the spring quarter, she (he) is first in her (his) class to be offered a top management job" (p. 115). Of the men 40 percent showed fear of success in their stories, compared with 30 percent of the women. It is possible that business executives see their jobs as less sex stereotyped than medical students see their profession. Or it may be that attitudes toward women having careers had changed in the eight years between the two studies. Or the difference may result from the fact that the previous study used students and the latter study used adults working in the profession. These examples are good case studies of the use of alternative hypotheses in interpreting data. See Tresemer (1977) for an excellent discussion.

11. Brain Damage Sometimes Produces Obesity in Rats

The successful investigators were using female rats and the others were using males. Female rats consistently showed the obesity after the lesions, whereas the males showed it to a lesser degree (Valenstein, Cox, & Kakolewski, 1969).

12. Cognitive and Arousal Factors in Emotion

The experiment had never been replicated until Christina Maslach (1979) and Gary Marshall and Philip Zimbardo (1979) published the results of their work. Maslach replicated the study, except that she used posthypnotic suggestion to induce the state of arousal. Otherwise, the experiment was similar to the original. We may consider her experiment to be a systematic, rather than an exact, replication. Marshall and Zimbardo were prevented by their institution's human subjects committee from inducing the state of anger in their subjects, so their replication was a partial one. They produced the arousal using the original drug but only induced euphoria. Their control conditions were a placebo injection and a neutral confederate.

Neither experiment found evidence in favor of Schachter and Singer's hypothesis. Equally important, though, both papers assert that the data of the original experiment did not support Schachter and Singer's own hypothesis or conclusions. They claim that the original paper made inappropriate comparisons and drew conclusions on the basis of marginal effects. In rebuttal Schachter and Singer (1979) point to differences in procedure between the original experiment and the replications and to other experiments that they consider similar enough to constitute replications. The dust probably will not settle for some time, but we can note how long it may take for an influential experiment to be replicated and how difficult it may be to decide when an experiment is similar enough to constitute a replication.

13. Ulcers in Executive Monkeys

Because the animals were not randomly assigned to the executive position, it is possible that those that learned faster were predisposed to ulcers (Weiss, 1968, 1971). When Weiss replicated the study using the proper controls, he found that the executive animals developed *fewer* ulcers than the control animals. We should note that Weiss used rats instead of monkeys, so a possible species difference may exist. Nevertheless, the executive monkey study has joined the ranks of nonreplicable studies in the view of many researchers.

14. Size of Reward and Cognitive Dissonance

Natalia Chapanis and Alphonse Chapanis (1964) wrote an article that was critical of a number of studies in this area. Among other criticisms of this experiment, they suggested that $20 was an implausible amount of money to offer a student for something that would take less than an hour. Remember that the original experiment was done in the mid-1950s when $20 would represent a larger amount than it does today. Chapanis and Chapanis suggest that the subjects became suspicious when such a large amount of money was offered. Therefore when they rated the experiment for interest, they said it was neither interesting nor boring, as an evasion or to express their ambivalence about the study. Chapanis and Chapanis conclude that the difference between the ratings of the $1 group and the $20 group may not have been because of cognitive dissonance on the part of the $1 subjects but to the suspiciousness of the $20 subjects. It should be noted that although this particular experiment may have been flawed, other research has supported the theory of cognitive dissonance. This experiment is a good example of the point that a theory can be correct even though a particular experiment may not be a good test of it.

15. Subliminal Seduction

A reader of that issue of *Playboy* would have seen many other pictures of naked women but few, if any, other wreaths. Therefore the wreath would be a more distinctive stimulus than one more naked woman. Without clothes there are not many features that would distinguish one *Playboy* model from another. Certainly a blonde would not be unusual. The explanation in terms of subliminal perception of the fancied appearance of the wreath seems gratuitous in view of this explanation. Significantly, no reference to a scientific journal is given in which one might examine the evidence more closely. This case is typical of the rest of the evidence for subliminal perception cited in the book.

16. Thirst in Brain-Damaged Rats

Coburn and Stricker propose that the brain-damaged rats failed to respond to the intraperitoneal injections because these injections caused more stress than the other means of changing salt balance. There is evidence that rats with damage to this area of the brain are unable to react well to stress. In other words, these animals may have been too sick to drink. The other means of inducing changes in salt balance were not as stressful, and therefore the brain-damaged rats were able to respond normally. One consequence of this interpretation is that the lateral preoptic area may not be involved in the regulation of drinking in response to salt balance after all.

17. Memory for Words

It is not possible to assign words randomly to conditions in an experiment on memory. Some words are nouns, some are common, some are short, and so forth. Therefore it is necessary to select words that meet particular criteria. Thus experiments on verbal memory are quasi experiments, according to our terminology. In any quasi experiment it is possible that another variable is confounded with the variable on which you are selecting. In this case McCloskey eventually realized that the highly related words tended to be more familiar to the subjects as well: Robins and oaks are more familiar than penguins and mahoganies. McCloskey (1980) repeated his earlier study, this time measuring the familiarity of the words. He found that familiarity caused a large part of the effect he had previously found and had attributed to similarity. He was able to show, however, that similarity also played a role in the results, when familiarity was controlled.

18. Aggression and XYY Males

Stephan Chorover (1979) points out several problems with the study. First, the mothers were not told that the chromosome test was part of an experiment or that it was funded by an agency concerned with crime and delinquency. The experimenters implied that the chromosome test was part of the hospital's routine practice and that it was a service to the family. Second, the parents were told of their child's condition, which probably would have an effect on how they treated the child. They might consider that he had "bad seed" and was doomed to a life of crime, thus creating a self-fulfilling prophecy. Or, they might have been overly concerned to control his aggressive tendencies. The study was actually one on the effects of having the XYY condition *and* having the parents know that the child had the condition. A more adequate design would have included a group that was told that their child had the condition when the child did not. That design, of course, would introduce new ethical problems.

19. Obesity and Control of Eating

Hibscher and Herman hypothesized that once the habitual dieters had consumed a highly caloric preload, their resistance to eating other highly caloric meals would be reduced. This hypothesis is rather like saying once they had blown the diet for the day, they might as well eat all they wanted. Hibscher and Herman performed an experiment similar to the previous studies, except that they classified subjects into dieters and nondieters as well as obese and nonobese. They found that whether the subjects were dieters had a greater effect on the amount eaten following a preload than whether they were obese. In other words, dieters would eat more after the preload than nondieters, regardless of whether they were obese or not. Conversely, obese persons did not eat more after the preload unless they were dieters.

20. Electrical Inhibition of Aggression in a Charging Bull

Notice that the bull turned to one side when he stopped. The caudate nucleus is involved in the control of motor movements. The bull likely stopped because the involuntary movement to one side caused by the stimulation interfered with his charge. He may have been just as aggressively motivated as before but unable to carry out his intents (Valenstein, 1973).

21. The Physiology of Attention

If you have ever watched a cat, you may have noticed that it will orient to a novel sound. Later, when the cat has ascertained that the sound is of no significance, it will start to do other things, often going to sleep. The significance of the orientation of the cat to the sound is that any changes in the position of the head produce profound effects on the exact intensity of the sound that reaches the cat's ear. F. G. Worden (1966) made careful measurements of the sound levels that reached the cat's ear in such a setting. He found that the movement of the cat's head could account for all of the changes that Hernandez-Peon had found in the response of the cochlear nucleus and had attributed to physiological mechanisms. Researchers no longer believe that this part of the brain is involved in the mechanism of attention.

22. Clever Hans

Hans was picking up subtle cues from his questioners. Oskar Pfungst, a psychologist, found that Hans gave the correct answer only when the questioner knew the correct answer. Pfungst had one person think up a number and whisper it in Hans's ear. A second person did the same and asked Hans to add them up. Hans was at a complete loss in this situation. It was also necessary for Hans to be able to see the questioner. When blinders were placed on him, he struggled to view the questioner.

Pfungst knew by then that Hans relied on visual cues from the questioner, but what were they? Pfungst eventually noticed that all of the questioners made an extremely slight inclination of the head when a question was posed. This head movement caused Hans to start tapping. When Hans had made the correct number of taps, the questioner raised his head and Hans stopped tapping. Pfungst was able to cause Hans to start and stop tapping by merely moving his head without saying a word to Hans. So Hans was just an ordinary horse that had been well trained to respond to subtle visual cues.

Clever Hans was no isolated phenomenon. In addition to the potential for circus acts that such animals have, scientific interest has been created over whether chimpanzees are able to use sign language to communicate with people. Terrace (1979) concluded on the basis of his experiments that previous research that seemed to show that chimpanzees could communicate in this way was subject to the Clever Hans effect. Terrace's conclusions are controversial, but they show how difficult ruling out such subtle biases in research may be.

23. Orchestra Conductors Live Longer

People do not usually become conductors of major orchestras until they are middle aged. So, in order to become a conductor it is necessary, but not sufficient, to live to middle age. Therefore, it is not proper to compare the longevity of conductors to the standard mortality tables, which give the life expectancy of newborns. The proper comparison would be against the life expectancy of other middle-aged persons, which would be considerably longer than that of newborns. Another factor to consider is that in order to become a conductor, one must do more than live to middle age. One must be healthy and have enough vigor to achieve distinction in music. These factors would also predict longer-than-average life expectancy.

24. Antisocial Behavior under Hypnosis

This experiment has several problems. First, the experimental and control groups were different. Both of the experimental subjects were selected for hypnotizability. People who are hypnotizable probably are more willing to follow instructions than others. Second, both were students and would therefore tend to comply with the professor's request. We do not know much about the control subjects, but from the description we can surmise that they were not all students. Third, the situation was defined as hypnosis for the experimental group only. They may have known what was expected of them as hypnotic subjects. Therefore they may have been responding to the role demands of the situation. The control subjects were simply asked to pick up the artificial snake (which actually was a live snake). Theodore Barber and Martin Ham (1974) suggest that the hypnotic instructions, rather than the state of hypnosis, resulted in the subjects' attempting to pick up the snake. In one experiment subjects who were not hypnotized, but were given firm and emphatic instructions to pick up a snake, attempted to do so. Barber and Ham emphasize that people often will conform to instructions to do dangerous acts when urged to do so by an authority figure.

25. Life Events and Illness

The measurement of the life events in retrospective research by definition is done after the person has suffered the illness. Therefore it is impossible to measure the number of life events before the illness strikes. Having the illness is likely to influence the recall and interpretation of life events (Brown & Harris, 1978). People who are sad are known to recall more sad events from the past then people who are not sad. In addition, people seek to find consistency between the events that happen to them. They are likely to reinterpret past events so as to provide some explanation of their illness. For example, one study found that mothers of Down's syndrome children recalled more emotional shocks during pregnancy than did mothers of normal children. The fact that the syndrome is caused by a chromosomal abnormality, however, makes it impossible that emotional stress during pregnancy could be the cause. The mothers must have searched their memories for stressful events that might explain the abnormal offspring.

26. Yes, but Is It Significant?

There is a difference between the statistical significance and the importance of a result. Statistical significance simply means that the results were not likely to have been produced by chance. It does not mean that the results are important. After all, even though three people identified their own shirts, eight people identified the wrong shirt. This evidence is not the sort that one would like to see used as the basis for sending someone to jail for 20 years.

27. The Liberated Female Rat

Most of the researchers were males who let their biases toward human females determine how they looked at the behavior of rats. Notice that McClintock is a woman. In the female rat conception can occur only when the uterus is prepared by hormones that are triggered by sexual activity. Therefore the sexual behavior must be properly timed in order for a successful mating to occur. For this reason the female rat logically should be in control of the timing of sexual activity.

28. The Causes of Child Abuse

Pelton suggests that the idea that child abuse is unrelated to social class is politically convenient, both to mental health professionals and to politicians. The mental health professionals would like to see the problem of child abuse as part of their turf so they could benefit from funding available for the study and cure of child abuse. If child abuse is caused by poverty instead, the mental health profession receives no benefit. Politicians, for their part, may prefer to see child abuse as psychologically caused because that view permits them to seek a technological solution instead of resolving the more difficult causes of poverty itself.

APPENDIX B

SUGGESTED STEPS FOR A TERM RESEARCH PROJECT

The following section is a suggested series of steps for conducting a research project that will take a term to complete. It is intended to permit you to perform all of the steps in conducting a research project, except for actually collecting the data. I have had my classes follow this procedure several times, with considerable success. The advantages of this type of project are that since you are not going to do the actual data collection, you will be able to design more demanding and interesting studies than you would if you were to conduct the research. In addition, you can design a greater variety of studies using methodologies, populations, or techniques that ordinarily would not be feasible. The pace is deliberately slow at first to permit you to change problem areas if you find your original area unsuitable.

After you have designed your study, you present a data sheet to the instructor, who provides fake data. The instructor may arrange that the data either confirm or disconfirm the hypothesis and may introduce various problems of interpretation into the data.

The schedule suggested is designed for a 15-week term. A week is allowed between weeks 6 and 8 to give time for a midterm exam. The schedule is easily adaptable to meet other requirements.

It is helpful if all papers are submitted on 8½-by-11-inch unperforated paper and if they follow APA style. The length of papers suggested is for typewritten format; appropriate allowance may be made for handwritten papers.

Week 1: Choose an area that interests you enough to make it the subject of a research project for the term. Choose an area that is not so familiar that you will not have to think through the basic problems of validity, control, and design. Submit a one-page proposal.

Week 2: Make a preliminary list of three to ten references. Skim a few of these references to get an overview of the area. Submit the reference list.

Week 3: Carefully read the introduction and method section of *one* experimental article (rather than a review) in your list. Pay particular attention to the following questions: (a) the problem that the paper addresses, (b) the history and present status of the problem, and (c) what the experiment you are reporting on will contribute to the understanding of the problem. What are the independent and dependent variables? What are the controls for particular extraneous variables? What is the design of the experiment? How is the design carried out? How many subjects were used, how were they selected, what were the instructions or other manipulations, and so forth. Submit a five-page report.

Week 4: Study the results and discussion sections of the article you reviewed in week 3. What were the principal results? How were they graphed or tabulated? What effects were significant according to which statistical tests? In the discussion section note what the conclusions were, how they were qualified, what weaknesses may have been present in the experiment, what the implications of the study are for the problem addressed in the introduction. Prepare a five-page report.

Week 5: Pick a specific problem for which you wish to design a study. Survey the relevant literature. Identify major reviews or books in the area. What is the history and present status of the problem? What issues have been identified as unresolved? What controversies exist? Prepare a five-page report, including a reference list.

Week 6: Focus on theoretical questions you wish to address. Be as specific as you can about the hypothesis you wish to test, but do not focus on methods at this time. Turn in a three-page proposal.

Week 7: Break for test.

Week 8: After your problem has been approved, propose a specific situation in which you will test your theoretical question. Turn in a three-page proposal.

Week 9: After your research situation has been approved, design the study. Specify all details of design and methodology as if you were going to carry out the experiment, along with descriptions of equipment needed and estimates of expenses. Submit a four-page proposal. Include a blank summary data sheet that your instructor can fill in with data.

Week 11: After you have received the fake data, write the results and discussion sections of the paper. Submit a five-page report.

Week 13: Write your results as you would submit them to a standard psychological journal. The introduction will be based largely on your theoretical and experimental proposals (weeks 6 and 8). The report for week 9 constitutes your method section, and the report for week 11 constitutes the results and discussion sections. Integrate these into a single paper in APA style. The final paper must not exceed 15 pages, including references.

Week 14: Submit the revised report, taking into account any questions raised by your instructor.

APPENDIX C

SOME OF THE PRINCIPAL PSYCHOLOGICAL JOURNALS

General

American Psychologist. The official journal of the American Psychological Association; contains articles of broad interest, news, and analysis of trends in psychology; prints presidential addresses and covers professional affairs.

Annual Review of Psychology. Periodic reviews of the major areas of psychology.

Psychological Bulletin. Review articles in all areas of psychology.

Psychological Review. Theoretical articles (not reviews, as the name suggests) in all areas of psychology, most of them containing empirical data.

Psychology Today. A popular magazine covering the behavioral sciences; publishes articles by psychologists, as well as material of less scientific nature; useful, with discretion.

Science. The leading American journal of general science; publishes articles and brief reports on psychological topics; essential for news of interest to the scientific community.

Scientific American. Authoritative but readable articles on current topics in all areas of science; intended for a general audience, with articles often presenting the best statement of a researcher's work.

Experimental

Bulletin of the Psychonomic Society. Brief articles written by or sponsored by members of the Psychonomic Society.

Journal of Experimental Psychology: General. *Journal of Experimental Psychology: Human Learning and Memory*. *Journal of Experimental Psychology: Human Perception and Performance*. *Journal of Experimental Psychology: Animal Behavior Processes*. Four journals, previously the *Journal of Experimental Psychology*, that publish empirical articles in the areas indicated by their titles.

Journal of the Experimental Analysis of Behavior. Empirical and theoretical articles in the Skinnerian tradition.

Journal of Verbal Learning and Verbal Behavior. Experimental, theoretical, and review articles dealing with verbal processes, human memory, and psycholinguistics.

Physiological and Sensory

Journal of Comparative and Physiological Psychology. Empirical articles, primarily in physiological psychology.

Perception and Psychophysics. Empirical and theoretical articles in sensation, perception, and psychophysics.

Physiology and Behavior. Articles on the relationship between physiology and behavior when one variable is physiological and the primary emphasis and theoretical content are behavioral.

Developmental

Child Development. Interdisciplinary papers on child development; theoretical and empirical articles.

Developmental Psychology. Theoretical and empirical articles on developmental psychology, covering the life span.

Monographs of the Society for Research in Child Development. Longer articles on topics in child development.

Personality and Social

Journal of Abnormal Psychology. Research on causes of abnormal behavior.

Journal of Consulting and Clinical Psychology. Articles on diagnosis, treatment, and issues related to psychological testing.

Journal of Educational Psychology. Articles on learning and cognition in relation to problems of instruction; articles also on development, relationships, and adjustment of the individual.

Journal of Personality. Articles on individual differences and human personal functioning.

Journal of Personality and Social Psychology. Empirical articles on attitudes and social cognition, interpersonal relations and group processes, and personality processes and individual differences.

Quantitative

Educational and Psychological Measurement. Theoretical and applied articles on testing.

Journal of Applied Psychology. Articles on industrial psychology, personnel and leadership topics.

Journal of Educational Measurement. Articles on the theory of testing.

Psychometrika. Primarily theoretical articles on quantitative methods.

REFERENCES

Adorno, T. W., Frenkel-Brunswik, E., Levinson, D. J., & Sanford, R. N. *The authoritarian personality.* New York: Harper & Row, 1950.

Allan, W. UCLA scientist probes psychic events' reality. *Pittsburgh Press,* 10 January 1975, p. 5.

American Psychological Association. APA ethics code. *APA Monitor,* November 1979, p. 17.

American Psychological Association. *Ethical principles in the conduct of research with human participants.* Washington, D. C.: Author, 1973.

American Psychological Association. *Publication manual of the American Psychological Association* (2nd ed.). Washington, D.C.: Author, 1974.

Antelman, S. M., & Caggiula, A. R. Tails of stress-related behavior: A neuropharmacological model. In I. Hanin & E. Usdin (Eds.), *Animal models in psychiatry and neurology.* Oxford: Pergamon Press, 1977.

Antelman, S. M., & Szechtman, H. Tail pinch induces eating in sated rats which appears to depend on Nigrostriatal Dopamine. *Science,* 1975, *189,* 731–733.

Aronson, E., & Carlsmith, J. M. Experimentation in social psychology. In G. Lindzey & E. Aronson (Eds.), *Handbook of social psychology* (2nd ed., Vol. 2). Reading, Mass.: Addison-Wesley, 1968.

Aserinsky, E., & Kleitman, N. Regularly occurring periods of eye motility, and concomitant phenomena, during sleep. *Science,* 1953, *118,* 273–274.

Association for the Advancement of Psychology, Administration intensifies attack on social science research. *Advance,* August 1981, pp. 3, 5.

Babich, F. R., Jacobson, A. L., Bubash, S., & Jacobson, A. Transfer of a response to naive rats by injection of ribonucleic acid extracted from trained rats. *Science,* 1965, *149,* 656–657.

Bachrach, A. J. *Psychological research: An introduction.* New York: Random House, 1962.

Bacon-Prue, A., Blount, R., Hosey, C., & Drabman, R. S. The public posting of photographs as a reinforcer for bedmaking in an institutional setting. *Behavior Therapy,* 1980, *11,* 417–420.

Barber, T. X. *Pitfalls in human research: Ten pivotal points.* New York: Pergamon Press, 1976.

Barber, T. X., & Ham, M. W. *Hypnotic phenomena.* Morristown, N.J.: General Learning Press, 1974.

Barnes, R. D., Ickes, W., & Kidd, R. F. Effects of the perceived intentionality and stabilty of another's dependency on helping behavior. *Personality and Social Psychology Bulletin,* 1979, *5,* 367–372.

Baum, A., & Davis, G. E. Reducing the stress of high-density living: An architectural intervention. *Journal of Personality and Social Psychology,* 1980, *38,* 471–481.

Blass, E. M., & Epstein, A. N. A lateral preoptic osmosensitive zone for thirst in the rat. *Journal of Comparative and Physiological Psychology,* 1971, *76,* 378–394.

Boring, E. G. The nature and history of experimental control. *American Journal of Psychology,* 1954, *67,* 573–589.

Boring, E. G. Perspective: Artifact and control. In R. Rosenthal and R. L. Rosnow (Eds.), *Artifact in behavioral research.* New York: Academic Press, 1969.

Bower, G. Mood and memory. *American Psychologist,* 1981, *36,* 129–148.

Bower, G. H., Gilligan, S. G., & Monteiro, K. P. Selectivity of learning caused by affective states. *Journal of Experimental Psychology: General,* 1981, *110,* 451–473.

Brady, J. V., Porter, R. W., Conrad, D. G., & Mason, J. W. Avoidance behavior and the development of gastroduodenal ulcers. *Journal of Experimental Analysis of Behavior,* 1958, *1,* 69–72.

Bramel, D., & Friend, R. Hawthorne, the myth of the docile worker, and class bias in psychology. *American Psychologist,* 1981, *36,* 867–878.

Breland, K., & Breland, M. The misbehavior of organisms. *American Psychologist,* 1961, *16,* 681–684.

Brennan, W. M., Ames, E. W., & Moore, R. W. Age differences in infant's attention to patterns of different complexities. *Science,* 1966, *151,* 354–356.

Brown, G. W., & Harris, T. *Social origins of depression.* New York: Free Press, 1978.

Byrne, W. L. (Ed.). *Molecular approaches to learning and memory.* New York: Academic Press, 1970.

Byrne, W. L., et al. Memory transfer. *Science,* 1966, *153,* 658–659.

Campbell, D. T. On the conflict between biological and social evolution and between psychology and moral tradition. *American Psychologist,* 1975, *30,* 1103–1126.

Carlsmith, J. M., Ellsworth, P., & Aronson, E. *Methods of research in social psychology.* Reading, Mass.: Addison-Wesley, 1976.

Carr, E. G., & McDowell, J. J. Social control of self-injurious behavior of organic etiology. *Behavior Therapy,* 1980, *11,* 402–409.

Chapanis, A. Prelude to 2001: Explorations in human communication. *American Psychologist,* 1971, *26,* 949–961.

Chapanis, N. P., & Chapanis, A. Cognitive dissonance: Five years later. *Psychological Bulletin,* 1964, *61,* 1–22.

Chari, C. T. K. Some generalized theories and models of psi: A critical evaluation. In B. B. Wolman (Ed.), *Handbook of parapsychology.* New York: Van Nostrand, 1977.

Chorover, S. L. *From genesis to genocide.* Cambridge, Mass.: MIT Press, 1979.

Coburn, P. C., & Stricker, E. M. Osmoregulatory thirst in rats after lateral preoptic lesions. *Journal of Comparative and Physiological Psychology,* 1978, *92,* 350–361.

Cochrane, P. Sex crimes and pornography revisited. *International Journal of Criminology and Penology,* 1978, *6,* 307–317.

Collett, P., & Marsh, P. Patterns of public behavior: Collision avoidance on a pedestrian crossing. *Semiotica,* 1974, *12,* 281–299.

Colligan, M. J., & Stockton, W. The mystery of assembly-line hysteria. *Psychology Today,* 1978, *12*(1), 93–99, 114–116.

Cook, T. D., & Campbell, D. T. The design and conduct of quasi-experiments and true experiments in field settings. In M. D. Dunette (Ed.), *Handbook of industrial and organizational psychology.* Chicago: Rand McNally, 1976.

Cook, T. D., & Campbell, D. T. *Quasi-experimentation: Design and analysis issues for field settings.* Chicago: Rand McNally, 1979.

Coombs, C. H., Raiffa, H., & Thrall, R. M. Some views on mathematical models and measurement theory. *Psychological Review,* 1954, *61,* 132–144.

Cotman, C. W., & McGaugh, J. L. *Behavioral Neuroscience.* New York: Academic Press, 1980.

COURT, J. H. Pornography and sex crimes: A re-evaluation in the light of recent trends around the world. *International Journal of Criminology and Penology*, 1976, *5*, 129–157.

CRUMBAUGH, J. C. A scientific critique of parapsychology. *International Journal of Neuropsychiatry*. 1966, *2*, 523–531.

DANZIGER, K. The social origins of modern psychology. In A. R. Buss (Ed.), *Psychology in social context*. New York: Irvington, 1979.

DARLEY, J. M., & LATANE, B. Bystander intervention in emergencies: Diffusion of responsibility. *Journal of Personality and Social Psychology*, 1968, *8*, 377–383.

DELGADO, J. M. R. *Physical control of the mind*. New York: Harper & Row, 1969.

DOTY, R. L. Influence of menstrual cycle on volunteering behavior. *Nature*, 1975, *254*, 139–140.

ENDLER, N. S. The role of person-by-situation interactions in personality theory. In I. C. Uzgiris & F. Weizmann (Eds.), *The structuring of experience*. New York: Plenum, 1977.

EVANS, C. Parapsychology—what the questionnaire revealed. *New Scientist*, 1973, *57*, 209.

FANTZ, R. L., FAGAN, J. F., & MIRANDA, S. B. Early visual selectivity. In L. B. Cohen & P. Salapatek (Eds.), *Infant perception; From sensation to cognition*, Basic visual processes (Vol. 1). New York: Academic Press, 1975.

FESTINGER, L., & CARLSMITH, J. M. Cognitive consequences of forced compliance. *Journal of Abnormal and Social Psychology*, 1959, *58*, 203–210.

FESTINGER, L., RIECKEN, H. W., JR., & SCHACHTER, S. *When prophecy fails*. Minneapolis: University of Minnesota Press, 1956.

FISHER, W. A., & BYRNE, D. Instrumentation and female indifference to arousing stimuli. *Journal of Personality and Social Psychology*, 1978, *36*, 117–125.

FRIEDMAN, M. I., & STRICKER, E. M. The physiological psychology of hunger: A physiological perspective. *Psychological Review*, 1976, *83*, 409–431.

GOFFMAN, E. *Relations in public*. New York: Basic Books, 1971.

GOULD, S. J. Morton's ranking of races by cranial capacity. *Science*, 1978, *200*, 503–509.

GOULD, S. J. The father of Jensenism (review of Hearnshaw). *Psychology Today*, 1979, *13*(7), 104–106.

GREELY, A. M. The sociology of the paranormal: A reconnaissance. *Sage Research Papers in the Social Sciences*, 1975, *3* (Series No. 90-023).

HAMM, R. J., & MATTSON, J. C. Additive summation following intradimensional discrimination training. *Journal of the Experimental Analysis of Behavior*, 1978, *29*, 505–510.

HANSEL, C. E. M. *ESP: A scientific examination*. New York: Charles Scribner's Sons, 1966.

HAWKES, N. Tracing Burt's descent into fraud. *Science*, 1979, *205*, 673–675.

HEARNSHAW, L. S. *Cyril Burt, psychologist*. Ithaca, New York: Cornell University Press, 1979.

HELSON, H. *Adaptation level theory*. New York: Harper & Row, 1964.

HERNANDEZ-PEON, R., SCHERRER, H., & JOUVET, M. Modification of electrical activity in cochlear nucleus during "attention" in unanesthetized cats. *Science*, 1956, *123*, 331–332.

HERSEN, M., & BARLOW, D. H. *Single case experimental designs*. New York: Pergamon Press, 1976.

HIBSCHER, J. A., & HERMAN, P. C. Obesity, dieting and the expression of "obese" characteristics. *Journal of Comparative and Physiological Psychology*, 1977, *91*, 374–380.

HOLDEN, C. Ethics in social science research (news and comment). *Science*, 1979, *206*, 537–540.

HORNER, M. S. Sex differences in achievement motivation and performance in competitive and noncompetitive situations. Doctoral dissertation, University of Michigan, 1968.

JOHNSON, M. Comments. *Journal of Parapsychology*. 1976, *40*, 151–154.

KEY, W. B. *Subliminal seduction*. Englewood Cliffs, N.J.: Prentice-Hall, 1973.

KIRK, R. E. *Experimental design: Procedures for the behavioral sciences*. Belmont, California: Brooks/Cole, 1968.

KRATOCHWILL, T. R. (Ed.). *Single subject research*. New York: Academic Press, 1978.

KUHN, T. S. *The structure of scientific revolutions*. Chicago: University of Chicago Press, 1962.

KUTCHINSKY, B. The effect of easy availability of pornography on the incidence of sex crimes: The Danish experience. *Journal of Social Issues*, 1973, *29*, 163–181.

LAUDAN, L. *Progress and its problems: Towards a theory of scientific growth*. Berkeley and Los Angeles: University of California Press, 1977.

LEPPER, M. R., GREENE, D., & NISBETT, R. E. Undermining children's intrinsic interest with extrinsic reward: A test of the "overjustification" hypothesis. *Journal of Personality and Social Psychology*, 1973, *28*, 129–137.

LETTVIN, S. Y., MATURANA, H. R., MCCULLOCH, W. S., & PITTS, W. H. What the frog's eye tells the frog's brain. *Proceedings of the Institute of Radio Engineers*, 1959, *47*, 1940–1951.

LORENZ, K. Z. The evolution of behavior. *Scientific American*, 1958, *199*(6), 67–78.

MARKS, D., & KAMMANN, R. *The psychology of the psychic*. Buffalo: Prometheus Books, 1980.

MARSHALL, G. D., & ZIMBARDO, P. G. Affective consequences of inadequately explained physiological arousal. *Journal of Personality and Social Psychology*. 1979, *37*, 970–988.

MARSHALL, J. F., & TEITELBAUM, P. Further analysis of sensory inattention following lateral hypothalamic damage in rats. *Journal of Comparative and Physiological Psychology*, 1974, *86*, 375–395.

MASLACH, C. Negative emotional biasing of unexplained arousal. *Journal of Personality and Social Psychology*, 1979, *37*, 953–969.

MCBURNEY, D. H., & GENT, J. F. On the nature of taste qualities. *Psychological Bulletin*, 1979, *86*, 151–167.

MCBURNEY, D. H., LEVINE, J. M., & CAVANAUGH, P. H. Psychophysical and social ratings of human body odor. *Personality and Social Psychology Bulletin*, 1977, *3*, 135–138.

MCCLINTOCK, M., & ADLER, N. T. The role of the female during copulation in wild and domestic rats (*Rattus norvegicus*). *Behavior*, 1978, *68*, 67–96.

MCCLOSKEY, M. The stimulus familiarity problem in semantic memory research. *Journal of Verbal Learning and Verbal Memory*, 1980, *19*, 485–502.

MCCLOSKEY, M., & GLUCKSBERG, S. Decision processes in verifying category membership statements: Implications for models of semantic memory. *Cognitive Psychology*, 1979, *11*, 1–37.

McCONNELL, J. V. Memory transfer through cannibalism in planarium. *Journal of Neuropsychiatry*, 1962 *3* (Supplement 1), 542–548.

McCONNELL, R. A. A parapsychological dialogue. *Journal of the American Society for Psychical Research*, 1977, *77*, 429–435.

McGINNIES, E. Emotionality and perceptual defense. *Psychological Review*, 1949, *56*(5), 244–251.

MILGRAM, S. Behavioral study of obedience. *Journal of Abnormal and Social Psychology*, 1963, *67*, 371–378.

MILLER, G. A. The magical number seven plus or minus two: Some limits on our capacity for processing information. *Psychological Review*, 1956, *63*, 81–97.

NISBETT, R. E. Determinants of food intake in human obesity. *Science*, 1968, *159*, 1254–1255.

OLDS, J. Commentary. In E. S. Valenstein (Ed.), *Brain stimulation and motivation*. Glenview, Ill.: Scott, Foresman and Company, 1973.

OLDS, J., & MILNER, P. Positive reinforcement produced by electrical stimulation of septal area and other regions of rat brain. *Journal of Comparative and Physiological Psychology*, 1954, *47*, 419–427.

ORNE, M. T., & EVANS, F. J. Social control in the psychological experiment: Antisocial behavior and hypnosis. *Journal of Personality and Social Psychology*, 1965, *1*, 189–200.

PELTON, L. H. Child abuse and neglect: The myth of classlessness. *American Journal of Orthopsychiatry*, 1978, *48*, 608–617.

PHILLIPS, D. P. Motor vehicle fatalities increase just after publicized suicide stories. *Science*, 1977, *196*, 1464–1465.

PHILLIPS, D. P. Suicide, motor vehicle fatalities, and the mass media: Evidence toward a theory of suggestion. *American Journal of Sociology*, 1979, *84*, 1150–1174.

RAO, K. R. On the nature of psi: An examination of some attempts to explain ESP and PK. *Journal of Parapsychology*, 1977, *41*, 294–351.

ROSENTHAL, R. *Experimenter effects in behavioral research* (enlarged ed.). New York: Irvington Publishers, 1976.

ROSENTHAL, R., & FODE, K. L. The effect of experimenter bias on the performance of the albino rat. *Behavioral Science*, 1963, *8*, 183–189.

ROSENTHAL, R., & ROSNOW, R. L. *Artifact in behavioral research*. New York: Academic Press, 1969.

ROSS, L., LEPPER, M. R., & HUBBARD, M. Perseverence in self-perception and social perception: Biased attributional processes in the debriefing paradigm. *Journal of Personality and Social Psychology*, 1975, *32*, 880–892.

ROWLAND, L. W. Will hypnotized persons try to harm themselves or others? *Journal of Abnormal and Social Psychology*. 1939, *34*, 114–117.

RUBIN, L. B. *Women of a certain age: The mid-life search for self*. New York: Harper & Row, 1979.

SCHACHTER, S. *The psychology of affiliation*. Stanford, Calif.: Stanford University Press, 1959.

SCHACHTER, S., & RODIN, J. (Eds.). *Obese humans and rats*. Potomac, Md.: Erlbaum, 1974.

SCHACHTER, S., & SINGER, J. Cognitive, social and physiological determinants of emotional state. *Psychological Review*, 1962, *69*, 379–399.

SCHACHTER, S., & SINGER, J. E. Comments on the Maslach and Marshall-Zimbardo experiments. *Journal of Personality and Social Psychology*, 1979, *37*, 989–995.

Shaffer, J. B. P. *Humanistic psychology*. Englewood Cliffs, N.J.: Prentice-Hall, 1978.

Sharpe, R. S., & Johnsgard, P. A. Inheritance of behavioral characters in F. mallard x pintail (*Anas platyrynchos L. x Anas acuta L.*) hybrids. *Behaviour*, 1966, *27*, 259–272.

Sidman, M. *Tactics of scientific research*. New York: Basic Books, 1960.

Singh, N. N., Dawson, M. J., & Gregory, P. R. Suppression of chronic hyperventilation using response-contingent aromatic ammonia. *Behavior Therapy*, 1980, *11*, 561–566.

Skinner, B. F. Are theories of learning necessary? *Psychological Review*, 1950, *57*, 193–216.

Skinner, B. F. A case history in scientific method. *American Psychologist*, 1956, *11*, 221–233.

Smith, M. J., Colligan, M. J., & Hurrell, J. J., Jr. Three incidents of industrial mass psychogenic illness. *Journal of Occupational Medicine*, 1978, *20*, 399–400.

Sternberg, R. J. *Writing the psychology paper*. Woodbury, N.Y: Barron's Educational Series, 1977.

Sternberg, S. High-speed scanning in human memory. *Science*, 1966, *153*, 652–654.

Stevens, J. C., & Rubin, L. L. Psychophysical scales of apparent heaviness and the size-weight illusion. *Perception and Psychophysics*, 1970, *8*, 225–230.

Terrace, H.S. How Nim Chimpsky changed my mind. *Psychology Today*, 1979, *13*(6), 65–76.

That numberless presidential chart. *New York Times*, 2 August 1981, p. F–17.

Tresemer, D. *Fear of success*. New York: Plenum, 1977.

U.S. Department of health, Education, and Welfare. *Guide for the care and use of laboratory animals* (Rev., NIH 78-23). Washington, D.C., 1978.

U.S. Bureau of the Census. *Statistical abstract of the United States: 1979* (100th ed.). Washington, D.C., 1979.

Valenstein, E. S. *Brain control*. New York: Wiley, 1973.

Valenstein, E. S., Cox, V. C., & Kakolewski, J. W. Sex differences in hyperphasia and body weight following hypothalamic damage. *Annals of the New York Academy of Sciences*, 1969, *157*, 1030–1046.

Wagenaar, A. C. Effects of raising the legal drinking age on traffic accident involvement of young drivers. Paper presented at the American Public Health Association, November 1981a.

Wagenaar, A. C. Effects of the raised legal drinking age on motor vehicle accidents in Michigan. *HSRI Research Review*, 1981b, *11*(4), 1–8.

Wagenaar, W. A. Note on the construction of digram-balanced Latin squares. *Psychological Bulletin*, 1969, 72, 384–386.

Wandell, B. A., & Pugh, E. N. A field-additive pathway detects brief-duration, long-wavelength incremental flashes. *Vision Research*, 1980, *20*, 613–624.

Webb, E. J., Campbell, D. T., Schwartz, R. D., & Sechrest, L. *Unobtrusive measures: Nonreactive research in the social sciences*. Chicago: Rand McNally, 1966.

Weisberg, H. F., & Bowen, B. D. *An introduction to survey research and data analysis*. San Francisco: Freeman, 1977.

Weiss, J. M. Effects of coping responses on stress. *Journal of Comparative and Physiological Psychology*, 1968, *65*, 251–260.

Worden, F. G. Attention and auditory electrophysiology. In E. Stellar and J. M. Sprague (Eds.), *Progress in physiological psychology* (Vol. 1). New York: Academic Press, 1966.

Zimmerman, D. H., & West, C. Sex roles, interruptions and silences in conversation. In B. Thorne and N. Henley (Eds.), *Language and sex: Difference and dominance*. Rowley, Mass.: Newbury House, 1975.

Zimmerman, D. H., & West, C. Strangers when they meet: A study of same-sex and cross-sex conversations between unacquainted persons. Unpublished manuscript, 1978.

NAME INDEX

SUBJECT INDEX

Italic entries refer to "Reading Between the Lines."